4/29/11 - gift

Upper: *Cryptolopha nigrorum*; **Lower:** *Abrornis olivacea*, **the two species of flycatchers from the Island of Negros, Philippines, named by Moseley.**

(*The Ibis*, Sixth Series 3: 46, 47, pl. II. 1891; Stuckey Collection)

Edwin Lincoln Moseley
(1865–1948)

Naturalist, Scientist, Educator

By

Relda E. Niederhofer

Bowling Green State University
Firelands College
Huron, Ohio

and

Ronald L. Stuckey

The Ohio State University
College of Biological Sciences
Columbus, Ohio

1998

EDWIN LINCOLN MOSELEY (1865-1948):
Naturalist, Scientist, Educator

By Relda E. Niederhofer and Ronald L. Stuckey

Published in the year of the fiftieth anniversary of Professor Moseley's death.

Designed and edited by Ronald L. Stuckey; Indexed by Relda E. Niederhofer; Word processing and page layout by Ricki C. Herdendorf.

Printed by Thomson-Shore, Inc., 7300 West Joy Road, Dexter, MI 48130.

Distributed by Ronald L. Stuckey, RLS Creations, P. O. Box 3010, Columbus, OH 43210.

A contribution from the Department of Natural and Social Sciences, BGSU, Firelands College, Huron; and the Herbarium and former Department of Botany, OSU, Columbus.

Citation: Niederhofer, Relda E. and Ronald L. Stuckey. 1998. Edwin Lincoln Moseley (1865-1948): Naturalist, Scientist, Educator. RLS Creations, Columbus, Ohio. xxvi, 292 pp.

Copyright © 1998 by Relda E. Niederhofer and Ronald L. Stuckey. All rights reserved. Printed in the United States of America. Except as permitted under the United States Copyright Act of 1976, no part of this book may be reproduced or transmitted in any form or by any means, electronic or mechanical, including photocopying, without permission in writing from the copyright owners.

ISBN 0-9668034-2-6

Edwin Lincoln Moseley
Science Teacher, Sandusky High School.

(Taken sometime before 1898; Sandusky Library Archives)

FOREWORD

Ohio has had its fair share of early natural scientists, including such notable scholars as Caleb Atwater, Jared P. Kirtland, William S. Sullivant, and James M. Wheaton. Not the least of these nationally renowned individuals was Edwin Lincoln Moseley, the naturalist, scientist, and educator from northwestern Ohio, whose lifetime of accomplishments is likewise legendary.

As a professional naturalist, also born and reared in northwestern Ohio, I have always felt a special kinship with Moseley. I only wish I could have been personally acquainted with this learned field naturalist. He was especially well versed in ornithology, zoology, geology, and botany. Two of his classic botanical works, "Sandusky flora" and "Flora of the Oak Openings," remain invaluable benchmark references for the flora of this region of Ohio. I have learned a great deal from studying his works. Consequently, I almost feel as if I did know this man who frequently traversed the woodlands, dunes, and wetlands of the western lake plain two generations before my time.

Moseley was much more than a remarkable naturalist. He was also a meticulous scientist driven by an insatiable need to know the reason for things. For several decades, milk sickness, the scourge of the western frontier during the nineteenth century, took countless lives while the best medical minds of the times struggled to determine its cause. The final credit goes to Moseley, who was the first to discover scientifically that milk sickness was transmitted to humans when dairy products were consumed from cows that had grazed upon white snakeroot, a common woodland plant. Many lives were saved as a result of Moseley's years of painstaking research.

Above all else, Moseley was the consummate educator. He was a skilled teacher with a mastery of several disciplines including geology, astronomy, physiology, English, Latin, mathematics, and, of course, biology. Moseley's entire life was devoted to his students and the art of teaching. He was always first and foremost the teacher.

Moseley's published works give insight to the professional side of this man, but not the man himself. Now, for the first time, the work of Relda E. Niederhofer and Ronald L. Stuckey is a marvelous contribution acquainting the reader with Edwin Lincoln Moseley, the man as well as the naturalist, scientist, and educator. It is a captivating account of this remarkable and somewhat eccentric individual who made major contributions to our present-day understanding of the natural history of Ohio. Clearly, the world is a much better place for his having been here.

Guy L. Denny
Chief, Division of Natural Areas and Preserves
Ohio Department of Natural Resources
July 1996

Foreword: *Guy L. Denny* iv

Contents v

Reader Guidelines viii

Preface I: *Relda E. Niederhofer* ix

Preface II: *Ronald L. Stuckey* xi

Dedication to T. Richard Fisher xiii

Introduction: *Ronald L. Stuckey* xv

Chronology of Edwin Lincoln Moseley (1865-1948): *Ronald L. Stuckey* xvii

Highlights in the History of Bowling Green State University,
  Bowling Green, Ohio: *Ronald L. Stuckey* xxv

Section I. Personality & Career 1

   1. Educator of Many Students .... *Josephine True*   3

   2. Formative Years in Michigan .... *Relda E. Niederhofer*   11
      Knowledge: Oration Delivered at
        High School Graduation *by Edwin L. Moseley* 16

   3. Lauded by University President .... *Homer B. Williams*   19

   4. The Inquiring Mind of a Teaching Scientist ..... *Frank J. Prout*   29

   5. Interviews with Students and Friends .... *Relda E. Niederhofer*   39

   6. Field Excursions for Moseley's Classes .... *Relda E. Niederhofer*   67
      Science Field Excursions 71
      Botany Field Trip to Vermilion
        and Oberlin *by Ralph H. McKelvey* 72

   7. Family History .... *Relda E. Niederhofer*   77
      Chart Showing Intermarriages of Moseley and Bingham Families 88

Section II. Contributions & Achievements 89

    8. Recollections of a Contemporary Naturalist .... *Milton B. Trautman*   91

    9. Scientific Presentations and Publications .... *Ronald L. Stuckey*   99
        Membership in Scientific Organizations and
        Publications in Periodicals 123

    10. Forecasting Long-Range Weather Conditions .... *Ronald L. Stuckey*   127
        Long-Range Weather Man *by Moran Tudury* 138
        Evaluation of Moseley's Rainfall Predictions 141

    11. Books and Science Education .... *Ronald L. Stuckey*   145

    12. The High School Museum .... *Relda E. Niederhofer*   165

Section III. Writings & Legacy 177

    13. Selected Letters from Correspondence .... *Edwin L. Moseley*   179

    14. Sandusky's Scientific and Economic Advantages .... *Edwin L. Moseley*   189
        List of Moseley's Lectures at the
        Sandusky High School 207

    15. Illness, Death, and Funeral .... *Ronald L. Stuckey*   209

    16. Estate Trust Fund of Benefit to Students .... *Relda E. Niederhofer*   215
        The Will of Edwin Lincoln Moseley 220
        Commentary on Moseley's Will by *Sentinel* Editor Canary 223

    17. Tributes from Former Students 225
        I. My Greatest Teacher *by Donald M. Love* 225
        II. A Great Man *by R. E. Dillery* 227
        III. Friend, Teacher, and Naturalist *by Seymour Van Gundy* 228
        IV. No Fear of Bald-Faced Hornets *by Richard S. Phillips* 230
        Students who Assisted Moseley in His Research Projects 235

18. Commentaries by Natural Science Writers	237
I. Gone But Not Forgotten *by Louis W. Campbell*	237
II. An Eccentric Genius *by Roger Conant*	238
III. An Appraisal *by Harold F. Mayfield*	240
19. Commemorated in Names .... *Ronald L. Stuckey*	245
20. Recognitions and Tributes .... *Ronald L. Stuckey*	257
A Final Summation	271
List of Publications about Moseley by the Authors	273
Publication Notes	275
Libraries Consulted	278
Photograph and Archive Credits	279
Acknowledgments	280
Index .... *Relda E. Niederhofer*	282
About the Authors	291

Reader Guidelines

I. Duplicate Topics

The reader will soon discover the repetition of certain topics appearing in several of the chapters throughout the book. This situation emerged because various authors have written different chapters. We are well aware of these duplicated topics, but rather than attempt to remove most of them as part of the editorial process, we have chosen to retain these duplications in order that each author's contribution remains intact mostly as originally prepared. In essence, each chapter is a complete unit in itself and can be read with understanding without having to read earlier chapters first.

II. Chapters with Supplemental Topics

Certain chapters contain supplemental topics similar to an appendix. These items are either original short essays or lists of information presented in smaller type to enhance those chapters where they are placed. These supplements are identified under the chapter title in the Contents. They occur in Chapters 2, 6, 7, 9, 10, 14, 16, 17, and 20.

III. Topics Requiring Further Explanation

Certain topics in various chapters require further explanation or documentation. These situations usually are marked in the text with asterisks, and explanations are presented in the form of explanatory remarks introduced by the word note or notes. These notes may be located at the bottom of a page or at the end of a chapter. In some situations, mostly because of space restrictions, certain topics requiring further explanation are marked in the text with a capital letter and a page number. For these explanatory notes, it is necessary to refer to the numbered page provided.

IV. Omission of Passages and Paragraphs

In those chapters credited to other authors, portions of their text may have been removed as part of the editorial process. Large passages or entire paragraphs that were eliminated are indicated by three large black dots centered on the page [for example, see Chapter 4, pages 30, 31, 34, and 35]. Omission of short passages or a few words from a sentence are marked with an ellipsis.

PREFACE I

Professor Edwin Lincoln Moseley visited the Bowling Green State University campus occasionally after his retirement in 1936. Stories about his unusual life were common on campus in the late 1940s when I was there as an undergraduate. I had a brief glimpse of him from a second-story window of the Science Building, but unfortunately I never met him. At the time of his funeral I remember hearing the organ music amplified through the bell tower on campus.

Money was very scarce when I was an undergraduate, so when Dr. Everett C. Myers, Moseley's successor as curator of the museum, put a help-wanted notice on the bulletin board, I applied for the job. Myers hired me to clean some of Moseley's museum specimens. For 50 cents an hour I removed large coiled snakes from gallon jars, filtered the formalin, cleaned the jars, and returned the specimens to the containers with fresh preservative. I typed Moseley's handwritten notes to make new labels for each container. I got fairly good at deciphering his illegible writing.

When I taught biology at Sandusky High School from 1957-1965, I found more specimens from Moseley's museum. He left shark's teeth and preserved porcupinefish. The one large item left there when he moved the museum to Bowling Green State University was a human skeleton he had used to teach high school human anatomy and physiology. I used it for the same purpose. In 1985 Sandusky High School gave it to Bowling Green State University, Firelands College at Huron, where I used it again when teaching college-level human anatomy and physiology.

Sandusky was an excellent area to begin my research of Moseley. The stories I had heard as an undergraduate were not very complimentary to him, and I thought there must be much more to this man's life. Helen Hansen at the Follett House Museum in Sandusky directed me to their file on Moseley. To get a better perspective of him, she suggested I talk with his former students who lived in the community. They were eager to share their memories, especially his work on mapping Sandusky Bay and his research on milk sickness. Each person would refer me to someone else who might have another anecdote. When I met Helen Stockdale, she told me that Dr. Ronald L. Stuckey was also collecting information about Moseley. In 1974 I had taken Stuckey's class in aquatic plants at the Franz Theodore Stone Laboratory on Gibraltar Island in Lake Erie. When I contacted Stuckey he encouraged me to prepare a written record of the interviews. In 1982 I took a course at Charminade University in Honolulu, Hawaii. While there, I went to visit a church, museum, and library, which were outgrowths of the Children's Mission School that Moseley's maternal grandparents, missionaries Hiram and Sybil Bingham, started in Honolulu in 1820. In 1983 I visited the Bentley Historical Library at The University of Michigan, Ann Arbor, in search of information about Moseley. Before returning to Sandusky I traveled the extra 75 miles to Moseley's birthplace in Union City, Michigan, to obtain information about his boyhood.

Several departments at Bowling Green State University were able to supply information and photographs about Moseley. The University Archives maintains four file boxes on him, which I used extensively. The Department of Public Relations supplied a number of photographs as well. The Department of Biological Sciences, then chaired by Dr. T. Richard Fisher, did not maintain a file on Moseley. Fisher, however, encouraged me to share my findings with the Department in the form of a seminar, which I held on 17 October 1984. Fisher has been very supportive of my work, and urged me to print it. My paper appeared in a campus publication in 1985. My association with Fisher began in 1968, when he recommended that the Firelands College hire me to teach as a full-time biology instructor. At that time Firelands College was a branch campus of Bowling Green State University relying heavily on the main campus for guidance.

Firelands College hosted its 29th annual recognition banquet on 17 April 1998. The event recognized students, community members, faculty and staff for their academic and service contribution to the college and the community. Dean Darby Williams of Firelands College presented the Dean's Special Recognition Award to me for my "exceptionally meritorious contributions" supporting the college's mission. A list of my publications about Moseley appears on page 273.

I thank my husband, James W. Niederhofer, and my daughter, Sandra Douglas for their patience and understanding during the many years of research and writing.

Relda E. Niederhofer
July 1998

PREFACE II

Edwin Lincoln Moseley, a pioneer in outdoor natural science education, is now, 50 years following his death, probably remembered by only a few scientists and his former students. Between 1914 and his retirement in 1936, and until his death in 1948, Moseley served Bowling Green State Normal College, now Bowling Green State University, as its first professor of science. His title was truly accurate for he was a one-man science department and member of the institution's original faculty. Here he taught all of the sciences and some related subjects, including astronomy, biology, chemistry, geography, geology, hygiene, physics, philosophy, and sometimes courses in English, Latin, and geometry.

My interest in Moseley has been an informative study during my entire professional life. Having grown up in northern Ohio, my mother, Leora Irene Shuey (1903-1966), who attended Bowling Green State Normal College during 1920-1922, often spoke of Moseley. Although I do not recall her saying that she had any classes with him, examination of her grade record reveals that she took a class in geography which was one of the courses that Moseley taught. Three photographs taken with her brownie camera on the campus are reproduced in this book [see pages xxvi and 163].

I first became aware of Moseley as a botanist when in the early summer of 1959 I attended the Franz Theodore Stone Laboratory on Gibraltar Island in Lake Erie, while an advanced undergraduate student from Heidelberg College. At the Laboratory, I studied Field Botany, a course taught by Dr. T. Richard Fisher, plant taxonomist of the Department of Botany and Plant Pathology, The Ohio State University. Reference to Moseley was made from time to time in the course, both orally and from the literature.

My interest in Moseley was heightened further, when soon after coming to The Ohio State University in 1965, I began studying his "Sandusky flora" (1899) in connection with my research on the terrestrial flora of the islands in Lake Erie, and on the changes in the aquatic and wetland flora in and along the shoreline of Lake Erie. I also became intrigued with the diversity of scientific disciplines in which Moseley wrote papers, and consequently I began assembling a bibliography of his scientific papers and books.

In the spring of 1967, my brother, Darwin Wendell Stuckey, who was then a graduate student in chemistry at Bowling Green State University, helped me obtain information from the campus library. Since then I have had considerable help from librarians and friends in Bowling Green, Columbus, Fremont, Sandusky, and Toledo, who have provided me access to materials relevant to Moseley's life and accomplishments. In the fall of 1981, I prepared a four-page typewritten summary of Moseley's life and scientific achievements for a *Biographical Dictionary,* which was published in 1997.

I have long anticipated that a collection of papers about Moseley, along with excerpts from his popular and scientific writings could be collected together in a book. In that connection, Dr. Milton B. Trautman, an authority on Ohio fishes and birds and a close friend of Moseley, prepared for me in November 1981 an eight-page typewritten account of his recollections. At about that same time, Mrs. Relda E. Niederhofer wrote to me that she was conducting interviews with Moseley's former students and friends. Niederhofer and I have continued working on Moseley's life in a cooperative effort, with the goal of preparing a book-length manuscript that would capture his personality and scientific achievements.

Perhaps my greatest surprise in developing this book came in the summer of 1996. At that time, I learned, in a visit with our family's long-time friend, Grace Myers (b. 1905), then of Sycamore, Ohio, that she had attended Moseley's botany class at Bowling Green State Normal College in 1924 [see lower-right photograph, page 163]. She considered Moseley a demanding teacher who tried to have students be more productive. Although she did not particularly care for him as a teacher, she had great respect for him as a scholar and scientist. My study of Moseley's work now seemed complete, for by the time we finished our conversation she gave me her 1924 college yearbook that contains Moseley's photograph. A list of my publications about Moseley appears on page 273.

Ronald L. Stuckey
April 1998

T. Richard Fisher, plant taxonomist specializing in *Heliopsis, Silphium,* and other related genera of the Compositae, served as chairman of the Department of Biological Sciences at Bowling Green State University (1968-1983). Born 1921 in Brownstown, Illinois, Fisher received his B. S. from Eastern Illinois University (1947) and the Ph. D. in botany under Charles B. Heiser, Jr., at Indiana University, Bloomington (1954).

He held teaching and research professorships at Appalachian Teachers College (1954-1956), The Ohio State University (1956-1968), and Bowling Green State University (1968-1988). He taught field botany courses at the Franz Theodore Stone Laboratory (1957-1965, 1967-1968, 1975). Author of Volume 2 of the *Vascular Flora of Ohio: Asteraceae* [Compositae] (1988), Fisher is the former executive director of the non-profit Schedel Foundation, which maintains a public 26-acre garden and arboretum at Elmore, Ottawa County, Ohio.

DEDICATION

T. Richard Fisher
Our friend and colleague.

(Taken in 1980; Photo Service, BGSU; Stuckey Collection)

The two buildings where Moseley taught his classes.

(Post cards; Stuckey Collection)

INTRODUCTION

"...*there is much good done to a man by a little praise.*" E. L. M.

"Whole books could be written about Edwin L. Moseley, who was probably the most widely known (and the most colorful) member of the original faculty," wrote James Robert Overman (1888-1978) in his *History of Bowling Green State University* (1967). Overman, a professor of mathematics and part-time assistant to the president, was, like Moseley, a member of the original faculty who would have known him and therefore could write with some personal authority. Overman, later the first Dean of the College of Liberal Arts and the first Dean of Faculties, devoted four paragraphs to Moseley's contributions to the University community, covering both his professional achievements and his personal eccentricities. He recognized Moseley's wide scientific qualifications, his popular and numerous field trips, his frugal habits, his financial support of students, and the many legends generated about him. These attributes of Moseley have become the focus of this book.

Until now, no book has been written on the life of Edwin Lincoln Moseley (1865-1948). Unlike most educators or scientists whose biographies are written in a chronological sequence, this book presents Moseley's life by topics. These topics are developed in 20 chapters. Information for some of the chapters was selected from writings by his contemporaries, who either knew him personally for a long time or who interviewed him before writing their published essays. Primarily for the reasons just stated these essays were selected for preservation here because they provide firsthand information about the person. Using the writings of various authors introduces an unevenness of quality, resulting in different writing styles and levels of complexity, duplicated information, and variable accuracy of statements. These potential difficulties are solved to a certain extent by a critical editing of these essays. Where authors have made mistakes or given incomplete information with respect to persons, places, or dates, these items have been corrected when detected. Sentence structure and punctuation have been edited to clarify the original by replacing inadequately chosen words or correcting inaccurate or incomplete statements. Some information is of necessity repeated in two or more chapters, although efforts have been made to eliminate extensive repetitious information. Because of the topical organization employed, determining the order of events in Moseley's life can at times be confusing. This situation is remedied by having a list of noteworthy events in his life arranged in a chronology following this introduction. The topical organization further allows the reader to understand the contents of each individual chapter without having to read one or more chapters preceding it.

This book, apportioned into three Sections, focuses on Moseley's personality and career in Section I, his contributions and achievements in Section II, and his selected writings and legacy in Section III. The topics comprising Chapters 1 through 7 in Section I are written by individuals once associated with Sandusky High School or Bowling Green State University. For the most part they reveal Moseley through their acquaintance with him.

Chapter 1 should be considered an introduction because it highlights Moseley's life as an educator but with little chronological reference. Chapter 2, composed mostly of fragments of information from several biographical sources, provides a sketch of his early life in Michigan. Chapters 3 and 4, originally presented as speeches by administrators under whom Moseley worked, are fully praiseworthy and may contain inflated statements not totally accurate, but which have been toned here when necessary, if detected. Chapter 5 gives an insight as to how his former students and associates viewed him in the 1980s. Chapter 6, descriptions of field excursions with Moseley, is highlighted with a description of a botany class trip written by one of his high school students in Sandusky. It provides an account of how these events were conducted and what occurred on them. More information is learned about the trip than about leader Moseley himself. Chapter 7 tells of his family history and heritage.

The topics comprising Chapters 8 through 12 in Section II are written mostly by individuals not associated with the schools in which Moseley was employed. These writers, in addition to myself, are in a position to reveal his contributions and achievements in a more objective context. The topics chosen for focus in Section II are his contributions as a field naturalist and classroom teacher in Chapter 8, his scientific presentations at meetings and publications in diverse periodicals in Chapter 9, his nationally known popular research on weather predictions, in part as told by him in an interview in Chapter 10, his writings of science educational textbooks and methods of teaching natural science in Chapter 11, and his development of an extensive natural history museum in Chapter 12.

The topics comprising Chapters 13 through 20 in Section III belong in two categories. Selections from his own writings in personal letters and reported research comprise Chapters 13 and 14, respectively. The remainder are mostly writings, events, or situations recognizing Moseley's life achievements, as viewed since his death 50 years ago. These individual accounts involving memorials, tributes, recognitions, and commemorations have become his legacy, as reported in Chapters 15 through 20. Those commentaries provide a comprehensive summation of his life.

With these useful guidelines at hand, a factual account of Moseley's life can be appreciated. At the same time, this account is punctuated with his eccentricities that should make this journey also amusing.

Ronald L. Stuckey

Edwin Lincoln Moseley
(1865–1948)

I. The Formative Years in Michigan
(1865–1889)

1865. Born 29 March 1865, Union City, Branch County, Michigan.

186?–1880. Attended the public schools of Union City, Michigan; influenced in the third grade by a teacher who took students on field trips and identified plants.

1876. Suffered from an illness he called "malaria" and was away from classes for some time.

1880. Graduated from Union City High School; at age 15 years, was the youngest member by two years of the first graduation class of 14 students.

1881. Continued for an additional year in high school and engaged in research, because of being under age for admission to The University of Michigan.

1882. Enrolled in The University of Michigan, Ann Arbor.

1885. Graduated with degree Master of Arts from The University of Michigan; the youngest member of the class of 82 students.

1885. Began career of teaching science and mathematics at Central High School, Grand Rapids, Michigan.

1885. Joined Kent Scientific Institute and was appointed curator of its natural history collections.

1887. Published first paper, a small pamphlet titled, *Lists of the Birds, Mammals, Birds' Eggs and Desiderata of Michigan Birds in the Museum of the Kent Scientific Institute, Grand Rapids, Mich[igan]*. Grand Rapids, Michigan. 32 pp., 1 pl.

1887. Resigned teaching position at Central High School, Grand Rapids, Michigan.

1887. Invited on the Steere Scientific Expedition to the Philippine Islands for 12 months under the leadership of Professor Joseph B. Steere of The University of Michigan (August 1887-July 1888).

1888. Traveled widely in China and Japan.

1889. Returned to Michigan and tutored private students.

II. *The Science-Teaching Years in Sandusky High School (1889–1914)*

1889. Appointed teacher of science, Sandusky High School, Sandusky, Ohio (September).

1890. Toured Europe with Dr. Charles Graefe, president of the Sandusky Board of Education, to obtain ideas for a natural history museum.

1891. Described two new species of flycatchers (birds) from the Island of Negros, Philippines (*The Ibis* 3: 46-47).

1891. Opened a museum of natural history in the Sandusky High School, as approved by the Board of Education [see Chapter 12, page 165].

1891. Began study of the local flora with students listing 448 species of plants growing wild within 10 miles of the school; gave prizes the following spring to students that autumn to stimulate botanical study and increase the list of plants.

1892. Left for Chicago en route to Denver, Colorado, to be a part of a camping party for several days in the Rocky Mountains (3 August). His story, "Long's Peak at sunset and a night on the mountain" was printed in the *Sandusky Daily Register*, 25, 26, 28, 29 November.

1894. Took botany class to obtain plant specimens on South Bass and Green Islands in Lake Erie; had picnic dinner in park grove at town of Put-in-Bay (June).

1894. Presented first paper, "Attractions for a scientist in the vicinity of Sandusky" at an Ohio State Academy of Science Meeting, Columbus, Ohio; elected secretary of the Ohio State Academy of Science (28 December).

1895. Conducted the excursions of the summer field meeting of the Ohio State Academy of Science, touring sites of interest in the vicinity of Sandusky (2,3 July).

1895. Took botany class on excursion to Vermilion and Oberlin, Ohio, as described by Ralph H. McKelvey (October) [see Chapter 6, page 67].

1895–1903. Served as secretary of the Ohio State Academy of Science.

1897. Donated 200 vascular plant specimens from northern Ohio to the Herbarium of The Ohio State University, Columbus (February).

1898. Explored, with the help of two students, the caves on South Bass Island (March).

1898. Offered position as teacher of natural history in the Toledo Public Schools, to which he declined (July).

1898. Began tracing the submerged valleys of the preglacial streams through Sandusky Bay.

1898. Published evidence that water in western Lake Erie was deepening because the land was subsiding at 2.14 feet per century (*Lakeside Magazine* 1(9): 14-20).

1898. Visited the Oak Openings west of Toledo, Ohio, for the first time.

1899. Published "Sandusky flora. A catalogue of the flowering plants and ferns growing without cultivation in Erie County, Ohio, and the peninsula and islands of Ottawa County." *Ohio State Academy of Science, Special Papers*, No. 1. 167 pp. [see Chapter 9, page 104].

1901. Left for Buffalo to spend remainder of vacation at the Pan-American Exposition (10 August).

1901. Traced pattern of currents in Sandusky Bay (October).

1901-1904. Surveyed Sandusky Bay to determine the natural river valley, using 100 high school boys, to probe the area when covered with ice.

1902. Presented two lectures at the Lake Laboratory of The Ohio State University, Sandusky Fish Hatchery, Sandusky (summer). The titles were "Physiographic Features of the Sandusky Region" and "Collecting in the Philippine Islands."

1902. Traced course of preglacial Huron River valley in Erie County, with help of high school students.

1903. Elected president of the Ohio State Academy of Science (27 November).

1904. Studied the geology and flora of Cedar Point, Ohio [see Chapter 9, page 107].

1904. Delivered Presidential Address, "Formation of Sandusky Bay and Cedar Point," at the annual meeting of the Ohio State Academy of Science, Cleveland, Ohio (25 November).

1905. Began, with the help of students, to determine the cause of milk sickness.

1906. Toured Europe to obtain specimens for Sandusky High School Museum (July).

1906. Determined that the white snakeroot plant, *Eupatorium rugosum*, was the cause of milk sickness [see Chapter 9, page 110].

1910. Completed report of the routes of the river valleys in Sandusky Bay; later the report was destroyed by fire when the City Building burned.

1912. Wrote story of his being "Lost" on the day after Christmas in Pioneer, Louisiana, which was printed in *The Fram* 12(3): 6-8. 1913. January.

1913. Attempted studies fail to determine outlet of Bellevue's sink holes and underground river; suspected to be at Castalia Blue Hole.

1914. Resigned position as science teacher of Sandusky High School (June).

III. The Science-Teaching Years at Bowling Green College (1914–1936)

1914. Became a one-man science faculty in the newly founded Bowling Green State Normal College, (September); taught the biological and physical science courses.

1916. Appointed to the Board of Health, Bowling Green, Ohio (12 January).

1917. Reported to have published *Nature Study*, a textbook for junior high and grammar schools. World Book Co., Yonkers, New York; book probably not published, as no additional information about it has been located. (see "Edwin L. Moseley," pp. 269-270, In Charles S. Van Tassel, ed. 1917. *The Ohio Blue Book, or Who's Who in the Buckeye State: A Cyclopedia of Biography...*).

1918. Elected an Associate of the American Ornithologists' Union.

1919. Published *Trees, Stars, and Birds: A Book of Outdoor Science*. World Book Co., Yonkers-on-Hudson, New York. 404 pp.

1922. Saw the Great Salt Lake for the second time en route to San Francisco and Honolulu, Hawaii, for two months (June, July); while there visited his sister Clara (Moseley) Sutherland; wrote first will.

1922. Studied marine life on the Hawaiian Islands; discovered a new fish; a year later it was named *Gonorhynchus moseleyi* by David Starr Jordan and John Otterbein Snyder.

1923. Began teaching only biological science courses; physical science courses taught by newly hired Dr. Clare S. Martin (1888-1982).

1923. Obtained additional data toward mapping the preglacial valley from near Huron, across Erie County, and into Huron County (August).

1924. Studied birds for five days in northeastern Louisiana with host Robert Oldham (January).

1927. Published *Our Wild Animals*. D. Appleton and Co., New York. 310 pp.

1928. Began study of tree rings and their relation to rainfall [see Chapter 10, page 127].

1928. Published "Flora of the Oak Openings West of Toledo." *Proceedings of The Ohio Academy of Science* 8: 79-134. *Special Paper*, No. 20.

1929. Had not missed a day from classes as a student or teacher in 50 years, because of illness (reported, *Sandusky Register*, 21 July 1929; *Toledo Times*, 10 May 1936).

1931. Received recognition from U.S. Biological Survey for contributing reports on bird migration for 45 years; Moseley continued the work until 1943, 57 years.

1932. Opened to the public for the last time, the Museum in the Sandusky High School then was moved to attic storage (December).

1932. Served as vice-president of the Wilson Ornithological Club.

1933. Published *Other Worlds*. D. Appleton and Co., New York. xi, 231 pp.

1934. Spent vacation in West Carroll Parish, Louisiana (December).

1935. Visited museums in Chicago and attended scientific meetings in St. Louis (December).

1936. Designated Professor Emeritus of Biology upon retirement from teaching; named Curator of the University Museum (June).

1936. Traveled to Pacific Coast by way of North Dakota and Montana, and returned by way of southern California and Kansas (*Papers Michigan Academy of Science, Arts and Letters* (1943) 29: 23-29. 1944).

IV. The Emeritus Years as Curator of the Museum (1936–1948)

1937. Honored at banquet for his 72nd birthday and upon becoming the University's first Professor Emeritus; address delivered by President Homer B. Williams (30 March) [see Chapter 3, page 19].

1937. Announced for the first time that 46-year weather cycle existed based on studies of growth rings in tree stumps; statement made at retirement banquet (30 March).

1938. Moved natural history museum of 17,000 specimens from Sandusky High School to display cases in the Science Building at Bowling Green State University.

1939. Read paper on predicting rainfall 90 years into the future based on width of growth rings in tree stumps and lake water levels; presented at annual Michigan Academy Meeting (17 March); information so intriguing that it was reported in the *New York Times*, 19 March, 10 August.

1939. Received wide publicity for predicting the wet summer of 1943 in Michigan and Ohio.

1939. Presented invited paper on "Long-time Forecasts of Ohio River Floods" to The Ohio Academy of Science.

1941. Published *Milk Sickness Caused by White Snakeroot*. Ohio Academy of Science and The Author, Bowling Green, Ohio. iv, 171 pp.

1943. Awarded Doctor of Humane Letters by Bowling Green State University, first faculty member to be so honored (13 August).

1945. Predicted drought in midwestern United States for 1947 (September).

1946-1947. Spent time during winter months in Mexico at Monterrey and Mexico City.

1948. Predicted future droughts for 1950 and 2037 (4 January).

1948. Traveled to California with William Love family of Louisville, Ohio.

1948. Traveled to Mexico via Louisiana and Texas; was staying in Ohio in late April with friends, Kelley Hale, M.D., Wilmington, and Carl Schmidt, Dayton, when illness came.

1948. Died 6 June 1948 of a coronary thrombosis in Johnston Hospital, Bowling Green State University; funeral at Young's Memorial with burial in Oak Grove Cemetery, Bowling Green, Ohio (8 June) [see Chapter 15, page 209].

Aerial view of the Bowling Green State University campus, about 1930.

The names of the buildings, progressing in an inverse U arrangement from the lower left to the lower right are: Shatzel Hall; Williams Hall; Men's Gymnasium (upper left corner); the Administration Building (top center) with the Science Building (Moseley Hall) attached to the left and the Teacher Training School Building (Hanna Hall) attached to the right; the Power Plant, behind the Administration Building; the Library at center right; and the President's House farther to the right. The streets were removed in 1958.

(*The Key*, BGSU, 1960, p. 44; Stuckey Collection)

Highlights in the History of Bowling Green State University, Bowling Green, Ohio

1907. The town of Bowling Green, Ohio, began efforts to secure a state normal (teacher training) school for its community.

1910. Governor Judson Harmon signed the Lowrey Bill for state support to establish additional normal schools, including one in northwestern Ohio; Bowling Green officially was chosen as the site (10 November).

1911. First Board of Trustees appointed by Governor Harmon for the new normal school at Bowling Green (17 May).

1912. The Board of Trustees chose the name, Bowling Green State Normal College (16 February) and offered the Presidency to Homer B. Williams, superintendent of schools in Sandusky, Ohio (accepted 23 May).

1914. The College adopted a curriculum for teacher training, and classes were taught by the original 10 faculty members and four critic teachers, all selected by President Williams; without buildings, portions of the nearby Armory Building were rented for class instruction.

1916. The Science Building (later named Moseley Hall) was completed in the spring and housed classes in science, agriculture, industrial arts, and the four upper grades of the teacher training school.

1929. Name was changed to Bowling Green State College and the degrees of Bachelor of Arts and Bachelor of Science were established upon passage of the Emmons-Hanna Act (2 April), President Williams having drafted the original text of the bill. This Act also changed the school from a two-year to a four-year degree-granting institution.

1935. Name changed to Bowling Green State University, with establishment of the Colleges of Liberal Arts, Education, Business Administration, and a graduate program leading to the Master of Arts.

1937. President Williams at age 70 retired (1 July) and was succeeded by Roy E. Offenhauer, superintendent of schools in Lima, Ohio, and formerly principal of Sandusky High School and superintendent of the Erie County schools.

1938. President Offenhauer died as a result of a truck-automobile accident (29 December); was replaced by Williams as acting president until April 1939.

1939. Frank J. Prout, superintendent of schools in Sandusky and the immediate past-president of the University's Board of Trustees, was appointed as its third President (April).

1948. Over the campus loud speaker, President Prout announced the death of emeritus faculty member Edwin Lincoln Moseley (6 June), his longtime friend whom he first met at age 15 on a farm south of Sandusky.

—Compiled by RLS primarily from James Robert Overman. 1967. *The History of Bowling Green State University*. Bowling Green University Press, Bowling Green, Ohio. 234 pp.

The Administration Building completed in 1915 on the Bowling Green State Normal College campus.

(Taken by Leora I. Shuey, 1922; Stuckey Collection)

Personality & Career

Section I

Faculty of 1908, Sandusky High School.

Back Row: l. to r., **Edwin L. Moseley**, R. D. Crout, W. A. Richardson.

Middle Row: Bessie Taylor, Elsie Denham, Charlotte Field, Clyde Holt, Clara Frick.

Front Row: unidentified, Edwina Black, Homer B. Williams, Augusta Erckner, George C. Dietrich.

(*The Fram*, June 1908; taken by Wildenthaler; Sandusky Library Archives)

**Moseley in his laboratory at BGSU,
where he studied cross-sections of tree trunks.**

(Josephine True, *Nature Magazine* 38: 37. 1945;
Photo Service, BGSU; Stuckey Collection)

Educator of Many Students

CHAPTER ONE

Josephine True [1945]

Josephine True, a senior student in education at Bowling Green State University, wrote this article in 1945 based on interviews she had with Professor Moseley. She was a special reporter and managing editor of the Bee Gee News *(1943–1944).*

In *Ripley's Believe It or Not!*, a few years ago, a sketch appeared of Professor Edwin Lincoln Moseley, one of Ohio's patriarchs of natural science, with the statement that he had taught school for 48 years without missing a class. The 79-year-old professor who established this outstanding record is now Professor Emeritus of Biology and Curator of the Museum of Natural History at Bowling Green State University. Moseley pioneered in the teaching of natural science by the experimental method. During 25 years at the high school in Sandusky, Ohio, followed by 22 years at the college in Bowling Green, Ohio, he has taught more than 6,000 young men and women.

Moseley is more than a teacher. He is a practical scientist, and only recently have some of the significant contributions of his painstaking and continuous research become fully apparent. As a young high school teacher of 22, Moseley began a program of research that he has followed conscientiously to the present. Early in his teaching career he applied the stimulus of practical scientific problems to the classroom and encouraged his students to join him in research.

Although nearly 80, Moseley continues his work with characteristic vigor. In recent years he has devoted much time to perfecting theories of long-range weather forecasting by means of tree rings. Daily he is in his laboratory or working with his extensive museum collection on the Bowling Green campus. He has become one of the inspiring figures, a slight, erect, old gentleman with a white beard, an absorbed manner, and intense, observing eyes.

• • •

While teaching at Central High School in Grand Rapids, Michigan, Moseley began to use an experimental method of teaching natural science to high school students. Later, at Sandusky, Ohio, he put his ideas into practice. It was not an uncommon sight to see the young teacher taking his students over many miles to view some phenomenon of nature, or to display or experiment with some fact that had been learned in class. They went by electric car, by horse and buggy, by train, and by boat. No phase of natural science was too challenging for Moseley to bring before his students. They visited quarries, where they studied rock formations; they observed constellations; they identified plants, animals, birds, and all wildlife.

Dr. Frank J. Prout, President of Bowling Green State University, and once one of Moseley's students, said, "I doubt that very many students have had the opportunity to be guided in scientific thinking during high-school days by as fine a thinker as Dr. Moseley."

During Prout's days at the Sandusky High School, Moseley was tracing the submerged valleys of Sandusky Bay, which is today one of the most important loading and unloading areas on Lake Erie. At the time Prout's teacher began his study, it was extremely difficult for deep-water vessels to enter and leave, because of the shallowness of the Bay.

By a consistent and thorough survey of the depth at different areas, Moseley traced a channel out through the Bay that could, with a little blasting, be used for deep-water traffic. Members of his classes helped the young teacher with this work. They would drill holes through the ice and measure the depth of the water and thickness of the soft mud under the water. Boys and girls of his classes thus learned how preglacial ledges were formed, where to expect them, and other information concerning rock formation.

Chapter 1 • Educator of Many Students

It was at Sandusky that the scientist began his collection of wild plants, which in time included the largest number of indigenous species ever to be obtained from such a small area. This research was embodied in a paper, "Sandusky flora," published by the Ohio State Academy of Science in 1899. Some specimens for the collection were brought by interested students, who were offered small rewards for each new addition to the collection.

In 1904 Moseley was elected president of the Ohio State Academy of Science after having served as secretary of that organization for the previous nine years. In that year he read his paper on the formation of Sandusky Bay and Cedar Point. This paper was later used for study in several colleges.

• • •

During his 25-year stay in Sandusky, Moseley applied himself to a number of other major research problems. The scourge of milk sickness was then a mystery to all who studied it, and Moseley, after years of the most painstaking effort, identified it with the white snakeroot, a plant on which cattle grazed. Much of the poison in the plant entered the milk of the cows that had eaten it. Abraham Lincoln's mother had died of milk sickness, and many other lives were taken by the disease during the days of the pioneers.

Milk sickness affected both men and cattle, being called the "trembles" in the latter. Various superstitions were attached to it, which made the problem of tracing the cause more difficult. Moseley spent years traveling to farms in regions where the disease was reported, questioning, observing, experimenting, until he finally determined the answer. While relatively rare today, the disease occasionally is reported, and Moseley journeys to any point to confirm that the cause is the wild snakeroot plant.

Moseley's collection of natural-history specimens at Bowling Green State University was begun at Sandusky. By travel, by trading with other museums, and by consistent collecting year by year, he added to it until today it is one of the high points of scientific interest at the University. Included are a botanical collection of more than 3,000 species, more than 600 mounted birds from all over the world, interesting minerals and fossils, mounted mammals from the north-central states, a large number of marine invertebrates, and a collection of reptiles and marine fishes. Natural-history specimens collected by him may be seen in considerable numbers in the British Museum, London; National Museum, Washington, D.C.; American Museum, New York City; Museum of Natural History, Chicago; and other museums.

Dr. Homer B. Williams, who had been superintendent of schools in Sandusky, was asked to accept the presidency of the new Bowling Green State Normal School when it was established in 1912. With him he brought Moseley to head the science department. For 22 years Moseley conducted classes at Bowling Green, watching the growth of a small normal school to a state university. Here he continued his work with milk sickness along with a new major project, long-range weather prediction. By a study of tree rings and their relative widths, he determined that a 90.4-year precipitation cycle existed. He knew that tree-ring widths are controlled mainly by the precipitation in the growing season of the year when the ring was formed. He began by collecting cross-sections from ancient tree stumps from a wide area, often going into the woods himself to work with saw and axe. His laboratory is filled with polished sections from mighty trees brought from many states.

It is a tedious task to count rings made by trees because of their somewhat indefinite demarcations and variations in width. Complicating the problem is the fact that precipitation is not the only factor that determines their growth. Soil, location, amount of sunlight, attacks by parasites, and fire affect the growth of the tree.

The manner in which Moseley conducted his study of about 350 stumps from nine different states was as follows: First he located the ring for 1890 and set a pin on its outer border. Then he would count 45 rings toward the center (half of the 90.4-year cycle) and set another pin, and so on as far as he could go toward the center. Moving to the outside, he would set the pin next to the 1890 ring in the 1935 ring. It was essential to know when the tree was sectioned.

Once he had the trunk divided into periods, he could relate the thicknesses to each other, and has been able to determine, with surprising accuracy to date, the rainfall picture for the next 90.4 years. Moseley's work presents many practical angles to farmers, who already have begun using the information in crop planning. Professor Andrew E. Douglass, director of the Steward Observatory at the University of Arizona, had pioneered in tree-ring studies, and it was from his publications that Moseley gained much insight into this approach for research.

Moseley was a good teacher as well as a competent scientist. Probably the one word that would best account for his success is meticulousness. If genius is "the infinite capacity for taking pains," then surely the title goes to Edwin L. Moseley.

Moseley says the cardinal principle in teaching nature is to have the courage and curiosity to take students out-of-doors and let them study for themselves. At the third-grade level he became interested in botany through the efforts of a teacher who took her pupils on outdoor field trips and introduced them to plants that they should know. This approach opened an entirely new world to the small boy, and he believed that it provided a firm foundation of curiosity and interest for his later work along these lines. If the natural sciences are taught to boys and girls, he contends, they will early learn to appreciate and be familiar with their natural environment. They will realize why things happen as they do, and will not have their conceptions hampered by foolish ignorance and superstitions.

In an article written for the college newspaper, the *Bee Gee News*, 20 January 1921, Moseley said, "The educational processes commonly employed rely too much on books and recitations. In order that the child may understand, he must use his hands and senses as well as his brain." He gave several examples of people's being grossly ignorant of unusual phenomena just "over the hill" from them. In one instance a Canadian friend had lived for several years only a few miles from Niagara Falls and had never seen the cataract. Moseley thinks this is one of the worst of sins that man can commit against himself. If he taught his students nothing else, the professor showed them how to see and understand.

On 29 March 1937, Moseley celebrated his 72nd birthday. At a banquet given in his honor, the educator was named the first emeritus professor at Bowling Green State University, and at the same time was designated Curator of the University Museum. That evening, he stated in his after-dinner speech that he had but one regret, that he had not given enough praise to pupils who had earned it.

In 1943, Professor Moseley at the age of 78 was awarded an honorary degree of Doctor of Humane Letters by the University he had served so many years. He is the first faculty member of the University to be so honored. At 79 years of age, after teaching for 48 years, Moseley remains a student, ever seeking new knowledge. He was one of America's outstanding authorities on plant and animal life.

Chapter 1 • Educator of Many Students

—Modified and edited by RLS from Josephine True. 1945. "Edwin Lincoln Moseley: The biography of an educator." *Nature Magazine* 38: 37-39.

Josephine True, Managing Editor, *Bee Gee News* (1944).

Jean Harshman (seated).

(*The Key*, BGSU, 1944, p. 136)

Josephine True, a native of Willard, Huron County, Ohio, graduated with a B. S. in education from Bowling Green State University (1944). As a sophomore transfer student, she became a staff member of the *Bee Gee News*, served initially as a news reporter, then special reporter, columnist, and managing editor during her senior year. She was a teacher in the high school at Shelby, Ohio, before enrolling in The Ohio State University, where she earned an M. A. in English Literature (1946). Most of her college teaching career was in Cleveland at the Cuyahoga Community College, where she taught English literature. Under her married name of Dehn, she received a Ph. D. from Kent State University in 1985. During the same year, she retired from teaching.

Front entrance to the Science Building on the campus.

(*The Beegee*, Yearbook of the State Normal College, Bowling Green, 1918, p. [16])

Graduating Class of Union City High School, 1880.

Standing: l. to r., A. Harshman Harrison, Lorenzo D. Cochran,
 Webster Cook (teacher), Elma F. Lynn, M. V. Rork (superintendent),
 Norris A. Cole, Anna West (teacher), **Edwin L. Moseley**.

Seated: William H. Brumfield, Robert H. Baker, William H. Bauer,
 Elbert L. Page, John D. H. Wallace, Ward C. Walker,
 George E. Willitts.

Seated in Center: Edward C. Wisner, Jay P. Lee.

(M. Glesmann and D. Evert, Union City, Michigan; Niederhofer Collection)

Formative Years in Michigan

CHAPTER TWO

Relda E. Niederhofer

Born 29 March 1865, 11 days before the end of the Civil War, Edwin Lincoln Moseley was named for the wartime president, Abraham Lincoln. He was the last of nine children born to William and Sophia (Bingham) Moseley of Union City, Branch County, Michigan. His parents came to this small town in the 1840s, undoubtedly choosing this location because William's cousin, Col. Thomas Moseley, originally of Pittsfield, Massachusetts, had located in the village to operate the Union Iron Company.[10]

Edwin was a serious, studious child, a born scientist. Before learning to read, he could count to a very high number. Merchants in his home town often asked him to solve problems which puzzled them, and his family envisioned the time when he would possibly be a professor of mathematics.[7] During his early youth, he was inspired by meeting and hearing such people as Edward Everett Hale, Henry Ward Beecher, Mark Twain, Frances Willard, John B. Gough, and J. T. Sunderland.[9] In later life, he credited his enthusiasm for science to his third-grade teacher, who took her students on field trips and introduced them to the common plants. During boyhood days, he kept in his room specimens of wildlife, birds' eggs, and plants.[8]

At age 11, Moseley suffered from an illness he called malaria, and he missed classes for a while but from that time until retirement, he never missed a class, either as a teacher or student, a fact which prompted Ripley in 1934 to include a note about him in his famous series of features.

Chapter 2 • Formative Years in Michigan

In high school Edwin studied zoology, physiology, philosophy, Greek, and Latin. He read all 12 books of Virgil's *Aeneid*.[7] Family member Mrs. Elizabeth (Brown) Brooks speculated that two of her books that had been owned by family members may have been available to Edwin before he entered The University of Michigan. *Adventures in Patagonia* by Titus Coan was sent to Sophia Moseley in 1880. Titus Coan, who was married to Lydia Bingham, Sophia's sister, wrote a chapter in the book about Charles Darwin and the voyage of the *Beagle*. Another book was the *Private Journal of the Voyage to the Pacific Ocean* and *Residence at the Sandwich Islands in the Years 1822, 23, 24, and 25* by C. S. Stewart. Both books contain vivid descriptions of the voyages and observations of nature.[11]

At 15, Moseley was the youngest student in his high school class when he graduated in 1880.[7] This class, the first to graduate from Union City High School, had 13 boys and one girl.[10] At graduation, the local newspaper, *The Union City Register* of 10 July 1880, recorded:

> ...not one member uses tobacco in any form or drinks malt or alcoholic beverages. In fact, it is just such a class as our citizens will often refer to when future classes come upon the stage. Each individual member of this class is intellectually strong, as a reading of their orations will show, and we have a perfect right to expect of them that they will write their names high up on the scroll of the nation's best, bravest, and wisest men....

Each member of the graduating class presented an oration that appeared in the *Union City Register*, 10 July 1880. Moseley's presentation[1] is reprinted at the end of this chapter.

Too young by a year to be accepted by The University of Michigan, Moseley took postgraduate courses and did much personal research in the high school the year

Union City High School, Union City, Michigan, about 1880.

(M. Glesmann and D. Evert, Union City, Michigan; Niederhofer Collection)

following graduation. He then entered The University of Michigan, where his scholastic record was so brilliant that he received a master's degree after four years instead of the usual bachelor's degree. He was then only 20 years old, and again, he was the youngest of 83 students in the graduating class, and one of two receiving a master's degree.[10] Moseley quickly learned to be thrifty and was able to accomplish much for himself by selling magazines, eventually purchasing a fine foot-power saw with which he fashioned brackets, photograph frames, and fancy ornaments for sale.[7] Except for $150 which he had when he entered, he earned his way through the University.[10]

For two school years, 1885-1887, Moseley taught science and mathematics in Central High School at Grand Rapids, Michigan. At the same time he became an active member of the Kent Scientific Institute of that city and curator of its natural history collections in the high school building. He had printed in 1887 a 32-page booklet listing the birds, mammals, and birds' eggs in the Museum of the Institute in Grand Rapids.[2]

With some hesitation Moseley relinquished his position at Central High School to accept an invitation of Joseph B. Steere (1842-1940), Professor of Zoology at The University of Michigan, to accompany him on a scientific expedition to the Philippine Islands.[6] This expedition, which had been contemplated for several years, gave Moseley an opportunity for extensive travel, enabling him to see life in nearly every part of the Philippine Archipelago, as well as Japan and China. Moseley was a member of a party of five that left in 1887 and spent from two to six weeks on each of the 15 large islands. More than 50 new species of birds and mammals were discovered in the Philippines.[3] Among them from the Island of Negros were two birds, *Cryptolopha nigrorum* and *Abrornis olivacea*, both flycatchers, that Moseley named and described as new to science.[5] A new species of kingfisher from the Island of Negros was named by Steere as *Actenoides moseleyi* in honor of his student companion.[4] Many of the specimens were distributed to museums throughout the world.

During the latter portion of the trip, Moseley visited Japan and China on his own before returning to Michigan in 1888. He then took a year tutoring students privately.[7] A position for a teacher of science became available in Sandusky, Ohio and upon leaving Michigan in 1889, Moseley taught at the Sandusky High School for the next 25 years.

CHAPTER 2 • FORMATIVE YEARS IN MICHIGAN

Steere expedition to the Philippines, 1887.

Seated: l. to r., **E. L. Moseley**, J. B. Steere, other man unidentified.
Standing: all unidentified.

(Bentley Historical Library)

Joseph Beal Steere.

Professor of Zoology
The University of Michigan.

(Taken in 1877, by Bigelow; Bentley Historical Library)

References

1. 1880. Anonymous. "The Orations." *Union City Register*, 10 July, p. 4.

2. 1887. Edwin L. Moseley. *Lists of the Birds, Mammals, Birds' Eggs, and Desiderata of Michigan Birds in the Museum of the Kent Scientific Institute, Grand Rapids, Mich[igan]*. Grand Rapids, Michigan. 32 pp., 1 pl.

3. 1890. Joseph B. Steere. *A List of the Birds and Mammals Collected by the Steere Expedition to the Philippines, with Localities, and with Brief Preliminary Descriptions of Supposed New Species.* The University of Michigan, Ann Arbor. 30 pp.

4. 1891. Joseph B. Steere. "Ornithological results of an Expedition to the Philippine Islands in 1887 and 1888." *The Ibis*, Sixth Series 3: 301-306, pls. VII, VIII.

5. 1891. Edwin L. Moseley. "Descriptions of two new species of flycatchers from the Island of Negros, Philippines." *The Ibis*, Sixth Series 3: 46,47, pl. II.

6. 1893. Anonymous. *Annual Report of the Board of Education of the City of Sandusky, Ohio for the School Year Ending August 31st, 1893*. I. F. Mack & Bro., Printers, Sandusky, Ohio. 340 pp. (see pages 130,131).

7. 1937. [Ivan E. Lake]. "Biographical sketch of Prof. Edwin L. Moseley." *Daily Sentinel-Tribune*, Bowling Green, 31 March, p. 5.

8. 1943. Moran Tudury. "Long-range weatherman. An Ohio scientist with a remarkable record of accuracy, gives C. G. readers a forecast of dry and wet periods in years ahead." *Country Gentleman* 113(11): 12, 38, 40. November.

9. 1945. Josephine True. "Edwin Lincoln Moseley: The biography of an educator." *Nature Magazine* 38: 37-39.

10. 1980. Mary Alaniz. "Union City graduate achieves success as a professor at Bowling Green University." *Coldwater Daily Reporter*, 9 July, p. 3.

11. 1981. Mrs. Elizabeth Brooks. Letter to Relda E. Niederhofer, 18 November.

"Knowledge"
Oration Delivered by Moseley at High School Graduation [1880]

Deprive man of what he knows, and what would he be? Think of a man that does not know he perceives, does not know he is. Since knowledge makes the chief difference between man and the brute, of what importance is knowledge.

Let us consider knowledge as connected with the acquirement of property. A number of the very rich men of the world were once poor. They first obtained an education and after that made a rapid acquisition of wealth. But wealthy men are not always well educated. Indeed the great men, the wise men, are never very wealthy, for they aspire to something higher than money. But no man has acquired wealth without at least a knowledge of the particular business from which he has obtained it.

Turn to the manifestation of knowledge in art. View this building, behold its arches and its proportions. Is there not beauty in it? Stand close to its wall and look up its towering columns. If there were no greater, you would even call it grand. Go to Europe. Visit the magnificent palaces, the majestic cathedrals. Go to Egypt. Behold the rising pyramids. Then you will say there is beauty and grandeur in architecture.

Conceive yourself to be in an art gallery. Here in marble is Columbus before Isabella, her delicately embroidered robe wrought out in marble while his face portrays the hope of his soul. Here again he stands on America, a happy man whose knowledge and perseverance made him the discoverer of this fair continent. Here on canvas before Galileo stands the poet of poets and the great astronomer through his telescope shows to Milton the moon. Here before the fireplace sits a boy studying by the light of the fire. Here kneels a negro looking forth into the future with fear and hope, his fetters of slavery stricken off. Beside him stands the boy of the last picture, now a man, whose earnest face tells you it is Abraham Lincoln. Passing on we behold a bust dug from the ruins of Rome, supposed to be one of the Caesars, and the mind wonders if it is the great Julius. Thus looking at paintings and statues we think of the knowledge and patience of the artist that can execute such fine work, portray the expression in the face of the feelings in the soul, and convey to us so much thought.

Next let us take up knowledge which is generally acquired in schools. Literature is the first thing to which the student devotes his attention. A knowledge of literature is of great importance since with the exception of speech it is the best known method of expressing thought, and the greater the knowledge of it the more easily and accurately thought is expressed. . . .

The study of mathematics is a source of greater discipline than the study of English. The lower mathematics are generally taught by those who do not understand them, the pupils being expected to solve problems by rule with the single view of getting the answers. The young student thus spends many years in an unsuccessful attempt to understand that which might be acquired in much less time. But while the methods of teaching mathematics differ widely, mathematics principles are eternal and upon mathematical demonstration the mind rests with a feeling of security.

Next in order is the interesting study of nature. In this the scientist takes delight and the world comfort. The various machines for changing the direction of force, the watch, the sewing machine, and the reaper, the few grains of powder that heave up huge rocks as the giant would toss a pebble, the telegraph by which men hold lightning under their thumbs and hurl it from place to place to do their bidding, are all the deductions of scientists from the laws in accordance with which forces govern matter. It is in the study of vegetable and animal life and the forces in matter that the mind of the honest man is convinced of the existence, greatness, and goodness of God.

What a vast store of knowledge do we find in history. Let the student of this reflect upon the results of his study; think of the nations that have risen, become corrupted, and fallen; of the civilization of cities, and the greatness of individuals; let him think of the untold millions that have lived and died, and be now one born like the rest. Since from history we learn the experiences of men and nations which have preceded, the study of history is a fit precedent to that of civil government and political economy which seek the highest welfare of the country.

• • •

Let us look for a moment at the cost of knowledge then finally at its value. To get knowledge takes time and through eternity the acquisition of knowledge will go on. Pecuniarily knowledge costs but little. He who spends one thousand dollars a year getting an education gets no better and generally not so good an education as he who spends two hundred. The question is asked, "If everyone devoted a considerable portion of his time to study, who would do the work necessary to satisfy the demands of the body, or in other words could we become a nation of students?" Think of the six hundred million dollars that this nation spends annually for liquor alone, think of the vast amount spent for tobacco and the luxuries of the table and of dress, think of the great loss from the impairing of health and the dulling of the senses and mental faculties produced by these things, think of the time misused at the billiard table, at cards, and in many other ways. On the other hand, think of the gain received from useful inventions, which constantly increases as we become more enlightened, and having carefully considered these things, you will agree with me in saying everyone might devote the greater portion of his time to study. If we can as a nation, we who will can as individuals. Without knowledge there is no happiness and, other things being equal, the more intelligent man is the happier he is. With history behind, conscience within, eternity before, man can ever advance and steadily ascend the successive steps of an unending progression.

Portrait of Moseley at his desk.

Painted by former student, Ralph H. McKelvey, and presented by an anonymous donor to BGSU on the occasion of the professor's retirement and birthday dinner, 30 March 1937.

(Archives, BGSU)

Lauded By University President

CHAPTER THREE

Homer B. Williams [1937]

Homer B. Williams (1865-1943), first president of Bowling Green State University (1912-1937), presented this address at the banquet dinner, 30 March 1937, honoring Professor Moseley upon his retirement from a lifetime of teaching many different courses in the sciences. Williams had been the superintendent of the Sandusky High School (1898-1913), where Moseley was the science teacher (1889-1914).

• • •

It has been my privilege to be closely associated with Professor Edwin Lincoln Moseley for the past 39 years, certainly long enough to know him well. I readily admit that he is *sui generis*; by that, I mean that I never knew a man just like him. Some people may think him peculiar. I would say he is different, but I have always found that he has "a good reason for the faith that is in him." He may have politely declined to partake of a late lunch as a guest in the president's home, or to remain after his regular hour for retiring, but it was done in such a way as to arouse one's admiration for his loyalty to his hygienic principles. He is the only man I have ever known of whom I can consistently say that he lives as well as he knows. I know, too, that for a man of rather frail physique, he has done a prodigious amount of work, and in all these years I have never known him to miss a class on account of illness. Possibly the rest of us might have accomplished more if we had been willing to follow his regimen.

I know also of his generosity to his students in their hours of illness and financial need, but he never let his left hand know what his right hand did, much less publish his benefactions. For example, Stuart Hamilton, a student, started to the Kansas harvest fields by "riding the rods" and was stricken with an attack of acute appendicitis at a railroad center in Bloomington, Illinois. Moseley hurried to him, engaged the best surgeon available, nursed the patient to health, and paid the bills, because the boy had no money and no credit. That boy is known today both at The University of Michigan and at the University of Chicago as a former prominent member of the faculty, and so I might mention other cases of like import for "their name is legion."

One only needs to read Palmer's *Ideal Teacher* or a more recent book, Bliss Perry's *And Gladly Teach*, to be impressed with the wonderful opportunities growing out of the relation of teacher and pupil. If the reader is a great teacher himself he may well become ecstatic over the possibilities. Emerson said he would travel ten miles anytime for a new idea. I cannot think of any achievement comparable to that of passing on to another mind a great truth of nature or principle of human relations in a way that will cause it to penetrate into the realm of appreciation and remain there forever. If you know anything more wonderful, what is it?

Within the past few days a collection of letters from Moseley's former students has come into my hands. I might in this address pay tribute to Moseley's ability as a teacher, but I would not be able to portray it so clearly and forcibly as does the testimony in these letters. . . . But here and now I should like to say in a sentence or two what I have always admired in him, and what I would continue to emphasize before prospective teachers or those not yet masters of the subjects they undertake to teach. It is this: Mastery of subject-matter is the *sine qua non* of teaching, and it should not be necessary to translate this Latin phrase before a college group. It means an indispensable condition. I say it without exaggeration: Moseley is the best exemplar of exact and thorough scholarship in his field that I have ever known in any type of school. I would say it has been the open sesame to his pedagogical greatness.

The third essential of the efficient life is one's contribution to progress. In this field of endeavor, Moseley ranks abreast to the best scholars of his day. I can take time to give only one illustration. For nearly a century, the people living in the vicinity of Castalia, Ohio, have been stricken at intervals with a disease called trembles in animals and milk sickness in human beings. The best medical authorities in the country were unable to ascertain the source of the trouble or treat the malady successfully. Moseley went to work on the problem. Everyone knew that human beings contracted the disease from the consumption of dairy products, but where did the cows get it? No one knew. Of Moseley's part in the study of trembles, I quote from an article by the botanist Albert A. Hansen of Purdue University which was published in the *Ohio Farmer* of 10 September 1927:

> One of the first scientists to establish definitely the relationship of a common plant to the disease was an Ohio man, Professor E. L. Moseley, now connected with Bowling Green State University. Although he worked with limited facilities, to him belongs the honor and credit of conducting the first satisfactory experiments to demonstrate that trembles in animals is due to grazing on a common woodland plant known as white snakeroot and that the poison enters the milk, causing human milk sickness.

Walter G. Sackett, of the Department of Hygiene and Bacteriology in the University of Chicago, wrote in the *Journal of Infectious Diseases* of March 1919: "Moseley in 1905 was the first to undertake anything in the way of a systematically organized study of trembles, according to our modern idea of what such experiments should be." It is not overestimating the pioneer efforts of Moseley in this field to rank his work as a distinct contribution to the public welfare. The prevalence of milk sickness extended to many sections of the United States. There need not be a recurrence of this serious malady anywhere, if the health authorities and public take proper precaution.

Another achievement illustrative of Moseley's influence directed toward the improvement of conditions in the freshwater fishing industry is worthy of particular mention. While living in Sandusky, Moseley became acquainted with the different species of fishes in Sandusky Bay and Lake Erie. Here was one of the largest freshwater fish markets in the world. When Leland Stanford Junior University ichthyologist David Starr Jordan (1851-1931) and members of the International Fish Commission were planning a visit to Sandusky several years ago, Jordan wired me some days before their arrival to arrange for Moseley to join his party in their study and investigation of conditions for freshwater fishes in and around Sandusky. Thus Jordan, the leading authority of his time on freshwater fish, sought Moseley's assistance in the important work of his Commission. This opportunity again was a fine tribute to Moseley's service to a great international problem [see publication note A, page 275].

Chapter 3 • Lauded by University President

In my professional experience, I have never known an educator, public school or university man or woman, who succeeded in popularizing his department in a community such as Moseley did in Sandusky. The following incident as related by Superintendent Roy E. Offenhauer now of Lima, Ohio, explains his achievement in this respect:

> When I came to Sandusky as principal of the high school, the high school assembly room was located on the second floor of the high school building. This building had four stairways, one in each corner. The laboratory was on the third floor. The assembly room was equipped with an elevated platform on which the teacher in charge sat during the study periods. At this particular period the teacher on duty was in the reference library in an alcove of the study hall and the platform was vacant. I mounted it to survey the study hall. The door to the stairway diagonally across the hall from the platform was open, and what did I see but a live snake ambling down the stairway and headed for the open door into the study hall. My first impulse was to rush across the room and close the door ahead of the snake, but I decided that might cause more consternation than the snake itself, and of the two evils, I would choose the lesser. His snakeship entered the room, crawled along to the fourth row of seats, selected a vacant seat, entwined his body in the openings in the cast-iron frame, projected his head several inches above the desk, and looked, as I thought, for other worlds to conquer. I confess I was scared stiff. This [moment] was the denouement of the plot. A girl across the aisle turned her book with the open side down on her desk, took hold of the reptile, untangled its folds from the iron part of the desk, caught it by the neck and carried it wriggling, that is, the snake did the wriggling, to the laboratory where she gave it to Professor Moseley, who, I fancy, rejoiced more over the one snake that was lost and found than over the ninety and nine that were safely in the fold. That incident, I do not believe, could have happened anywhere else in the United States. It was a harmless fox snake and the pupils knew it. No farmer in that locality would kill a fox snake, for Professor Moseley had taught the residents of the entire countryside that snakes of this variety were valuable aids on the farm and in the garden in destroying, as they do, small animal pests.

This estimate would be incomplete did I not include some mention of the versatility of Moseley. His breadth of scholarship and culture is not limited to science. I brought him here as a member of the original faculty. We could not afford a head for the several branches of science in which we attempted to offer courses in those early years, but owing to Moseley's command of so many fields of science, we got along quite admirably and at the same time developed standards of thoroughness that furnished a substantial background specialization and finer differentiation as the departments were separated and headed by specialists. In this University Moseley has taught courses in geography, hygiene, biology, physics, and other subjects which do not now occur to me. In the Sandusky High School, when regular teachers were absent, he taught geometry, astronomy, physiology, geology, English, and Latin, and taught them well. Because of his familiarity with so wide a range of science and because of his scholarly standards, he has rendered a service to this University which few men could have done so well.

Another characteristic of Moseley deserving of mention is *his devotion to science*. It is said of Alexander the Great that he died because no more worlds were available to conquer. The idea is unthinkable, but I have often wondered whether Moseley could continue to live if all scientific material were annihilated. In my mind I have always compared him with Louis Agassiz, to whom nothing in nature failed to make its appeal. Near the end of a mild winter many years ago, Moseley said to me, "Have you observed that dandelions have bloomed every month this winter on the high school campus?" Of course, I admitted that I had made no such observation, but they had. No man has ever lived with eyes more optically perfect to see animal and plant phenomena, or shall I rather say that such phenomena were in his soul and his eyes just reacted to the instincts of his soul? I think the latter is the better way to put it. In the great naturalist there is something akin to the poet. He sees so much that is only a blur to the prosaic eye.

Shakespeare has said, "Some men achieve greatness and some have greatness thrust upon them." By his industry, by his ability, by his love of nature, and by his singleness of purpose, Moseley has achieved high renown among scholars and the love and gratitude of thousands of students who have enjoyed the high privilege of sitting under his tuition. And now, Moseley, as a group of your colleagues and former students, we salute and congratulate you.

—Modified and edited by RLS from Homer B. Williams. 1937. "Dr. Williams lauds Moseley: teacher, author, scientist honored this week." *Bee Gee News* 21(26): 1, 2, 4. 31 March.

CHAPTER 3 • LAUDED BY UNIVERSITY PRESIDENT

Homer B. Williams.

(*The Key*, BGSU, 1960, p. 47)

Homer B. Williams (1865-1943), first president of Bowling Green State University, began with only the authority to establish a two-year teacher's program identified as Bowling Green State Normal College (1912), later renamed Bowling Green State College (1929), and Bowling Green State University (1935). He organized the courses of study that became the College of Education, selected the original faculty of 14, and submitted a plan for the buildings to the Board of Trustees. A Liberal Arts College was added (1929), and the College of Business Administration and Graduate School was organized (1935). He retired with a faculty of 173 individuals, 12 buildings, and 1,200 students. In June 1938, for his service to the public schools of Ohio and to the building of a credible University, Williams was awarded an honorary Doctor of Laws degree by Bowling Green State University.

Born 16 October 1865 on a farm near Mt. Ephraim, Noble County, Ohio, Homer B. Williams lived his entire life in the state, and received a B. A. from Ohio Northern University (1891), Ph. B. and M. A. from Baldwin Wallace College (1912), M. A. from Columbia University (1914) and Ph. D. from Ohio Northern University (1913) and Miami University (1914). He was a teacher in the rural and village schools (1885-1889), and superintendent of schools in Caldwell (1889-1892), Kenton (1892-1894), Cambridge (1894-1898), and Sandusky (1898-1913). Death came at 78 years, 22 September 1943, in Toledo, Ohio, following an illness of six weeks. Moseley served as one of his pallbearers; burial was in Oak Grove Cemetery next to the University campus in Bowling Green.

Chapter 3 • Lauded by University President

Roy E. Offenhauer.

(*The Key*, BGSU, 1960, p. 47)

Roy Ernest Offenhauer (1891-1938), second president of Bowling Green State University (1937-1938), adopted a tenure policy for the school during his short administration. As told by Williams in this Chapter, Offenhauer gave him the story of the snake entering the assembly room in Sandusky High School.

Born 10 August 1881 in Montezuma, Mercer County, Ohio, Offenhauer received a B. S. from Marion Normal College in Marion, Indiana (1903), B. A. from Otterbein College (1905), additional study at Miami University (1906) and Harvard University (1909), M. A. from Columbia University (1917), and an honorary D. Ped. from Ohio Northern University (1934). His teaching (1899-1902) and administrative (1905-1907) career began in the rural schools of Mercer County, following which he became principal of the high schools in Mount Vernon (1907-1909) and Sandusky (1909-1914). He then served as superintendent of the Erie County Schools (1914-1918), principal (1918-1924) and superintendent (1924-1937) of Lima High School, before becoming president of Bowling Green State University. His presidency was short-lived, as death came at 57 years, 29 December 1938, in a Findlay, Ohio, hospital following a tragic truck-auto accident on route 31 south of the town. Offenhauer presented a tribute to Moseley [see Chapter 20, page 258].

CHAPTER 3 • LAUDED BY UNIVERSITY PRESIDENT

References for Biographical Sketches

1917.   Charles S. Van Tassel, ed. "Roy Ernest Offenhauer," p. 180; "Homer B. Williams," p. 403. In *The Ohio Blue Book, or Who's Who in the Buckeye State: A Cyclopedia of Biography of Men and Women in Ohio.* Charles Summer Van Tassel, Toledo, Ohio. 479 pp.

1938.   Anonymous. "Dr. R. E. Offenhauer fatally hurt when truck-auto crash." *Sandusky Register*, 30 December, p. 1.

1943.   Anonymous. "Dr. Williams, former school head, stricken." *Sandusky Register-Star News*, 23 September, pp. 1, 10.

1943.   Anonymous. "Services for pioneer president were held Saturday afternoon. Dr. Williams dies in Toledo Hospital after long illness." *Bee Gee News*, 29 September, p. 1.

1943.   Editors. "Roy Ernest Offenhauer," p. 912. *Who Was Who in America.* A. N. Marquis Co., Chicago. vol. 1 (1897-1942): 1396 pp.

1967.   James Robert Overman. *The History of Bowling Green State University*, Bowling Green University Press, Bowling Green, Ohio. 234 pp.

1985.   Jim Nieman. "Williams saw BG through its beginning." *Daily Sentinel-Tribune*, Bowling Green, 23 August, p. A-4.

1985.   Jim Nieman. "Accident cut short Offenhauer's tenure." *Daily Sentinel-Tribune*, Bowling Green, 23 August, p. A-11.

CHAPTER 3 • LAUDED BY UNIVERSITY PRESIDENT

Residence of Homer B. Williams, first president of Bowling Green State University, on the campus in Bowling Green, Ohio.

(Archives, BGSU)

Moseley recording data in notebook; plant press beneath notebook.

(Taken 26 August 1924, by Mrs. Ruby G. Engle, Gibsonburg, Ohio; Niederhofer Collection)

The Inquiring Mind of a Teaching Scientist

Frank J. Prout [1959]

CHAPTER FOUR

Frank J. Prout (1883-1967), third president of Bowling Green State University (1939-1951), delivered these remarks at the dedication ceremony, 14 April 1959, during the presentation of a commemorative plaque and an oil portrait of the late Professor Moseley at the Sandusky High School. President Emeritus Prout was selected for this role because of his fifty years association with the Professor.

On the first October Saturday afternoon of 1898, as a youngster of 15 years I was gathering elderberries on the north end of our farm eight miles south of Sandusky. A stranger, gaunt and a bit disheveled by walking in the heat of this warm day, joined me. He introduced himself as Mr. Moseley of the Sandusky High School. I had read and heard of him. He had come to Sandusky in late August of 1889 as an applicant for a science teaching position. With considerable reluctance after a lengthy debate about whether he would make a good teacher, the Board of Education hired him. He soon became popular in the classroom, in the city, and in the county. This particular afternoon he had found on the nearby Ross Ransom farm a mammoth's tooth. He gave me the scientific story of that prehistoric age in which such monster animals lived. They were destroyed by the glaciers which pushed huge piles of rocks southward from the Arctic to mid-Ohio. In one of these piles of debris he had located this tooth. It was an interesting story, and it was my introduction to Professor Edwin Lincoln Moseley.

Chapter 4 • Inquiring Mind of a Teaching Scientist

Early on a Sunday afternoon, just a half century later, the telephone rang in my office at the University in Bowling Green. The message was from the head nurse at the University hospital. Moseley had just died. Through the loudspeaker on top of the administration building I transferred this message to the city and surrounding area. The local news editor put the story on the wires of the Associated Press. In ten minutes the editor of the *New York Times* called for confirmation. A similar inquiry came from the *San Francisco Chronicle*. These inquiries gave proof to the recognized greatness of the man.

I sat back in my chair for a few moments of deep, almost tearful reverie. I recalled that first meeting out on the farm. I thought how interesting it would have been if that October afternoon somehow I could have looked down the road of time and have had the proof that this gaunt and rather unpromising man would become known and famous the breadth of this land.

• • •

We loved his peculiarities. He was very economical, even stingy. He came to Sandusky wearing a reddish-colored suit of excellent quality, the gift of a friend in Grand Rapids, Michigan. He wore this suit, except in the hot summer months, for probably 10 years. He ate little or no meat. A bachelor, he cooked most of his meals in his room. Occasionally he went to a restaurant and would eat the untouched biscuits, pancakes, or other food left by the acquaintances with whom he sat. He would ask the waiter for a cup of hot water, then add catsup from the bottle on the table. This mixture was a tasty cup of tomato soup.

Moseley was not interested in women. They were no part of his social life. We know of only one exception. One evening he took a teacher to the Biemiller theater in Sandusky. When the play was over, he forgot she was with him and went home without her.

Moseley was very devoted to his students and they to him. He urged his talented students to go to college and helped them financially when help was needed. A very gifted orphan boy, Stuart Hamilton, in the summer before his senior year found a job in Kansas. Stuart became seriously ill with what we now know as appendicitis. In those early days we called it bowel complaint. It often resulted in peritonitis. Perhaps 90 percent of the cases were fatal. When Moseley learned of

Stuart's serious illness he hurried to his bedside, placed him in a hospital, employed a good physician, paid all bills, and brought him back to Sandusky.

• • •

I have said that Moseley was devoted to his students. In full measure they returned his devotion. They strove to please him. Establishing this fact is an incident that happened on the second floor of the high school about 2:30 in an early June afternoon of 1902. In his nature classes Moseley emphasized that our harmless snakes make a real contribution to us. The small garter snake destroys insect pests in the garden, and the four-foot-long fox snake lives on rats and mice. This snake was so destructive of these rats and mice that the federal government published a small pamphlet describing its value and urging its protection. Each spring Moseley was sure to have one or more of these fox snakes in his third-floor laboratory. The girls, as well as the boys, were taught to handle this snake and be friendly to it. On this warm June afternoon, one of these fox snakes got out of its cage, and came down the southwest stairway to our second-floor study hall. Between the first and second rows of seats it started up to the front of the room. Students, busily getting ready for the next day's lessons, looked at it and went back to work. Finally, one of the girls closed her book, stepped into the aisle, and picked up the snake right back of its head. It wound itself around her arm and she carried it back to its cage. Not one of the 120 students made any disturbance. No one would have been scolded if she had screamed and rushed out of doors. Not a murmur! When the dismissal bell rang, I asked the young lady in front of me why there had been no demonstration. Her reply was, "That would have displeased Moseley." I believe that could not have happened in any other place in America.

Moseley's greatness as a teacher lay in his emphasis on always searching for the reason of things. This technique led one of the students one day to ask where the water came from in the Castalia Blue Hole. Moseley promptly replied, "I wish we knew. Perhaps it comes from the underground river that flows under Bellevue." Then it was explained that Bellevue had no sewer system. The waste of that city was emptied into this underground river through holes bored straight down. Said the inquiring student, "Is there any way we can prove that?" Moseley took from one of his supply cases a bottle of red cochineal solution, each drop of which would color red perhaps a million drops of water. "If you will furnish a horse and buggy and go with me tomorrow afternoon to Bellevue, we will empty this solution into one of the vertical sewers." They made the trip. Then Monday after school they drove to the Blue Hole. They were delighted. The water was red. Thus did he ever emphasize the importance of searching for the reason of phenomena.

On weekends Moseley would take his classes on trips to study birds, flowers, plants, and trees. He had one of the most complete private herbaria in the state and a very extensive bird collection. They visited Kelleys Island and the stone quarries around Berea to study geology. These were popular and exciting excursions. An appropriate extract comes from a letter recently written to me by Mrs. Charles Kiefer:

> *I graduated from Sandusky High School in the class of 1905. I have many pleasant memories of the classes which Moseley taught. He made his students appreciate the wonders of nature in our field trips, which were always interesting. The geology class saw him tie a large fox snake to the picnic table at Cedar Point, which was later used in class. We made a trip to the glacial groves at Kelleys Island, where he explained their origin to us. In the evenings we studied with him the stars. There surely never will be another teacher like him. I am fortunate to have been one of his pupils.*

Truly, may it be said of him, "He was a great teacher." But his greatness was not confined to his classes. In all of the years after college, he was doing research work outside of high school. We must note four distinct achievements. 1. He was the first man scientifically to discover the cause of milk sickness. 2. He discovered and charted the preglacial rivers of Erie and adjoining counties. 3. He proved that the Cedar Point peninsula was on a clay foundation and safe from storm. 4. By a study of tree rings he was able to foretell periods of heavy rainfall and periods of drought.

1. *His discovery of the cause of milk sickness.* This illness was a scourge of the pioneer days. It was prevalent in Ohio, Indiana, Illinois, Kentucky, and Tennessee. President Abraham Lincoln's mother died of it. Cows would get the trembles and very often die. Human beings drank the cows' milk, developed the "trembles," and often died. It was quite virulent in Erie County. Several of its victims are buried in the cemeteries at Castalia, Sand Hill, and Bloomingville. Nobody knew the cause. Dr. Carpenter of Castalia at first thought the cows got the disease from drinking the spring water of the village. Later, he thought it might be due to eating of the "White Snake Root Plant." Dr. Deyo of Bellevue agreed. Many others

over the county were inclined to agree with them. But there was no certainty. The evidence was erratic. The farmers through the century were confused and uncertain. Therefore they did not destroy the white snakeroot plants nor did they fence areas where the plants grew.

In 1904, Moseley began to study the plant in his laboratory. By using an ether extract he secured a yellow, syrupy liquid. When this extract was given by hypodermic to animals, they developed the full symptoms of milk sickness. Thus the uncertainty was removed. On 2 December 1905, before the Ohio State Academy of Science, Moseley read his first paper on the topic. It carried the title, "The cause of trembles in cattle, sheep, and horses, and of milk-sickness in man." Moseley continued his study of milk sickness until he discovered the very complex chemical formula for the white snakeroot poison. He merits, indeed, the credit for this study and discovery [see Chapter 9, page 110].

2. *His discovery of preglacial rivers.* I have told you of Moseley's carrying the mastodon's tooth he had found in the Ross Ransom farm. It had been there because 10,000 years ago a huge mountain of ice had moved down from the arctic area where the mastodon creatures had lived, and it had carried this tooth to the Ransom Farm in the piles of drift and rock which had been pushed before it.

Long centuries before this glacier, rivers had worn their gullies down through soil and rock and made their river beds of that early day. But the glaciers filled those river beds with the debris they pushed before them. When finally the ice melted, the resulting waters began to form new rivers—the rivers of our day—as they flowed to the oceans. Moseley and his classes wished to locate those preglacial, buried river valleys. He did it this way. In his field trips out over the country, he and his student groups would stop at the farm houses for a drink of water. Always the farmer was asked, "In digging this well, how far down did you go before you struck rock?" The answer would be, "About 15 feet." Often the farmer would volunteer the information that one of his nearby neighbors found the rock down 30 feet. Moseley made a record of these deep places. When the survey was completed, with his lead pencil he connected the 30-foot dots and thus located the preglacial river. One of these rivers flowed from the location of the village of Venice to 200 yards into Sandusky Bay.

Another project for his boys was then made. In the winters of 1901 and 1902 when the ice was thick, with steel bars the boys broke through the ice and found that rock was about 12 feet down, except that at times the rock was more than 30 feet down. In that manner the preglacial river was traced from Venice through Sandusky Bay into Lake Erie [see Chapter 9, page 107].

This river had flowed northeast where now the coal loading docks are located. It flowed past them, then to the right, and past the end of Cedar Point into Lake Erie. In that preglacial river, long since filled with glacial deposits, was a 30-foot channel without rock. In towards the Sandusky shoreline the Federal Government had blasted out of the rock a 24-foot channel, some 50 feet wide. The cost extended into the millions of dollars. When this costly channel was completed, barges could be loaded with the coal brought by the Pennsylvania Railroad and destined for Duluth via the Great Lakes. This was in 1918. Moseley in 1905 had left in the mayor's office the full information about this wonderful natural channel 30 feet deep and a fourth of a mile wide. It would cost very little to pump out the sediment. The city building burned in 1910, and this report probably was lost in the fire. In 1936, from some source, the city engineer learned of this outer channel and had the sediment cleaned from it. Since 1939 it has been the exit route for all of the ships heavily loaded with coal destined for Lake Superior. Today it is referred to as the "outer channel." It rightly should bear the name, Moseley Channel [see Chapter 19, page 253].

• • •

3. *His proof that Cedar Point was safe from storms.* One morning in the fall of 1902 a heavy northeaster rolled on Lake Erie. The waves were reaching the crest of the bank at Cedar Point and occasionally were sweeping across the Marblehead Peninsula into Sandusky Bay. The storm became a subject of discussion in Moseley's senior class. He told of the very high level of Lake Erie's waters and the destructive storms of the preceding century, the years of 1859, 1860, and 1862. The storm of 1862 was of such force that it completely washed away Spit Island, directly across from Cedar Point. It was a sand island, no rock or clay foundation. Then, true to his teaching, one bright boy asked, "Why was not Cedar Point also destroyed?" Moseley said he would like to know. He asked the men students if they would help him on Saturdays. That fall and winter, 96 boys drove iron bars down in the eight-mile peninsula from Rye Beach to the end of Cedar Point. Always their bars were stopped in hard blue clay, very different from the sand foundation of Spit Island. These findings were the answer, an answer that made it possible to

consider Cedar Point with the Lake on one side and the Bay on the other as a prized residence area. Moseley had scored again [see Chapter 10, page 128].

• • •

4. *His study of tree rings.* In 1928 he began to study tree rings and their relation to periodical rainfall. He examined the tree rings in more than 500 stumps from all parts of the nation. Two of them a few miles from Marion were small trees when Columbus discovered America. Each year a tree records its growth in a tree ring. Some rings are narrow and close together; some are wide and farther apart. Moseley observed that the wide ones were developed in known years of heavy rainfall, the narrow rings in years of drought. Then came a second observation. These wide and narrow rings were at regular intervals, just before or in the years of recorded sunspot activity. That activity occurs each 90.4 years. Heavy rainfall follows this increased sun's heat and causes increased tree growth, resulting in wide tree rings.

On those 465-year-old tree stumps you can read the record of those five 90-year-apart sunspots. Our weather bureau recorded a very intense sunspot activity back in 1856; the expected wide ring was on that stump, 90 rings back. Then as you study towards the center, you find the wide tree rings of 1765, 1675, 1584, and 1494. All of these rings were there, 90 years apart. Very narrow rings indicating years of extreme drought preceded by two years each of those dates. By 1937, Moseley was forecasting severe drought in 1946 and heavy rainfall in 1948, the due 90.4 sunspot cycle date. We had the drought in 1946. . . . Then came the heavy rains in 1948. The farmers from New York to Oregon knew of his prophecy in their magazines and planted their crops accordingly. Following his death, our office was busy answering letters of appreciation and inquiry [see Chapter 10, page 127].

Moseley became a teacher whose classrooms widened with the years. He started with the conventional 30' x 40' room in the Sandusky High School and expanded to the county, state, and nation. Very few teachers have such a unique service record. Today we give it proper recognition.

—Modified and edited by RLS from Frank Jay Prout. 1959. "The inquiring mind of Mr. Moseley." *Bowling Green State University Magazine* 4(4): 16-20. November.

CHAPTER 4 • INQUIRING MIND OF A TEACHING SCIENTIST

Frank Jay Prout.

(*The Key*, BGSU, 1960, p. 47)

Frank Jay Prout (1883-1967), third president of Bowling Green State University (1939-1951), foresaw the coming increase in enrollments during the latter 1940s and prepared the University to meet this new challenge. At the same time the school shed its normal or teacher college image and became recognized as a growing university. Prout was responsible for the development of the graduate school, the addition of many new academic programs and buildings, and the attainment of national accreditations. A very popular president, he rarely missed a social function or sporting event.

Born 4 January 1883 in the village of Prout, Erie County, Ohio, Frank J. Prout lived his entire life in the state, where he attended the Milan School, graduated from Sandusky High School (1902), and received a B. A. from Ohio Wesleyan University (1906) an M. A. from Ohio University (1907). He was an instructor in history at Ohio Wesleyan University (1906), a teacher in the Zanesville, Chillicothe, and Sandusky schools, serving as principal of the high school in Chillicothe (1912-1914), and superintendent of schools in Chillicothe (1914-1921) and Sandusky (1921-1939). Prout was awarded honorary degrees from Ohio University (1919), Ohio Wesleyan University (1924), Miami University, and Bowling Green State University (1952). In retirement, he was advisor to his successor, President Ralph W. McDonald, and helped supervise the landscaping of the Bowling Green campus. Death came at 84 years, 28 March 1967, in Sandusky, and burial was made in the rural Sand Hill Cemetery.

References for Biographical Sketch

1967. Anonymous. "Frank Prout educator: BGSU President during expansion." *Toledo Blade*, 29 March, p. 6.

1967. Anonymous. "Frank J. Prout dies in Sandusky." *BG News*, 30 March, p. 1, 3.

1967. James Robert Overman. *The History of Bowling Green State University*, Bowling Green University Press, Bowling Green, Ohio. 234 pp.

1985. Jim Nieman. "Prout saw BG through war years." *Daily Sentinel-Tribune*, Bowling Green, 23 August, p. A-4.

Campus buildings among wild plants: Science Building (Moseley Hall) erected in 1916, the Administration Building completed in 1915, Teacher Training School Building (Hanna Hall) constructed in 1921.

(Post card with postal date of 1922; Stuckey Collection)

Moseley with a rare smile, dressed in his well-worn overcoat.

(Wilbert Ohlemacher, in his *Sandusky Register* article, 19 February 1984, p. A-4; Sandusky Library Archives)

Interviews With Students And Friends

CHAPTER FIVE

Relda E. Niederhofer

Only a very few times in a lifetime does one meet a person whose whole being revolves around his profession. Such an individual was Professor Edwin Lincoln Moseley, whose entire life was devoted to the study and teaching of science and nature. I never knew Moseley as a person; but as a teacher of biology in the area where he taught, I became interested in learning more about the life of this man. Subsequently I interviewed people who knew him and have summarized their comments.

Students described Moseley as a rather frail, gaunt man, who was not particularly handsome. He was dark-complexioned with almost a sallow skin and blue eyes. His tall thin frame, when covered with his long overcoat, caused some to compare him to Ichabod Crane. With his preoccupation in science, he was unconcerned about his personal appearance, and clothes became unimportant to him. Certainly, he must have thought that what a man did was more important than what he wore on his back. He frequently wore clothes given to him, rather than taking the time to buy new ones. His former students observed that he wore the same rust-colored winter overcoat for years, as well as the same light-tan topcoat in the summer. One of his favorite outfits was a blue serge suit that he wore so long that the wool became very shiny.

Moseley apparently remained thin by exercising and controlling his diet. Walking was his favorite form of exercise. He cooked many of his meals on a hotplate in his room. Several of his favorite foods were bananas, graham crackers, and boiled eggs. He is said to have been a vegetarian; however, one of his former students indicated an exception. Even in old age, weight was not a problem for him. His 1943 War Ration Book gives a brief description of him at age 75: Height 5'9", weight 110 pounds, blue eyes, and gray hair.

Former students described Moseley as a teacher who was very scholarly; all business in the classroom. He was very demanding in his requirements for good grades, and resorted to embarrassing a student who did not know the answer. Several students indicated they were afraid of him, which meant they were fearful of being embarrassed, but not of any physical punishment he might inflict on them.

Individuals Interviewed

Lelia Bittikofer	41
Howard Braithwaite	41
Clarence Clark	44
Ralph W. Dexter	46
Lewis Hause	46
Ruth (Milkey) Holzhauser	48
Inez (Reinheimer) Koch	49
Ervin Kreischer	50
Clare Martin	52
Wilbert Ohlemacher and Helen Ohlemacher	53
Cynthia (Otis) Witte	56
Charles Otis	56
Edna Scheid	57
Louis Schultz, Sr.	58
Hazel Stockdale	58
Rose (Steiner) Tschantz	62
Anonymous I, II	63

Several former students have referred to Professor Moseley as "Pete." Apparently this nickname originated in Sandusky and later spread to Bowling Green. Although many students used it in their conversations about Moseley, it was not said in his presence. Hazel Stockdale indicated that the nickname came from his discovery of peat in the marsh at Old Woman Creek.

Mrs. Ruth Holzhauser had another theory as to why Moseley was referred to as "Pete." Nicknames were common terms of reference used by college students in place of their correct names. The college boys thought Moseley looked like St. Peter, or at least what they imagined St. Peter ought to look like. His tall figure and gaunt features helped add to the illusion. If anyone guarded the gates of heaven, he must certainly look like Moseley.

Lelia Bittikofer (1899-1992), who came to Sandusky High School in 1923 to teach biology, knew of Moseley's reputation. She had mixed feelings about how to follow such an outstanding man. She quickly overcame that sense of uncertainty by deciding not to be like him, but to be herself. Using her own methods, she taught biology for 37 years. She was one of the most gentle, loving women this author has ever had the pleasure of knowing. At Sandusky High School, she gave her students patience and understanding, no matter how long it took them to comprehend a particular principle. Many of her former students also attribute their appreciation of nature to Miss Bittikofer.

When Moseley went to Bowling Green Normal College in 1914 he left his vast museum collection in Sandusky. He returned periodically to conduct museum open houses at Sandusky High School. In preparation for these exhibits he contacted Miss Bittikofer by post card explaining when and what to have ready for him when he arrived. Moseley had so much to write he frequently filled the card in one direction then turned it a quarter turn to write over his first message. Miss Bittikofer was left with the task of interpreting Moseley's writing as well as following his directions to set-up the open house.

Howard Braithwaite (b. 1913), was raised in Lakeside, Ohio, where his grandfather and father published the *Peninsular News*. After graduation from Bowling Green State University in 1935, he taught school in Brecksville and Olmstead Falls, both a part of the Cuyahoga County system. In 1942 he took employment with the United States Civil Service Commission. This organization helped prepare him for a position in the newly formed National Aeronautics and Space Administration (NASA) in 1958, from which he retired in 1973. His work for NASA was in personnel, as a specialist in position classification and salary administration. Braithwaite lives in Silver Spring, Maryland.

Chapter 5 • Interviews with Students and Friends

Braithwaite remembered with respect Moseley's concentrated and intensive mastery of his field combined with a broad range of general information. Dominant also were his courtesy and refinement of person, his uncompromising standards of character strongly and positively equated with intelligence, along with his contempt, also strongly expressed, for those who abuse their bodies with tobacco or alcohol. Braithwaite always had a little pity for Moseley, in that he was alone and seemingly concentrated on his field to the exclusion of all else. With years Braithwaite can understand better how one can be so intensively identified with one's work as to find in it joy and contented happiness.

Braithwaite was a student in Moseley's botany and zoology college classes in 1932-1933. Students recognized Moseley as a dedicated scientist of the Darwin-Spencer school, although most of them at the time were not aware of Darwin or Spencer in the cultural evolution of the 18th, 19th and early 20th centuries. One day Moseley mentioned Herbert Spencer and got no reaction. "Doesn't anyone know who Herbert Spencer was? No! Well, I am amazed! Here you are in college and one of the greatest writers on modern science is *unknown* to you!" It was the first Braithwaite had heard the name, although he'd heard of Darwin, and it was not until many years later when he became interested in cultural history that he learned more about Spencer and his interpretation of Darwin.

Charles Otis (1886-1979) and Moseley each taught biology classes in the 1930s. Otis specialized in premedical classes, tissue culture, and experiments with live animals. Moseley's sections emphasized the phylogenetic study of animals and plants. Braithwaite and other students believed that if they bought autographed copies of Moseley's *Our Wild Animals* and *Trees, Stars and Birds*, they might get an "A" in his classes. Moseley, of course, was flattered that students purchased his books, but his grades were based strictly on the student's performance in class work.

The chairs in Moseley's classroom were divided into two sections with an aisle in the middle. Some 50 to 60 students occupied the chairs in the section next to the blackboard in front of the Professor's favorite Greek-style armchair, with the section next to the windows unoccupied. Moseley often lectured seated in his chair with his long arms dangling over the side. During one of his lectures he was interrupted by the wheezing of spittle and mist from one of his students in the front row. Moseley picked up his chair, and after dragging it across the room to the windows, sat down and said, "Mr. _____, anyone with a minimum of decency would use handkerchiefs and would stay away with a cold like yours!" He conducted the remainder of the class seated in front of the empty chairs.

Braithwaite recalled that he and other students enjoyed poking fun at the elderly professor they called "Old Pete." When Moseley left the campus for some professional meeting, Otis helped the students play a joke on Pete. The chimpanzee skeleton was borrowed from the museum and placed in Pete's favorite chair. Its long arms were draped over the sides to mimic the professor's style. To complete the picture Pete's old hat was placed on the chimp's cranium and a burned cigarette was shoved between the teeth ready for Pete's return the "Monday after."

Smoking and the use of alcohol were, Moseley said, evidences of poor intelligence, and "one who smoked or drank" could not get a grade above a C. If Moseley ever saw one of his students smoking on campus, the story was that it was a race between student and the professor for the registrar's office, one to reverse his estimate, and the other to defend his grade. This recollection may be just a story but all the students believed it.

One field trip was across the street and into the cemetery where the class crouched behind a hillock out of the wind. Moseley said, "Can anyone tell me why this cemetery was located here on this hill?" No one could. Grinning with yel-

Moseley at the shore.

(Gift of Mrs. Francis Koch; Sandusky Library Archives)

lowed, snaggled teeth at his inner joke, he said, "Well we are on an ancient sand dune, well drained, heh heh heh!" And then he lectured on that cemetery as an ancient sand dune in the old lake that later became part of the Black Swamp, a deeply fertile plain of Wood County.

Moseley reading at laboratory desk.

(Archives, BGSU)

Clarence Clark (b. 1912), graduated from Paulding High School in Paulding, Ohio, and went on to Defiance College, Miami University, and The Ohio State University. He completed his bachelor of science degree at Miami and master's degree in zoology at The Ohio State University. Clark taught school for a few years, but spent most of his professional career with the Department of Natural Resources, Division of Wildlife. He taught fish culture as a research professor at The Ohio State University, College of Agriculture. His research resulted in numerous scientific articles on fish, birds, mollusks, and water areas in Ohio. Clark is enjoying retirement in Arizona.

In the 1930s, Clark was enrolled in graduate school at the Franz Theodore Stone Laboratory, Put-in-Bay, Ohio. At lunch one day the director, Dr. Raymond C. Osburn, informed him that Moseley was coming to the islands to conduct a population study of the heronry on West Sister Island. Clark was delighted to have the opportunity to work with such a learned man as Moseley.

The skies were overcast when Moseley and Clark left the dock at Put-in-Bay for West Sister Island. When the boat sailed beyond the protection of the Bass

Islands into the open water of Lake Erie, a severe storm hit them. Their skipper, an experienced seaman who had sailed Lake Erie since his youth, was not about to turn back; instead he kept the bow headed into the wind and they rode out the storm. Moseley, who never had much to say was silent on this occasion. He sat out on the open deck where the spray from the rough sea soaked him. His knuckles became white from gripping the seat so tightly. Clark could see him gulping continuously, fighting back seasickness. Moseley's only comment after they landed was, "That was a new experience!" Their trip to West Sister Island was the beginning of a long friendship.

In one of their conversations Clark mentioned that as a high school biology teacher, he was familiar with the nesting sites of birds in the area. Moseley suggested that he come over sometime to see one of the heron rookeries nearby. Clark was pleased to be Moseley's host many times. Even after the Clark family moved to St. Mary's, Ohio, Moseley would come to visit them. Clark would meet Moseley at the bus station and provide transportation for him to various sites in the area. One of their big objectives was to estimate the number of black-crowned night herons in the rookery on Lake Loraine, Shelby County. They concluded that nearly 4,000 birds were seen.

During one of Moseley's visits, Clark mentioned he would like to buy a couple of Moseley's books; but his son was having an operation and some things had to be delayed. Moseley said nothing at the time; in a few days Clark received both books in the mail. He found a piece of yellow tablet paper tucked in one of the books with a handwritten note stating, "If and when you have the money, the price is $3.00." Moseley was especially generous with anyone who wanted to learn. Clark knew if he never had the money it would be satisfactory with Moseley.

Clark related a story told to him by a former superintendent of schools. It seems to be the only occasion on which Moseley did not pay special attention to someone who wanted to know something. The superintendent's daughter was a student in one of Moseley's college classes. On a field trip she picked up some little round balls, walked rapidly up to Moseley and asked, "What are these?" He took one look, turned his head away rather embarrassed as he walked a little faster. She persisted. On her third attempt Moseley put an end to her curiosity in a rather indignant way, "Miss, sheep have been here!"

Osburn told Clark about a walk he and Moseley took along the shores of Lake Erie one hot summer day in the late 1890s. They found a badly decomposed fish neither of them recognized. Moseley took out his handkerchief, carefully worked it under the rotten fish, wrapped it up neatly and stuck it in his pocket. They continued on along the beach for several hours in the intense heat. The rank smelling fish even remained in Moseley's pocket through lunch. Osburn gave Moseley credit for being a much more dedicated fisherman than he was.

One of Clark's friends, who lived in Bowling Green, told about how her small son had run into the house one day to announce, "Mother, Jesus just went past!" The mother tried to explain he was mistaken, but the child insisted he was right. The next time the child saw Jesus coming, the mother went to the door to see Moseley walking down the street.

Ralph W. Dexter (1912-1991), born in Gloucester, Massachusetts, received his Bachelor of Science degree from Massachusetts State College in 1934 and his Doctor of Philosophy in ecology from Illinois in 1938. An interest in ecology prompted his study of the life history of the chimney swift, as well as the history of American naturalists, which resulted in numerous publications. In 1982 he concluded his 45th year of teaching and retired from the Department of Biology at Kent State University.

Dexter and Moseley attended many of the same scientific meetings. Dexter remembered hearing some of Moseley's scientific papers read at the annual meetings of the Ohio Academy of Science. While the information in the text of Moseley's speech was usually very interesting, his method of presentation became very tiresome to the assemblage. He spoke in a low voice, and his monotone style was so boring it nearly put his audience to sleep.

Lewis Hause (1904-1984), who graduated from Bowling Green State University in 1929, taught elementary grades at Florence, Ohio, and classes at junior and senior high schools in Castalia, Ohio, before coming to the Sandusky public schools. In Sandusky he served as principal at Sycamore and Ontario Elementary schools and Adams Junior High. He retired in 1961.

Hause was in Moseley's college zoology and biology classes at Bowling Green. These classes went on field trips, which included such places as the Oak Openings near Toledo and the Waggoner Farm north of Fremont to the Great Blue Heron rookery. On one field trip to the Oak Openings, Moseley told the boys he would take the lunch. While bird watching, the boys anticipated a good-sized lunch after walking for several hours in the loose sand. When they stopped for lunch, Moseley gave them fig newtons and overripe bananas. It was not at all what the boys had hoped.

Moseley was hard on boys who smoked. Most of the boys learned to put their cigarettes out before going to class and not smoke on field trips. It was rumored around campus that Moseley might fail a boy whom he knew smoked.

Hause worked at the College Inn, where Moseley often ate dinner. When the boys saw Moseley coming, they would announce his arrival by calling back to the cook that the "monkey lunch" was here. The cook would know to whom they referred, and he would prepare the professor's vegetable plate.

Moseley needed transportation to Berlin Heights, so he offered to buy gas and oil if Lewis would drive him there. Lewis agreed and they left on a Saturday morning. They had just left town when Moseley started questioning Lewis, "Do you know what that tree is?"

Hause was somewhat fearful that he would be given many questions en route, so he decided to stop the test before it could get underway. Hause exclaimed, "When I drive, I don't have time to look at the trees!" Moseley realized it might put the safety of their trip in jeopardy, so he ended the quizzing and enjoyed the scenery.

In 1940, Hause and his wife were living in Sandusky. He saw Moseley downtown one Saturday and invited him to their home for dinner. Mrs. Hause served him an all-vegetable dinner with some homemade whole-wheat bread. She included all the items she thought he would like. When Moseley was ready to leave, he asked her if he could have two slices of bread. She graciously complied with his request. He was staying in town over the weekend and needed something for breakfast. When he returned to Bowling Green, he wrote a note of thanks for the nice dinner. He also told them his new book was out now, and if they would like to have an autographed copy, he would be glad to send them one for $1.75, the price of the book.

Ruth (Milkey) Holzhauser (1908-1997), a former college student of Moseley, graduated from Sandusky High School in 1926 and Bowling Green State University in 1930 with dual teaching certification. During her teaching career in the Sandusky public schools, she taught all levels: fifth and sixth grades in the elementary, junior high school, and English, history, and civics in the senior high school.

In a college zoology class, Ruth remembers seeing Moseley pace up and down the classroom in front of the windows. He was moving around the room trying to stay in the sunlight. He explained to the class that Vitamin D could be absorbed through the skin from sunlight. He did not believe in using medication, such as cough medicine. He thought it was far better for a person to get the natural protection of the sunlight.

One of Moseley's favorite teaching practices in zoology class was his spot-identification tests. Before class convened, he would hide several preserved birds in a box below his desk in the front of the room, well out of sight of his students. When it was time for the test, he would hold up one specimen at a time for just a few seconds. Students were required to name the birds quickly. Common names were acceptable, so it might be a starling or grackle, but he did not approve of referring to the bird as a blackbird. He explained there were too many black birds to use such a common term.

Ruth worked as an assistant in the college Department of English. When Moseley needed someone to proofread one of his manuscripts before it was sent to the publisher, he would ask Ruth and promise to give her a handsome reward for her time. After she had prepared her own work for the next day, she worked on the manuscript for several hours each night for about two weeks. After correcting his punctuation and sentence structure, she returned the manuscript to Moseley, anticipating her handsome reward. He was very pleased with her work. Ruth remembers how slowly he said, "T-h-a-n-k y-o-u, M-i-s-s M-i-l-k-e-y." With that, he wrote his name on a card and gave it to her. His autograph was to be her handsome reward. Ruth felt very disappointed at this expression of his gratitude, but she kept the card for a number of years.

On one occasion, Ruth's father, of Sandusky, drove to Bowling Green to take her, several classmates, and Moseley to Sandusky for the weekend. Halfway there, they stopped in Fremont to drop off William Miller. Everyone got out of the car to help unload the boy's luggage before they proceeded on to Sandusky. When they arrived in Sandusky, Moseley realized his straw hat was missing. He thought he had laid it on the car roof when they unloaded the luggage in Fremont. He wanted Milkey to return to Fremont at once to retrieve his straw hat. Milkey refused to travel the sixty miles round trip to look for his hat, especially since Moseley was not sure he had the hat with him when they left Bowling Green.

Inez (Reinheimer) Koch (1894-1986), a former student of Moseley, who after high school graduation in 1912, went to Western Reserve College in Cleveland for nurses' training. She worked as a volunteer nurse in Cleveland and Sandusky. After marriage, she and her husband moved to a farm on the outskirts of Sandusky.

Bartel Reinheimer, Inez's older brother, was one of Moseley's favorite students. After high school Bartel went to Kenyon College and became a minister. He eventually became a bishop in the Episcopal Church in Rochester, New York.

One other member in the Reinheimer household was Glen Cullen. He was from North Bass Island. Since there was no high school on the Island, Cullen needed a home in Sandusky. He roomed and boarded in the Reinheimer home so he could complete high school. Cullen eventually went to The University of Michigan, Moseley's Alma Mater. Later, he worked for a chemical company for many years.

Moseley visited the Reinheimer home often, both when Inez was a young girl, as well as later when she and her husband had the farm. After Moseley moved Sandusky's museum specimens to Bowling Green in 1938, he came often to rest and have dinner with them. He often took a nap on their sofa while she cooked dinner, which usually included his favorite banana cake. He always had time to take her children for a walk in the woods to show them the plants and animals.

When Inez was in high school, Moseley recognized how good her penmanship was. She often drew pictures of plants on the reports she handed in to be graded. She was a good artist. Moseley had Inez write many of the identification cards he

49

needed for his museum specimens. In preparing for museum openings, Inez dusted showcases and unpacked boxes. Then on Sunday after the opening, all the specimens were packed away again.

Inez indicated that Bartel was one of the boys who had helped Moseley survey the Sandusky Bay during the winters of 1901 and 1902. The boys made holes in the ice and used an auger with a long extension to probe the bottom. With the help of Moseley, it took them two winters to plot the submerged valleys through the Bay. Moseley used a sled with a box attached to carry supplies out on the ice. Since they were out nearly all day, it was necessary to carry lunch. Inez told of how Moseley fixed hot oatmeal to take along for the boys to eat. They wrapped it securely to keep it warm for lunch.

Bartel often traveled with Moseley. On one of their trips to Moseley's property in Louisiana, Bartel helped collect snakes which the professor brought back to Sandusky and then shipped to the New York Zoo.

Bartel and Glen helped Moseley when he was experimenting to prove white snakeroot caused trembles in animals. They ground up the dried white snakeroot and put it in the dog's food. They were trying to find out how much snakeroot it would take to kill the dog, as well as how soon it would kill the dog. The dog lived.

Ervin Kreischer (1906-1986), a 1930 university graduate, was employed as an administrator for many of his 30 years with Bowling Green State University. He refers to himself as a business manager; however, the University conferred the title of vice-president in charge of finance and treasurer on him. He helped revise legislation to permit state universities to issue revenue bonds on the open market to finance building construction. His colleagues referred to him as the "dean" of Ohio college business officers. At the time of his retirement in 1965, he had the distinction of having worked for all the University presidents from the first, Homer B. Williams to Hollis A. Moore. In 1967 the University honored him by naming the $6,500,000 residence hall, Kreischer Quadrangle.

In the 1920s, both Kreischer and his late wife, Marge, had been students in Moseley's college classes. Mrs. Kreischer enjoyed comparing stories with her husband about Moseley's eccentricities. When Kreischer would comment that, "Boys would fail Moseley's class if he caught them smoking," She would rebuff with,

"Yes, but if girls so much as wore rouge on their faces Moseley said they didn't deserve an A!"

Examining snakes in class was a particular dislike of Mrs. Kreischer. Fox snakes were often in Moseley's laboratory as teaching aids to illustrate their importance as predators in the balance of nature. Moseley wanted students, especially the squeamish girls, to handle live snakes, not only to identify their markings, but also to see that snakes were not wet and slimy, as they imagined, but dry and smooth. If Moseley could educate students to overcome their fear of snakes, they would be less likely to kill the harmless ones.

Kreischer remembered the rather strange way Moseley kept track of his winter mittens. When Moseley draped his woolen overcoat on the office halltree, it looked as if a person was standing in the corner hugging the pole. Dangling out of each sleeve was an attached mitten. To keep from losing his mittens Moseley had connected them with a string which extended up each sleeve and across the back of his coat; the same way a mother dresses a small child to go out and play in the snow.

Moseley pointing to growth ring.

(Photo Service, BGSU)

During the years of his retirement, Moseley collected tree sections to study the wet/dry cycles for predicting future weather patterns. On one of his trips out West, Moseley shipped a large number of sections to the University C.O.D., without notifying anyone of their arrival. When the sections were delivered at the University Receiving Department, much confusion existed, until someone called Kreischer to inquire if he should accept or reject the consignment. When Kreischer was told who sent the tree sections, they were accepted. During that summer, as more C.O.D. packages arrived they were stored in the basement of Hanna Hall, the teacher training school building where Moseley was given space to research the tree rings when he returned.

The 17,000 museum specimens that Moseley moved from the Sandusky High School to Bowling Green in 1938 have diminished through the years. In the early 1940s, many museum specimens that had been on display in the Science Building, later named Moseley Hall, had to be moved to the basement of the Practical Arts Building, Hayes Hall. Holt's geology collection had also been stored on the third floor of the Science Building. It was believed that the added weight was causing structural stress to the building, so many items were relocated. Unfortunately, the humidity was very high in the Practical Arts basement, and a number of museum specimens degenerated very rapidly. Mold and mildew formed quickly on a number of preserved mammals and birds which had to be discarded.

Classes were structured somewhat differently than they are today. Kreischer remembers that before the lesson of the day Moseley would review current events with the class. It became very evident to the class that Moseley believed in a Higher Being from his many Biblical quotations. No objection to religious teaching was evident in the classroom; in fact, students were required to attend chapel once a week. Kreischer said that he learned much about nature as a student in Moseley's 1927 biology and zoology classes.

Clare Martin (1888-1982), completed both his undergraduate and graduate degrees in chemistry at The Ohio State University. In 1923, with his Ph.D. freshly in hand, he took his first and only teaching assignment, at Bowling Green State Normal College. Moseley's chemistry laboratories had not been improved since he set them up in 1914. It was Martin's assignment to order new equipment and update the laboratories. He also worked actively with the community of Bowling Green and Wood County in the 1920s and 30s to improve health conditions. A number of cases of typhoid fever and tuberculosis had occurred throughout the area. He tried to teach the citizens that a real health hazard existed if disposed human sewage was too close to sources of drinking water. In 1959 Martin retired from Bowling Green State University after having been chairman for the chemistry department for 31 years. Martin died 1 November 1982, four months after this interview was granted.

Martin remembered that Moseley had a real talent for illustrating ideas to students. One day when Dr. Martin was cleaning out one of the large cases of stuffed birds in the Science Building he discovered a small box. Opening it he found some sand and a note which read, "There are as many grains of sand in this box as People in Toledo." Moseley had used this comparison to impress students with the much greater population of Toledo than that of Bowling Green.

Martin had worked with Moseley on several research projects in which Moseley had made keen observations. On one occasion Martin was having trouble working out the solution to a problem. Moseley studied the question a few minutes and then explained how he should proceed. When Martin tried Moseley's suggestion, it worked.

Martin indicated that Moseley occasionally attended the Bowling Green Presbyterian Church for at least twelve years. This reference is the first to Moseley's religious affiliation since his childhood. He liked the morality and discipline of the church. Moseley told Martin, "The Presbyterians are thinkers!"

Martin admired Moseley when he came to Bowling Green, so when the Professor invited him for a stroll he gladly accepted. Their walk to the fairgrounds, now the city park, became a nature hike. As they walked Moseley talked about the trees. He asked Martin, "What kind of tree is this?" Martin indicated, rather indignantly, he did not know since he was a chemist and not a botanist. "I'll teach you," Moseley replied, "Look at the leaf, if it has a thumb it is a sassafras." It was a botany lesson Martin never forgot.

Wilbert Ohlemacher (1892-1987) and **Helen Ohlemacher** (1895-1987), brother and sister, were former Sandusky High School students of Moseley. After

Wilbert's graduation in 1911 he continued his education at Case Institute of Technology in Cleveland, majoring in mechanical engineering and receiving his degree in 1915. Retirement came after 40 years as plant engineer at the American Crayon Company in Sandusky. Ohlemacher will be remembered in Sandusky for the column "The Elderlies" he wrote for the *Sandusky Register*. "The Elderlies" appeared about every other week for six years. His column recorded life in the early 20th century in nearly 150 stories. When Ohlemacher was no longer able to write the column, it was replaced with a similar column "Sandusky Revisited."

Helen Ohlemacher graduated from Sandusky High School in 1913 at the half-year ceremony. Her college education was spread over several years at such universities as Kent State University and Bowling Green State University. She completed her bachelor's degree at Columbia University. Helen taught in the county schools, then Huron and finally Sandusky, where she was a teaching principal at Monroe Elementary for 27 years and a full-time principal the last seven or eight years. Helen retired and lived with Wilbert in an old Victorian-style family home with the iron picket fence along the sidewalk. This white frame house had been their home since 1898. When Wilbert and Helen were unable to care for themselves, they entered the Fairhaven Home in Upper Sandusky where Wilbert died 2 January 1987 at age 94 and Helen died the next day at age 91. After Wilbert died it was as if Helen could die now too; she had cared for him to his death. They shared funeral services.

The Cedar Point Amusement Park has been Sandusky's number-one attraction since before the turn of the century. In the early 1900s the fastest access to the Park was by water, not roads. The steamship *Boeckling* was put into use about 1909 to carry passengers across the Bay from downtown Sandusky to the dock at Cedar Point. Students waited anxiously for the Park to open each summer. Wilbert remembered that several girls had planned a day at the Park. They left the house a little late and were running downtown to catch the *Boeckling* when they met Moseley, or "Pete," as he was known to his students. He greeted them and engaged them in a conversation about a fly that had just landed on his sleeve. The girls heard the bell sound for the final boarding, but could not break away from him. They wanted to get an early start to Cedar Point, yet not at the expense of being rude to their teacher. When he finished telling them about the fly, the big side-wheeler had pulled away from the dock. The girls had to wait until it returned about an hour later.

Wilbert remembered a story about a family who invited Moseley to have dinner with them. When everyone had finished eating, Moseley asked the cook if he could have another spoonful of mashed potatoes, explaining he did not want anything sweet left in his mouth, since he was trying to protect his teeth from decay.

Helen was in Bowling Green taking some courses in June 1924, when a severe tornado hit Sandusky. Property damage was extensive, telephone lines were down, and transportation into the city was impossible for several days. News of everyone's well-being was slow in filtering out of the city, so it was some time before Helen knew if her parents were all right. Crossing the campus one day she met Moseley, whom she thought would inquire about her parents; instead he was concerned about their property, "Are the four big maples and one birch tree still standing in your yard?" She replied that they were. As he walked off across the campus he seemed much relieved.

Moseley examining trunk of tree.

(Photo Service, BGSU)

Chapter 5 • Interviews with Students and Friends

Cynthia (Otis) Witte, daughter of **Charles Otis** (1886-1979), who was a former professor of biology at Bowling Green State University. The Otis family left Wisconsin in 1930 when University president Homer B. Williams offered Otis a teaching position in the biology department. As a young girl, Miss Otis was impressed with Moseley's kindness to her, as well as his eagerness to teach her about birds. She recalled his rosy cheeks and well-groomed beard, which gave him the appearance of a very distinguished gentleman.

The office which Otis and Moseley shared in the Science Building as teachers brought them together as friends. Their mutual love of nature fostered many weekend field trips in the vicinity of Bowling Green. Working on a limited budget for biological supplies made it important for them to collect as many specimens as possible on these trips, for their use in the laboratories. One particular depression along route 105 flooded each spring, when a branch of the Portage River overflowed, providing an ideal reservoir for organisms. They visited this small pool each spring for their stock of fairy shrimp.

Mrs. Witte recalled that her mother included many of Moseley's favorite dishes such as baked potatoes and fruit, when they invited him to come for Sunday dinner. Sometimes the Professor would surprise them with an unusual fruit for dinner, such as papaw, which he had collected during an Oak Opening's field trip. When Mrs. Witte set the table for her mother, she always put a cup of hot water at Moseley's place, because he never drank coffee or tea with his meal. On one occasion he taught Mrs. Otis how to prepare puffballs for a meal. He showed her how to clean and skin the puffballs before they were fried in butter and salt.

When Moseley died in 1948, Otis wrote his obituary for the *Ohio Journal of Science*. Mrs. Witte remembers the funeral, and how impressed she was with the beautiful red cherry casket. The wooden casket was very fitting for one who loved the beauty of nature so much.

Mrs. Witte graduated twice from Bowling Green State University, first in 1946 as a sociology major, and then in 1971 with a Bachelor of Science Degree in Education. She worked for Western Union in both Detroit and Toledo. She and her husband, James Witte, live in Scotch Ridge, about five miles from the University.

CHAPTER 5 • INTERVIEWS WITH STUDENTS AND FRIENDS

Edna Scheid (1890-1990), a student of Moseley, graduated from Sandusky High School in 1908 and Oberlin College in 1912. The Scheid name is familiar to Sanduskians, who have traveled on the south edge of Perkins Township. Her grandfather, William Scheid, owned a farm along what became known as Scheid Road. Edna honored the family name with a very impressive teaching career. Her first teaching assignment was Latin in Huron High School. In 1918 she moved to Sandusky and taught English at Sandusky High School. She retired in 1957 with 45 years of teaching experience. Moseley had moved to Bowling Green in 1914, so they were not on the faculty at the same time, but she remembered him quite well as her high school physics teacher.

Examples of hairbows and hat worn by young women in the early 1900s.

In these views, the hairbows and hat are worn by
Hazel B. Grunder (1891-1969), mother of Relda E. Niederhofer.

(Niederhofer Collection)

When Edna was in high school, it was fashionable for schoolgirls to wear large hair ribbons tied in a bow across the back of the head. In fact, they were so big the bow frequently extended for several inches beyond the side of the head. Moseley was not at all pleased with that current ribbon fad, and on one occasion he indicated his displeasure to the class. He looked directly at one girl who was wearing a large hair ribbon, and remarked, "The size of a girl's brains is inversely proportional to the size of her hair ribbon!" Shortly after this terse comment the young lady stopped wearing hair ribbons. Ironically, the one he selected to criticize later graduated from Smith College and was elected a member of Phi Beta Kappa. Certainly he chose the wrong girl to draw such an analogy.

Louis Schultz, Sr. (1882-1969), another high school student of Moseley, was one of about 100 boys who assisted Moseley in plotting the preglacial river valley through Sandusky Bay during the winters of 1901 through 1903. Perhaps in some small way that work on the Bay helped interest Schultz in his later occupation as a civil engineer and surveyor. Schultz died in 1969, but his son, Louis Schultz, Jr., has supplied a favorite story his father used to tell about Moseley.

When the elder Schultz was in high school, he and another boy decided to play a joke on Moseley. They decapitated two insects of different species and then carefully attached the head of one insect onto the body of the other insect. They took their new "pseudo-species" to the Professor for him to identify. He studied the strange-looking insect for a few minutes and then decided to go along with the joke. "W-e-l-l, b-o-y-s," he slowly drawled. "I-t-'s d-e-f-i-n-i-t-e-l-y a b-u-g. I-n f-a-c-t I'd s-a-y i-t-'s a h-u-m-b-u-g!" Moseley laughed and enjoyed the joke as much as the boys did.

Hazel Stockdale (1893-1989), a 1914 graduate, was in Moseley's class the last year he taught at Sandusky High School. After completing her teacher's training at The Ohio State University and the New York School of Physical Education, Stockdale taught in the junior high school at Birmingham, Ohio, for two years, then the same grade level at Oberlin, Ohio. Stockdale used Moseley's book *Trees, Stars, and Birds* when she taught general science. She retired from teaching in 1928 to pursue other occupations.

Miss Stockdale recalled high school excursions with Moseley. One trip in particular to Put-in-Bay was especially significant to her. The class met at the foot of Columbus Avenue to take the steamer *Arrow* to the Islands. It was approximately a two-hour boat ride with stops at Lakeside, Kelleys Island, Middle Bass Island, and then Put-in-Bay. The *Arrow* delivered passengers as well as mail and supplies to each of the isolated areas. Moseley and the students walked several miles visiting the vineyards, glacial grooves, and the state fish hatchery. As they walked, they looked for eagles' nests and tabulated the birds they saw. All along the road, in fields and woods, they helped Moseley collect plant specimens. They stopped for lunch in the woods near the Hotel Victory. The Hotel was closed at the time because of poor patronage. During their break, a few of the boys were playing catch with an orange. One boy missed a catch and fell down a rather steep embankment.

Believed to be a reunion of Moseley's Sandusky students and friends, about 1919 or 1920.

(Organized by Hazel Stockdale, seated at far left with Professor Moseley next to her; Sandusky Library Archives)

The group was quite concerned about his welfare. His bruises were minor so the group continued on its tour of the Island. Miss Stockdale's most outstanding memory concerned their visit to the caves. Moseley explained that the formations they saw in the Perry and Crystal Caves had been shaped by water. Hazel remembers asking, "How are they formed by water?" He gave her a brief answer at the time, but the next day he brought her a book on geology and a topographic map for her to study. He wanted her to use her natural curiosity to find the answers. One of the things that made his teaching so outstanding was that he constantly urged his students to search for the reason why things happened.

Many Saturday high school excursions were within a few miles of Sandusky to Milan, Norwalk, Monroeville, Castalia, or Berlin Heights by way of the Lake Shore Electric, the interurban streetcar. The trips were optional for students, but generally a group of 10 to 15 students would go each week. The students were instructed to bring two items, money for the interurban and a good-sized lunch. Departure was early in the morning from the interurban station in Sandusky. Even in bad weather the field trips generally were held. Hazel recalled one trip to Milan was exceptionally rainy, but the excursion was not canceled. Moseley and his students went to a farmer's old field to see a pumping ram, which was an electric pump for taking water out of a well. Moseley wanted students to see it operate. When it rained too hard, they stayed in the farmer's barn part of the day. When the rain subsided, they were on their way again. Moseley allowed his students to explore on their own, but when he found something of interest, he would summon them to gather around by blowing hard on the policeman's whistle he carried around his neck on a string. He also carried a vasculum to collect plant specimens as well as rocks, leaves, and flowers. However, he taught the students to leave the rare species in the field so they might become more abundant, and to respect the fine balance of nature in an ecosystem. Lunch was a time for sharing, because Moseley never packed a lunch. He relied on students to provide him with an extra apple or sandwich. One boy had carried his lunch in a shoebox, and during the rain he held it close to him to keep it dry. When he stopped for lunch, the only dry part of his clothes was a rectangle-shaped patch on his shirt where he had held the shoebox close to his chest. The trip ended with a ride back home on the interurban. Everyone joked all the way home about having enough mud on their shoes to go into the real estate business.

Moseley kept snakes in the laboratory. Their cages were not always at maximum security, so occasionally one would break loose and try to escape from the building. One time Hazel saw a black snake crawling into her English classroom. Terrified of the snake, students screamed and ran about in the room. Hazel picked it up behind the head as Moseley had taught, and took it wiggling and twisting back to its box in the laboratory. Moseley was grateful to get his snake back, and needless to say the English class was glad to get rid of the snake.

In 1914, Moseley moved to Bowling Green, Ohio, to teach in the new normal school there, but he never forgot his strong ties to Sandusky and his many good friends. He returned often to visit friends and go on field trips in the surrounding area. He never owned a car or learned to drive, probably because public transportation was easily available on the interurban, and he had good friends who would take him wherever he wanted to go. Streetcars operated about every hour and stopped on demand in many areas. On one trip in 1941 or 1942, Hazel picked him up at the interurban station in Sandusky. She drove him to New London to look for a heron rookery. He had studied the Great Blue Heron nesting habitats in the vicinity of Bowling Green, and he wanted to see the rookery he had heard about in New London. He located the rookery, but its location was so far inland that it disturbed Moseley. The parent herons feed fish to their young, and this rookery was too far from the water for that source of food. He had Hazel drive him to all the farms, up and down the road, so he could inquire about the herons. Finally, Moseley located an old farmer who remembered that when he was a boy, his grandfather told him about an old marsh where the cornfield existed now. The corn field was close to the rookery. This was the reason why the birds nested there; the marsh had provided enough fish to feed the young herons.

Part of their trip to New London was spent bird watching. A farmer had been plowing in a field nearby with a team of horses. They noticed the farmer approaching them on horseback. He was riding one horse and leading the other. He had seen Moseley and stopped to discuss a problem with him. The farmer complained that several of his horses had died of the trembles. Moseley explained that when the grass dies back in the hot summer, horses and cattle become short of food in the pasture, and they eat the white snakeroot which is poisonous. Moseley noticed young snakeroot growing in the farmer's pasture and asked permission to come back in the fall to collect some to take back to Bowling Green. The farmer indicated he would be glad to get rid of the white snakeroot. In the fall, Moseley did return to pick a whole basket of the dried white snakeroot. He used it to try to find an antidote for trembles. The disease was referred to as trembles when it affected the animals and milk sickness when humans got the disease from drinking milk from diseased cows.

In the later years of Moseley's life, Hazel gathered a large group of his former students and their families together for a field trip. Moseley led the group as before, but this time there were many young children in the group. His former students wanted their children to have the same unique experience that they had enjoyed years before. After the trip, they all returned to Hazel's home for a big potluck dinner.

Rose (Steiner) Tschantz (1905-1993), a graduate from Upper Sandusky High School in 1925, entered Bowling Green State Normal College that fall. After one year of training, she taught in the county schools, and continued on to complete her college education with numerous years of summer school and extension classes. After 38 years of teaching, she retired in 1971.

Mrs. Tschantz was a student in Moseley's college class in 1925. Part of the curriculum included astronomy which he taught using his own text *Trees, Stars, and Birds*. To augment a lecture on constellations, the professor set up a night field trip for star gazing. He chose a vantage point away from street lights which would obscure the view. The class of about 35 to 40 students met one winter night at the city post office in Bowling Green. The building had an inside stairway to take them up part way; then they were to go outside to climb up the slanted roof to a flat platform on the top of the building. Mrs. Tschantz remembers that she and her roommate had on their Sunday coats so they did not make the final climb up the icy slant, but they did observe the stars on that bright winter night.

As he went bird watching, Moseley was a familiar sight on the streets of Bowling Green. Mrs. Tschantz remembers that she and her roommate often met him there. Dressed in an ankle-length overcoat and woolen mittens, he was easy to recognize from a distance. He would be leaning way back, almost off balance, with his face upturned so he could watch for birds. If a student stopped and chatted, he would sometimes get a better grade.

Moseley was very mindful of the need for bird sanctuaries. Mrs. Tschantz remembers he owned a farm east of Bowling Green while he taught at the University. All the vegetation was left to grow so the birds could utilize it to the fullest extent for ground cover. Nothing was ever disturbed. This interest in ecology is very well documented in the University archival collection of his personal correspondence, which contains a letter with instructions to one of his farmer tenants to keep an uncut fencerow for the birds.

On one occasion, Mrs. Tschantz's entire class traveled to a forest south of Bowling Green on the interurban streetcar for a field trip. Moseley called it a forest primeval—no logging or farming. She was deeply impressed by this virgin land.

Mrs. Tschantz credits Moseley with her appreciation of nature and the universe. During her 38 years of teaching, she tried to pass that love of nature and the universe on to at least one child in each class. Certainly, this goal would have pleased Moseley.

Anonymous I. One of Moseley's former college students from a 1929 geography class, who asked to be interviewed anonymously, remembers his stern criticism of what he probably thought was eye makeup. The student had been having trouble with a slight skin irritation. Her eyelids were chapped which caused much itching, but a nightly application of vaseline relieved the pain. Apparently one morning she failed to remove the excess medication because Moseley remarked, "I can't see how anyone would have time to put something shiny on her eyes this early in the morning!" She was too embarrassed by his reprimand to explain that it was a medical problem, not a cosmetic beautifier. The following morning she was sure *all* of the vaseline was removed before she attended the Professor's eight o'clock class.

Moseley was fond of using a colorful metaphor to illustrate a point, much like the one-liners used by Henny Youngman. His comment on seeing a man hurrying down the street with his long coattails flying out behind him was, "The man ran so fast you could play a game of checkers on his coat tail!"

Anonymous II. The following stories were contributed by Moseley's former colleague, a woman still living in Bowling Green, who remembers him as tall, thin, fully bearded, and very deliberate in his speech. His colleagues recognized him as a very unusual man, and were often amused by his eccentricities but were always awed by his brilliant mind.

During a September faculty picnic on the shores of the Maumee River, when the air was clear and cool, the sky suddenly took on such a peculiar eerie glow that the watchers were not only startled, but some were even a little frightened. Curving bands of bright light were followed by flashing streaks of color until the whole sky was covered, and the people were dazzled and speechless. Taking advantage of the quiet, Moseley said, "Folks, we are seeing the Aurora Borealis." And his explanation was as spectacular as the Northern Lights themselves.

Frugal in his habits, Moseley practiced small economies wherever possible, as when he made tomato soup from hot water and ketchup or ate his table companions extra bread. He never owned a car but always managed to get rides for the field trips which he himself had planned.

The people of Bowling Green usually overlooked Moseley's poor appearance, out of kindness and respect for him. He spent very little money on his meager wardrobe, which was worn until threadbare and green with age. Along with other college faculty, Moseley had initiated a drive to collect warm clothing for the Russians left destitute after the revolution. When faculty wives were packing the donated items at an empty downtown store, Moseley came in to help. "He was pleased with the community's generosity and with the ladies' packing, and so he left—only to return almost immediately with the words—"HAS ANYBODY SEEN MY OVERCOAT?" No one remembered seeing the coat, but all suspected where it might be, and so they dug down into the box until they found it, the oldest, greenest one in the package. He was grateful, the ladies were amused, and the coat was again on its way for another season of use.

It was said that some landladies refused to rent a room to Moseley for fear he might bring a snake into the house, as he had been known to do just that. However, as a roomer, he was so quiet and private in his comings and goings that, when fire broke out in his rooming house, firemen had to probe with a long hook through the window in order to learn that he wasn't there. Meantime, observers on the street were very anxious.

One of his hobbies was watching and recording the annual flights of migrating birds. He knew when each type was expected and watched for it. However, once in a while an unexpected flock stopped in Bowling Green and was seen by people who then reported the sighting to Moseley. He was delighted with the information but wanted to know *exactly* when the birds were seen. If one could not tell him the exact date, the viewer was apt to be reminded, even by mail, that he should *try* very hard to remember *when he saw that special bird*. After one such experience, the viewer did not tell Moseley about seeing an unusual bird unless he knew exactly when the sighting took place!

Because he was a loner and eccentric, few knew Moseley very well. It was common knowledge that he owned a farm someplace, and that he had a nephew or two, but not many knew where he spent his vacations or his money. It was, therefore, a surprise at the time of his death to learn that he had left a remarkably large estate to Bowling Green State University, the money to be used for students. During President Prout's lifetime, he took pleasure in administering this fund, considering needs as small as fifty dollars for books. In perspective, Moseley's whole life now seems to have been shaped around his interest in knowledge and in young people, both worthy causes.

Steamer *Arrow*.

(Post card; Stuckey Collection)

Moseley with students, as if waiting on a streetcar, to leave on a botanical field excursion.

(Taken on the loading platform at rear of entrance of the Bowling Green Armory Building where classes were first held when the school opened (1914-1915); Gift of Wilbert Ohlemacher, Niederhofer Collection)

Field Excursions for Moseley's Classes

CHAPTER SIX

Relda E. Niederhofer

Edwin Lincoln Moseley at age 24, came to Sandusky in 1889 to teach all the science courses at Sandusky High School. For the next 10 years he involved his students in collecting and identifying the plants in the Sandusky area, with the project culminating in the publication of his "Sandusky flora" (1899). Class field trips a hundred years ago were different from today, because of the rapidity of travel in private cars on super paved highways. Moseley's means of travel was by public transportation, for example, the Lake Shore Electric, the interurban streetcar, which was readily available in Sandusky to go almost anywhere. The conductors knew Moseley, so they would stop on demand to discharge the Professor and his students wherever they wanted to go. When he traveled by water the Port of Sandusky had many steamers that made scheduled trips to the Erie Islands. Moseley was armed with a vasculum, whistle, and field glasses. He required his students to bring money for transportation and a large well packed lunch, because Moseley did not carry a lunch.

Moseley undoubtedly took many field excursions with his classes, but only a few are documented in the *Sandusky Register*. Those known reported excursions, a total of 15, are listed at the end of this account. The remainder of this essay is composed of descriptions from the newspaper reports on selected trips. The first known recorded trip, which involved his botany class, was 18 May 1891 to Johnson's Island in Sandusky Bay.[1] Two years later, on 19 May 1893,[2] the botany class sailed to Cedar Point, just across Sandusky Bay from Sandusky, in search of wild flowers, with the report that "Cedar Point abounds in botanical specimens, many of them not found in the woods on the mainland." On Saturday 20 May 1893, the class went to Castalia:

> ...the energetic botany class, in spite of threatening skies, took a much longer trip, . . .They started at eight o'clock in carriages and arriving at the Castalia blue hole, alighted to view that wonder. They then drove on to the remarkable rocky ridge beyond Castalia and spent the remainder of the forenoon in gathering flowers. After dinner they drove to [a] woods in Sandusky county. . . gathering flowers [and] looking and listening for the different birds and listening to Prof. Moseley's interesting remarks when anything new to the class was found. . . .All that went agreed that they had a very pleasant and instructive day.

The botany class, according to the newspaper account[2] for 1 June 1893 had taken trips to the woods on the bay shore west of the city, and the woods to the west and those southeast of the Soldiers' Home. These sites have each been visited on many different afternoons, several of them on school days, the class starting at the time that the botany recitation usually commences. Memorial Day, 30 May 1893, was decided to be the last excursion of the school year, this time to the Huron River, about two and one-half miles west of Milan. The river cuts through a rock formation of Huron shale, exposing a perpendicular wall 50 to 60 feet in height. In certain places, these walls support vegetation such as the hemlock tree and stonecrop which does not grow nearer Sandusky. Altogether the class obtained specimens of 30 or 40 species of plants, most of them with flowers. Among those that were new to the class were wild sarsaparilla, wild ginger, baneberry, blue cohosh, lance-leaved violet, sickle pod, Canada violet, tulip tree, and Greek valerian.

On Saturday, 19 May 1894, Moseley chartered the steamer *Erie* to take the botany class and their friends to Kelleys and Green Island. A second chartered excursion to the Islands on the steamer *Erie* was planned for 2 July 1894.[3] The departure time was 7:30 a.m. from the dock at the foot of Columbus Avenue in Sandusky. "Room will be reserved for graduates of the High School and seniors until 10 minutes before the boat starts when other students will be admitted." This trip was to Catawba, Green, and Rattlesnake Islands.

Seven girls and five boys of the senior class with Moseley departed on the nine o'clock interurban streetcar for Milan Saturday, 25 September 1897.[4] They were clad in their oldest time-worn clothes. Each carried a vasculum, tin or pasteboard boxes, bottles for bugs and things, a camera, and a huge butterfly net. At Milan they changed to a farmer's long wagon drawn by two horses. They were happy to have the farmer added to their party, because they were now 14 in number and not the dreaded 13, which meant that ill luck would follow them. Their wagon trip to the banks of the Huron River took them up and down hills, a most bumpy dusty ride of about two and one-half miles on a wagon without springs. They found concretions in the river bed, some complete and others broken. In some low places they were able to walk on the dry river bed, other impounded areas were good for collecting "living creatures" of crayfish, clams, crabs, and minnows. At some places along the bank masses of solid rock were almost perpendicular to the river bed. They stopped to eat their lunch at a place where a huge basswood tree had fallen providing a place to sit and rest. Their trip progressed through the woods collecting frogs, butterflies, and many kinds of asters and goldenrods. They climbed the steep embankment and slid down muddy slopes collecting and enjoying the beautiful scenery. They missed their 4:20 p.m. car that was to take them home, but the farmer gave them water and a basket of apples from his orchard for dinner. Assailed by pangs of hunger two boys went into Milan for grapes, but they were unsuccessful in finding any of them. The group sat watching twilight deepen and with nighttime coming the stars began to shine. After Moseley gave a lesson in astronomy, the longed for streetcar appeared, and by eight o'clock all were home again.

> Notwithstanding the discomforts after nightfall, should you ask any of the party how they enjoyed themselves they will tell you that they "would fall into the river ten times, spend an hour or so after the return in removing burrs and mud; [sun] burn their faces; skin their hands; wilt their collars; lose pocketbooks, knives and all (provided they found them again); be bitten by crabs [chiggers]; lose their dear little frogs and beautiful butterflies; suffer the pangs of hunger; and walk and walk and walk; endure all of these tribulations, yes, and even more for the pleasures of another such a perfect day. For that excursion," they will add, "truly paid."

—Modified and edited from a manuscript read at the annual meeting of the Ohio Academy of Science, 5 April 1997, on the campus of Bowling Green State University, see Relda E. Niederhofer. 1997. "Edwin Lincoln Moseley's botany class field trips." *Ohio Journal of Science* 97(2): A-24. Program Abstracts.

References

1. 1891. Anonymous. "[Trip to Johnson Island]." *Sandusky Register*, 19 May, p. 4.

2. 1893. Grace Farwell. "High School Column. [Botany class trip]." *Sandusky Daily Register*, 25 May p. 1; "[Botany class excursions]." *Sandusky Daily Register*, 1 June, p. 4.

3. 1894. Anonymous. "[Botanical tour of Kelleys and Green Islands]." *Sandusky Register*, 17 May, p. 8; "Natural history students. N. B." *Sandusky Daily Register*, 1 July, p. 5.

4. 1897. Anonymous. "Day on the Huron's banks. High school seniors took a trip that truly paid." *Sandusky Register*, 27 September, p. 5.

Sandusky streetcar station on DeWitt Avenue across from Soldiers Home.

(Sandusky Library Archives)

Science Field Excursions for Moseley's Classes, Sandusky High School (1891-1899)

This list of local field excursions taken by Moseley and his high school botany classes has been compiled from those reported in the *Sandusky Register*. They were all taken from 1891 to 1897, during the time when he was preparing his "Sandusky flora" (1899).

Mon.	18 May 1891	Johnson's Island, Ottawa County
Fri.	19 May 1893	Cedar Point, Erie County
Sat.	20 May 1893	Castalia Blue Hole, rocky ridge [Margaretta Ridge in Erie County] southeast of Castalia; woods in Sandusky County
Tue.	30 May 1893	Huron River, 2.5 miles west of Milan, Erie County
Sat.	30 Sep. 1893	Berlin Heights, Erie County
Sat.	19 May 1894	Kelleys Island, Erie County; Green Island, Ottawa County
Sat.	2 June 1894	Put-in-Bay Island [South Bass Island], Green Island, Ottawa County
Mon.	2 July 1894	Catawba, Green, and Rattlesnake Islands, Ottawa County [a special trip for students who had graduated and were interested in natural history]
Fri.	3 Aug. 1894	Catawba Island, Moss Island [Mouse Island]
Sat.	20 Apr. 1895	Berlin, Erie County [Notice of this field trip appeared in the *Erie County Reporter*, 25 April, p. 4]
Sat.	19 Oct. 1895	Vermilion and Oberlin, Lorain County
Sat.	25 Apr. 1896	Milan, Erie County
Sat.	9 May 1896	Put-in-Bay Island [South Bass Island], Ottawa County
Sat.	25 Sep. 1897	Banks of the Huron River, Erie County
Thurs.	13 May 1897	Margaretta Ridge, west end of Margaretta Township, Erie County

CHAPTER 6 • FIELD EXCURSIONS FOR MOSELEY'S CLASSES

Botany Field Trip to Vermilion and Oberlin: A Description by Ralph H. McKelvey [1895]

Ralph H. McKelvey (1877-1957), a student of Moseley's in Sandusky High School, provided a colorful description of one of Moseley's botany-class field trips taken in October 1895. His essay preserves one example of many field-class excursions that Moseley led during his lifetime of teaching natural history.

As some of us may know, the school year of 1895-96 commenced the first of last September, and with the opening of school came the joyful tidings from Professor Edwin Lincoln Moseley that the botany class was soon to go on an excursion.

Now botany excursions were quite frequent last spring, but no matter how often they were planned, their announcement was always greeted with the greatest enthusiasm and manifestation of joy. And to come down to the point they generally cost each person from 10 to 50 cents, according to the distance. And now when Moseley made the fearful announcement that the excursion in question was to cost a dollar and a quarter we were all filled with a wild desire to know when and where we were going. As to the when part of it we were soon satisfied: We were not to go until the twelfth of October. But where? To tell the truth, we never knew where we were going until about 10 seconds before we got off the train at our destination. One evening Moseley positively refused to tell us beforehand where he was going to take us.

Moseley told us everything about the trip except where we would go. The main object of the trip was to see scenery, in fact some of the finest scenery in northern Ohio. We were to go part way by train and then drive a long distance. We were especially urged to bring plenty to eat. We never knew until the afternoon before the twelfth on what railroad we would go, and then at the last moment we were requested to be at the Lake Shore depot at 5:30 the following morning.

We, who for a month had been unsuccessfully trying to find out where our trip would take us, immediately looked up timetables and found that the only train leaving the Lake Shore depot at 5:30 a.m. was one going east. This did away with wild conjectures on the part of some who believed that we were going to Ann Arbor or other places west of Sandusky. It was wonderful to observe the ideas some members of the class got for the purchasing power of $1.25. One boy even got excited enough over the affair to think that we were going to the Rocky Mountains and accordingly wrote to an uncle who lives in Denver, Colorado, to meet him at the train. Ten had expressed their intention of going, and on Friday night those 10 went to bed early, each one having stowed away an alarm clock under the pillow. Ten alarm clocks struck at 4:30 the next morning and 10 sleepy scholars awoke only to find the rain pouring down on the roof. We didn't go. The trip was postponed for a week, and at the end of that time we knew no more about where we were going than we did the week before. Nevertheless, six of the 10 who had originally intended to go got up when the stars were shining brightly in the sky, and after stowing away a hasty breakfast wended their weary way to the depot. Whether or not all six of them were weary or not I don't know. I was. I will say nothing of the experiences of that morning, nothing of the boy who climbed on another boy's roof to wake him up by yelling in the window and then had to hold up his hands to keep from being shot by the next-door neighbor, who took him for a housebreaker. Nothing of the girl who waited for a street car that didn't come and then had to run all the way to the depot. At last we found ourselves in a train full of people who had just awoke or who were still "insomno." They didn't seem to understand our mirth and evidently thought we were tin peddlers from the array of vasculums which we carried. But we didn't bother them long, for when the train drew up at Vermilion we knew for the first time that the metropolis of Vermilion township was our destination.

When we got off the train the natives about the station gazed on us in awe as we marched toward a vehicle which resembled a patrol wagon more than anything else, and which was to carry us on our long drive through the surrounding country. They evidently thought that a Salvation Army had struck the town and when they caught sight of the young ladies of the party all prepared to sign the pledge. Later on they must have changed their minds and thought us a delegation from the insane asylum when two of the three boys went around to the drygoods, furniture, and drug stores of the city in an effort to buy a pound of pretzels, which the young ladies felt they could not do without. Soon we started on our drive, following the winding course of the beautiful Vermilion River, crossing and recrossing it, now rolling along on the high banks, stopping here and there to fearfully glance over the perpendicular walls or to ramble among the trees, their leaves now painted by the autumn, and then, descending into the valley by some precipitous road, we gazed upon the walls of rock, the beautiful woods above, and the distant hills. Many were the scenes we looked on which might well be put on canvas and we all deplored the lack of a camera.

After a delightful time spent along the Vermilion River, at the suggestion of the driver, who had so kindly given us the use of his horses, we drove to South Amherst to see the deepest, or one of the deepest, sandstone quarries in the state. The little limestone quarries hereabouts are paled by the grand and magnificent scale on which this quarry is conducted. We judged it to be nearly half a mile long, and it was so deep that the men working on the bottom were thought by some of us to be small boys.

At this point some questions brought forth the fact that we were then only seven or eight miles from Oberlin, Ohio, the college town. The leader of the expedition had no intention of taking us so far, but Mr. Olds furnished so good a team of horses that we thought we could drive to Oberlin and still return in time for our train. We spent the next three or four miles eating our lunch, and soon we were aware that we were nearing Oberlin, for the air was fragrant with delicious odors of hash and ham fat, which viands are said to be the principal fare of the students. A lurking belief exists in my mind that this is imaginary, so I do not make the statement on my own authority.

We arrived at Oberlin, cold and dusty, and found the museum, the building which we made for first, locked up, but we managed to get in through a back door, and we somewhat hurriedly went through the fine collection, not giving it as much time as we wished. On the second floor of the same building we saw the library, and from there went to the old residence of the famous Mr. Finney, an early president of the College, which has been turned into a botanical laboratory and herbarium. Here we met Professor Kelsey, who seemed to consider it the greatest honor of his life to meet a party of Sanduskians. We also hurriedly visited the conservatory of music, ladies' hall, the chemical laboratory and the chapel, after which we left in high spirits for Vermilion, 20 miles away.

On this long drive we passed the time in sleep, at least the boys did. But the said sleep was of a peculiar nature. We slept under peculiar circumstances, to say the least. For example, one boy lay in the bottom of the wagon wrapped in an astrakhan horse blanket, while the other two sat on top of him and pounded him with repeated requests for him to dream. If the dream was not forthcoming he was pounded and smothered more until he had to dream or die. We also exercised our vocal talent and brought forth some truly beautiful music, entertaining the passersby to such an extent that they gave us the whole road, even turning into the ditch to do so.

At Vermilion we took leave of Mr. Olds, who had driven us forty miles or more and pointed out so many objects of interest. We were soon in Sandusky, as tired as when we started. The girls all said it was perfectly lovely, and the boys indicated that they had never had so much fun before in their lives.

—Modified and edited by RLS from Ralph H. McKelvey. 1895. "One of our excursions:" Essay read in the junior and senior literary class, Sandusky High School. *Sandusky Register*, 16 November, p. 6.

Ralph Huntington McKelvey (1877-1957), born in Sandusky, Ohio, 17 December 1877, was a graduate of Sandusky High School and Oberlin College (1901). He also studied at The Ohio State University and Stanford University. McKelvey became a self-taught artist and worked with artists and art organizations in Florida (1929-1957), as an artist in Mentone, France (1932, 1933), and had a one-man show in New York City at the Studio Guild (1939). During his earlier career, he was principally headquartered in New York City as the head of R. H. McKelvey & Co., Lumber Insurance. His works of art are in many private collections, including Oberlin College, in the United States and England. At age 80, McKelvey died 3 April 1957 in Bradenton, Florida.

CHAPTER 6 • FIELD EXCURSIONS FOR MOSELEY'S CLASSES

References for Biographical Sketch

19—. Anonymous. [Biographical Sketch of Ralph Huntington McKelvey]. Printed, one page. McKelvey File, Miscellaneous Biography, Sandusky Library Archives, Sandusky, Ohio.

1956. Dorothy B. Gilbert, ed. 1956. "Ralph Huntington McKelvey," p. 317. In *Who's Who in American Art*. R. R. Bowker Co., New York. x, 603 pp.

Three field sites where Moseley took his botany classes: Inscription Rock, Kelleys Island (upper left); Glacial Grooves, Kelleys Island (upper right); Blue Hole, Castalia (lower center).

(Post cards; Stuckey Collection)

75

Hiram and Sybil (Moseley) Bingham, Moseley's maternal grandparents.

(Portrait by Samuel F. B. Morse in 1820; published in the
Hawaiian Journal of History 9: opp. p. 8. 1975; Yale University Art Gallery)

Family History

Relda E. Niederhofer

CHAPTER SEVEN

Research into the histories of both the Moseley family and the Bingham family has revealed, in an unpublished manuscript by family member Lillian (Crocker) Brown[6,10] that its members were ministers, missionaries, teachers, statesmen, and writers. Among them were graduates from Yale, Harvard, Amherst, and Andover Seminary. Mrs. Brown wrote: "Some of the more outstanding are found through the distaff side. Most of them loved learning more than money and were able to get the higher education which they craved." [see publication note B, page 275].

The Moseley family can trace its genealogy back eight generations to Miles Standish, who came to this country in December 1620 on the *Mayflower*. Other ancestors included Thomas Dudley, one of the earliest governors of Massachusetts; Rev. Benjamin Woodbridge, who was the first graduate of Harvard and ordained as a minister at Andover; Ralph Wheelock, born in England 1600, who took a master's degree at Cambridge, fled to America because of his nonconformity to the Church of England, and became the first school teacher in Medford, Massachusetts; and Deacon Samuel Chapin, who founded Springfield, Massachusetts. Edwin L. Moseley's maternal grandparents, Hiram and Sybil Bingham, were missionaries in Honolulu where his mother Sophia was born. As a young girl of eight, Sophia was sent back to New England to be raised by an aunt in a more civilized area and to have a good education.

The first paternal American ancestor of Edwin L. Moseley was John Moseley, who came from Lancaster, England, in 1630, and settled in Dorchester, Massachusetts. His first maternal American ancestor was Thomas Bingham, who came to this country from Sheffield, England in 1659, and settled in Saybrook, Connecticut. They did not know each other, but in the next three hundred years the families met and married and merged more than once.

Ancestry of Moseley Family

John Moseley was among the first settlers in Dorchester, Massachusetts. By his first wife Elizabeth, he had three sons, Thomas, Joseph, and John, and a daughter Elizabeth. In 1636 the Moseleys, along with a large portion of the first inhabitants, moved west to a new settlement, Windsor, on the borders of the Connecticut River. A second wife Cicily and John, the father, both died in 1661.

The family history is traced through John and Elizabeth's youngest son, John who married Mary Allyn Newberry in 1664. This John was called Lieutenant Moseley then. He died in 1690 leaving large real estate holdings. John and Mary had ten children, of which two sons, Joseph and Consider, were direct ancestors of Edwin L. Moseley. Only the descendants of Consider are traced here because the compiler, Mrs. Lillian Brown, did not provide information about Joseph's descendants.

Consider Moseley married Elizabeth Bancroft and reared eight children. Most of John's children and Consider's eight children grew up in Westfield, Massachusetts. As the city prospered the Moseley families flourished, becoming leading citizens.

Consider's son Israel married Anna Maudlesley. Their son, Israel, Jr., married Abigail Chapin, and their son Chauncey Moseley married Harriet Bingham, Edwin's paternal grandparents. A second son of Consider Moseley, Daniel married Anna Abbott who was a grandmother of Sybil (Moseley) Bingham, Edwin's maternal grandmother [see Chart Showing Intermarriages of Moseley and Bingham Families, page 88].

Chauncey Moseley was a handful to his esteemed Westfield family and to his 10 children. He cared nothing for higher learning and still less for piety; he loved personal ease and pleasure. Harriet was a grand woman and devoted mother. Several of Chauncey's children were able to get an education, despite their father's resistance. A son, Samuel, was educated at Yale and became a minister. Son David became an editor of a religious paper in Hartford. Chauncey and Harriet's sixth child, William Augustus Moseley, Edwin's father, decided that the struggle to go to college, against his father's opposition, was too great. He ran away to Atlanta, Georgia, for a short stay, but returned to Westfield to marry 18-year-old Sophia. She and William later moved to Union City, Branch County, Michigan, about 75 miles west of Ann Arbor, where they raised nine children. The youngest child was Edwin Lincoln Moseley, born 29 March 1865.

Ancestry of Bingham Family

The Bingham family can be traced back to Sheffield, England, where the silver industry flourished. In 1614, Thomas Bingham was admitted as a master cutler and the trademark ₿ granted him. Thomas married Anna Stenton in 1631. A son Thomas was born in 1642, the first American ancestor by the name of Bingham. When he was 17 years old he sailed from England with parents, Thomas and Anna, for Saybrook, Connecticut, in 1659. It is assumed that Thomas, the father, died en route as no mention of him is given after the company landed. The widow, Anna, had property enough to buy in for herself and son as proprietors in a new colony. Anna soon married William Backus, a widower with grown children, and a year later they moved to Norwich, Connecticut.

Young Thomas married Mary Rudd in 1666 and they moved to Windham, Connecticut, where a large tract of land had been willed to a few of the Norwich colonists by a son of the very friendly Indian chief, Uncas. Tom and Mary had 11 children. Most of their children settled in Windham, but their eldest son, also named Thomas, remained in Norwich and succeeded to his father's property there. The second Thomas Bingham in America, married Hannah Backus and through two of their sons, Jabez and Joseph, the ancestral path leads down to both William and Sophia Moseley, Edwin's parents. From Jabez Bingham I and his wife Bethia Wood, the descent was through their son, Jabez Bingham II and Mary Wheelock, and their son, Jabez Bingham III and Mary Mitchell, and their daughter Harriet Bingham who married Chauncey Moseley and then to William Moseley, father of Edwin. From Joseph Bingham and his wife, Ruth Post, the descent was through their son, Calvin Bingham, and Lydia Denton, and their son Hiram Bingham and Sybil (Moseley) Bingham and then to Sophia Bingham, mother of Edwin [see Chart Showing Intermarriages of Moseley and Bingham Families, page 88].

Missionary Work in Hawaii

The most colorful of the Binghams were Hiram and Sybil, missionaries to the Hawaiian Islands (Sandwich Islands) in 1820-1841. Hiram was born in 1789 in Bennington, Vermont. He graduated from Middlebury College and then studied for the ministry at Andover Seminary. While at the seminary he and Asa Thurston, a fellow student, became interested and volunteered for foreign missionary work. The American Board of Commissioners for Foreign Missions (ABCFM) decided to send six young men with their wives, as a pioneer group to the Hawaiian Islands. Asa was married, but Hiram had not yet found a wife when they accepted the charge. It seemed desirable that Hiram should also have the help and companionship of a fine, capable wife. Hiram was refused his first proposal of marriage to Sarah Shepard, the daughter of the village clergyman, Rev. Samuel Shepard.[8] A month later at the time of his ordination, he was introduced to Sybil Moseley. She was charming, had a splendid education, had been teaching in a school in Canandaigua, New York, and was deeply interested in missionary work. They met in September and were married a month later in October 1819. Since the young couple would be away for a considerable length of time, the families wanted a remembrance of them. So their wedding picture was a portrait painted by the famous American painter and inventor of the Morse code and telegraph, Samuel F. B. Morse.[8]

They sailed with the other missionaries from Boston harbor, 23 October 1819, on the Brig *Thaddeus* and arrived in Honolulu 19 April 1820. The six months voyage around Cape Horn, South America, was an ordeal in the small sailing vessel. Sybil kept an account of the long tedious trip in her diaries and many letters.[8] Her entries indicate they were both sea sick much of the time. Sybil and three of the other young missionary wives became pregnant during the voyage.

Life in the primitive village of Honolulu was difficult for the frail young Sybil. She worked diligently, many hours a day with Hiram in his ministry. In November of that first year, Hiram acted as midwife for Sybil, delivering their first child. Not only was Sophia their first born, but she was also one of the first white children born in the Islands. As was the custom of most missionaries, Sophia was sent to New England to be educated. Sybil was heartbroken to let the little eight-year-old make the long trip back to the mainland. Six other children were born to Hiram and Sybil. Two of their sons died in infancy.

Sybil was beloved by the Hawaiians as well as her fellow missionaries. Her son Hiram, Jr. wrote a letter years after her death to his son, Hiram:

> *If ever there was in this world a woman who was noble, honest, generous, loving, tenderhearted and sympathetic, that woman was your grandmother, my own dear, sainted mother; and how sincere was her belief in those doctrines which I hold to be essential to salvations, and to earnest wholehearted service for our Lord Jesus.*[8]

Queen Kaahumanu thought so much of Sybil that she gave the Binghams a 224-acre tract on which she built a thatched cottage. As the years went by Hiram improved the cottage to make it more comfortable, and Sybil managed the building of a wall to keep the cattle from wandering into the home. The night-blooming cereus she planted on the wall remained for generations. Mrs. Lillian (Crocker) Brown, reported in the unpublished history that the night-blooming cereus had spread until the hedge surrounded two sides of the campus.[6] Mrs. Brown had seen them in bloom when it was estimated 12,000 blossoms were open at one time. Sybil also started sugar cane and banana plantations to help support the church.[8] The 21 years they labored as missionaries took its toll on Sybil's health.

Hiram was the strictest of Calvinist preachers. While his life was devoted to "saving the souls of the heathen," his manner was very abrasive. He assumed the

Sophia Bingham, eight-year-old daughter of Hiram and Sybil Bingham.

She was one of the first white children born on the Hawaiian Islands (Sandwich Islands), and later became the mother of Edwin L. Moseley.

(Taken about the same time that she was sent to New England for her education; Hawaiian Mission Children's Society Library, Mission Houses Museum)

position of self-appointed leader of the missionaries. One of Hiram's concerns was the degradation of the young native girls' morals. For years the "waninini" had met the sailing ships when they came into port. Hiram stopped this custom by teaching the girls that their behavior was immoral. In 1827, a whaling ship's crew bombarded a mission home on Maui because they were angry with the missionaries for denying them their customary visitation by the native girls. The particular incident was used in the movie version of James A. Michener's *Hawaii*, released in 1966.[8]

The natives had always worn very light clothing, indeed if any, in the tropics; skinny dipping was a common practice to cool off on a hot day. By contrast, the missionaries wore dark colored, heavy woolens and starched linens even in the summer. Every fall they followed their New England custom of putting on their "red flannels." Hiram tried to teach the Hawaiians to dress and act more civilized.[11]

With the help of the other preachers, Hiram developed a written language for the Hawaiians. They reduced the English alphabet to twelve letters to accommodate the sound of the spoken language. The missionaries translated the books of the Bible, elementary school books for the children, and hymnals into Hawaiian.[6,11]

Hiram did the architectural drawings, raised the money, and wheedled King Kamehameha III into supplying the land and a thousand laborers to build the stone church at Kawaiahao in Honolulu. The workers had considerable trouble digging down to bedrock and quarrying almost 14,000 coral slabs from the reef for its construction. Six years in building, it was finally dedicated in 1842. Hiram had planned to be its first pastor, but was called back to New England. King Kamehameha III was the first Christian King converted by the missionaries.[12]

Hiram was anxious to end his furlough in New England and to return to the Islands to continue educating the natives, but the ABCFM was receiving complaints about him. The board heard criticism ". . . about the domineering character of its pioneer missionary—not only from the Chinese trade merchants and whaling ship masters, on whose financial contributions they were heavily dependent, but even from the latter missionaries, who had determined Bingham's continuing assumption of leadership intolerably arrogant."[8]

Finally in 1841, Hiram resigned his position as missionary and returned to New England with his semi-invalid wife.[8] Hiram was confident that with a short rest Sybil would be well, and they would return to their evangelistic work. Sybil's health grew worse, though, and she died of consumption in 1848. The Mission Board had no intention of sending Hiram back to the islands with or without his second wife, Naomi. Hiram wrote the long history of their adventures, *A Residence of Twenty-one Years in the Sandwich Islands*. Although the book did not become the best seller he had hoped, it was used by James A. Michener to research the lives of the early missionaries. Michener used the missionaries as models for his portrayal of Abner Hale and Jerusha Bromley in *Hawaii*, his 1959 best seller. Abner Hale became a composite of Hiram Bingham and Asa Thurston, but he favored Hiram's domineering character a little closer. The beautiful heroine, Jerusha (played by Julie Andrews) was more like Lucy Thurston than the "plain conscience-ridden Sybil, if only because she too had written a book, while Sybil's story was locked in her diaries and many scattered letters. . . ."[8]

After the War Between the States, but before 1873, Hiram and Sybil's daughter Lydia started a girls' school in Honolulu across the street from the great stone church her father had established. A few years later her sister Lizzie joined her. Hiram, Jr. followed almost exactly in his father's footsteps. He was ordained, married, and then sailed from Boston to bring Christianity to the natives in the Pacific. It had taken Hiram, Sr. 25 days; Hiram, Jr. managed all of this in just 23 days.[8] Hiram, Jr. and his wife Clara were sent to the Gilbert Islands where they worked as missionaries for 34 years. Like his father, in 1890 Hiram, Jr. translated the Bible, but this time into Gilbertese. Hiram, Jr's. Gilbertese dictionary was published in 1908, and a Gilbertese hymnal and tune book in 1880. In 1875, Mrs. Bingham published *Bible Stories in the Gilbertese*.[4] Hiram Bingham III broke away from the missionary tradition. He distinguished himself as an explorer (directing the Peruvian expedition in 1912 and 1914-1915), as governor of Connecticut, and a United States Senator.[5]

Edwin L. Moseley's Parents

Mrs. Brown's history[6] continues when eight-year-old Sophia Bingham sailed out of the Honolulu harbor in 1828 destined for Boston. She carried with her not only the love of her missionary parents, but also a small wooden doll Hiram had made for her. She was met in Boston by her Aunt Lucy Whiting, Sybil's sister, who raised her as Hiram and Sybil wanted—in a more civilized environment.[15] She attended Miss Emma Willard's Seminary in Troy, New York.[6] Sophia did not see her parents again until they returned in 1841. By this time she had matured into a young lady and had married William Augustus Moseley.

Discouraged by his disapproving father Chauncey, William A. Moseley never received the college education he wanted. He married eighteen-year-old Sophia Bingham in 1839. They were apparently third cousins, as discussed previously. They lived in Hartford, Connecticut, for a year or two, but William wanted to go west as some relatives and friends had done earlier. Their first child, Mary Bingham, was born 9 November 1840.[1] A second daughter, Ella Sophia, was born 14 March 1842, just two months before the first baby died. After burying Mary Bingham in Hartford, the family moved to southern Michigan. William A., Jr. was born 12 May 1845 at Moscow, Michigan, but by 24 August 1847 when a second son, Hiram Bingham, was born they had moved to Union City, Michigan. William A., Sr.'s cousin, Colonel Thomas Moseley (1794-1865),[3] formerly of Pittsfield, Massachusetts, had come to Union City, Michigan, and established himself as a prosperous businessman in the manufacture of iron. Colonel Tom purchased considerable land and extensive business interests in the city. William conducted a mercantile business in the city for many years with varied success, where he sold everything from muslin to codfish.

The Moseley family continued to grow with the birth of their fifth child, Mary Whiting,[1] born 24 August 1849. Charles Albert, a sixth child was born 27 August 1853, just about a year before 12-year-old Ella Sophia died. Charles Albert died as a youngster of 11. Frank Hunnewell was born 28 January 1855; he died of consumption as a young man of 21. Frank was the fourth child to die before reaching adulthood. Clara Lydia, eighth child was born 14 June 1857. As a young girl of 16, Clara[15] went to Honolulu to help her aunts, Lydia and Lizzie, Sophia's sisters, who had started a girls' school, across the street from the stone church that their father, Hiram, Sr. had built. The 24-year-old Mary, had been chosen to go to the Islands, but Charles Crocker, their next door neighbor and William A., Sr.'s partner in the mercantile business, wanted Mary for his bride, thus Clara went in Mary's place. Edwin was the baby of the family, born eight years after Clara, on 29 March 1865. It became Edwin's responsibility to be executor for many of the wills of his older brothers and sisters. He was in a position to help in this regard, because he became the most educated family member, whose occupation was an innovative educator.[6,7]

In his advanced years William A., Sr.[14] was often seen on the streets advocating his views of prohibition. The articles William wrote for the *Coldwater Republican* (15 December 1885, 11 February 1887, and 17 April 1894) expressed his very ardent prohibitionist belief. The following reflects the feelings of William A., Sr.:

Remodeled home of William and Sophia Moseley in Union City, Michigan, where Edwin L. Moseley was born.

(Taken in 1983 by Relda E. Niederhofer; Niederhofer Collection)

One word of encouragement to men engaged in the liquor business: I will not call you my friends, because you are the enemies of my country, and your own worst enemies, because you have been deceived and led to engage in a business that is destructive and damaging to the morals of the people.[2]

In 1863, William and Sophia built their large home two doors from the Congregational Church on North Broadway in Union City, just a block or two from their general store.[9] The long porch with railing, baluster, and vertical spindles, extended across the entire front of the house with wooden steps at the center. The symmetrical design, with a window above another window or door, the Federal doorways with heavy cornice molding, all characterized its Federal style architecture. With a little imagination one can see the Moseley family seated behind the railing rocking on a Sunday afternoon in the shade of that fine porch roof.

The early Congregational Church records in Union City were destroyed by fire, but since William and Sophia lived two doors away I think we can assume that they were members of that church and had all the children baptized there.[13] The other reason for believing they were members of the Congregational Church is that Sophia's parents were missionaries for the ABCFM which was a Protestant group, primarily Congregational and Presbyterian. Mrs. Elizabeth Brooks, grandniece of Edwin, remembers family stories of how Sophia had no trouble getting Edwin to go to church, but did have difficulty getting the oldest son, William A. Jr. to attend services.[15] With their age differences, this seems understandable; William was twenty when Edwin was born.

References

1. Without Date. Anonymous. [Family list for William Augustus Moseley]. Genealogical Collection, Hawaiian Mission Children's Society Library. Mission Houses Museum, Honolulu, Hawaii.

2. 1892. Wm. A. Moseley. *How to Save the Nation*. Leaflet, published for the author, Union City, Michigan. 4 February. Archives, Bowling Green State University. 1 p.

3. 1893. Dwight E. Young. *Chronicles of Union City, Michigan*, D. J. Easton Printer, Union City, Michigan. p. 38.

4. 1929. Anonymous. "Hiram Bingham (1831-1908)", p. 277. In *Dictionary of American Biography*. vol. I. Charles Scribner's Sons, New York. 277 pp.

5. 1930. Anonymous. "Hiram Bingham," pp. 28,29. In *The National Cyclopedia of American Biography, Current*. vol. A. James T. White & Co., New York. 552 pp., index.

6. 1940. Lillian (Crocker) Brown. "Moseleys and Binghams." Unpublished history. 10 pp.

7. 1945. Josephine True. "Edwin Lincoln Moseley: The biography of an educator." *Nature Magazine* 38: 37-39.

8. 1975. Alfred M. Bingham. "Sybil's bones, a chronicle of the three Hiram Bingham's." *Hawaiian Journal of History* 9: 3-36. (page 8).

9. 1980. Mary Alaniz. "1880 Union City graduate achieves success as a professor at Bowling Green University." *Coldwater Daily Reporter*, 9 July, p. 3.

10. 1981. Mrs. Elizabeth Brooks. Letter to Relda E. Niederhofer, 18 November, from Wilmette, Illinois.

11. 1982. Mrs. Richard Lee. Personal conversation with Relda E. Niederhofer, June, from Honolulu, Hawaii.

12. 1982. Albertine Loomis. *The Ali'i of Hawaii at Kawaiahao Church, Honolulu, Hawaii*. Leaflet, 2 pp., June.

13. 1982. Mrs. Marjorie Glesmann. Personal conversation with Relda E. Niederhofer, 11 November, from Union City, Michigan.

14. 1982. Mrs. Marjorie Glesmann. Letter to Relda E. Niederhofer, 29 November, from Union City, Michigan.

15. 1983. Mrs. Elizabeth Brooks. Personal conversation with Relda E. Niederhofer, 13 August, from Wilmette, Illinois.

CHAPTER 7 • FAMILY HISTORY

Chart Showing Intermarriages of Moseley and Bingham Families

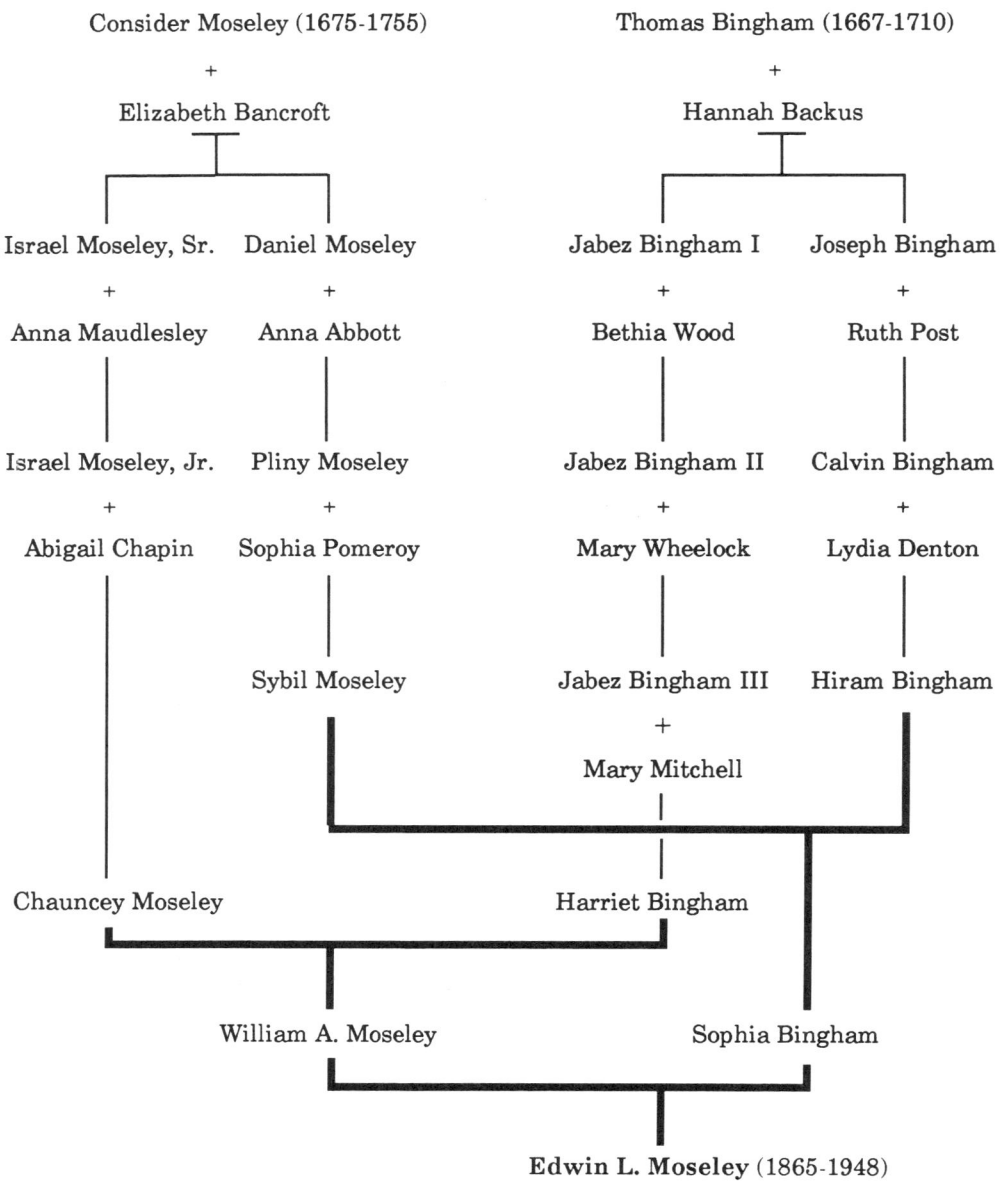

(youngest of nine children)

CONTRIBUTIONS & ACHIEVEMENTS

SECTION II

Faculty of 1909, Sandusky High School.

Back Row: l. to r., W. A. Richardson, Clara Feick, George C. Dietrich, R. D. Crout, **Edwin L. Moseley**, unidentified, Clyde Holt.

Front Row: Charlotte Field (music), unidentified lady with necktie, Homer B. Williams, Augusta Erckner, Bessie Taylor, Elsie Denham.

(*The Fram,* June 1909; Sandusky Library Archives)

Moseley with barn owl.

(Archives, BGSU)

Recollections of a Contemporary Naturalist

CHAPTER EIGHT

Milton B. Trautman [1981]

Milton B. Trautman (1899-1991), a self-taught Ohio field naturalist, wrote of his recollections of Professor Moseley for this project at the request of Ronald L. Stuckey, in 1981. Trautman related examples of his interactions with Moseley at scientific meetings and in the museum, in addition to accounts given him by Moseley's former students.

My earliest recollections of Professor Edwin Lincoln Moseley date from the Ohio Academy of Science annual meetings during the last half of the 1920s. At these meetings he was a conspicuous figure, partly because of his idiosyncrasies. Many undergraduates and recently graduated students usually failed to grasp the broad extent of his knowledge. In their eyes he had several strikes against him. He was eccentric, a bachelor, a nonsmoker, shy except when forgetting his shyness in his eagerness to instruct a student or anyone else. Because of his broad knowledge, he was considered to be a "naturalist," who was interested in everything relative to the natural world. Usually naturalists, now known as ecologists, were considered largely untrained in scientific methods and procedures. The younger generation was being trained to be ultra-specialists, to know much about a very narrow subject, such as the development of a part of a plant or animal, and then only in the laboratory. Research had to be "pure" and have no or little economic importance. They ignored such matters as the relation of Pleistocene geology to plant and animal distribution and abundance. During that period, to the average student, the day of unspecialization was past. Moseley was archaic, a relic of the past.

I was college untrained. I was interested in the natural world, a throwback similar to Moseley. As a minority, Moseley and I gravitated towards each other. Our discussions were on common grounds. Early on, I began saving up questions to be asked and discussed at the annual meetings. I became aware that his overpowering drive in life was to share his knowledge with others, especially the young. His inhibitions and shyness largely vanished when he began to discuss a subject, preferably with a student. Most students considered his actions unusual and funny, and tended to discuss and to be impressed by his eccentricities rather than his knowledge. When these students gave a paper before the Academy, one usually knew the narrow field they were going to discuss; often it was a progress report on the subject given previously. One always examined the program of papers to be presented, to learn what subject Moseley was presenting. The subject was largely unpredictable. It might concern past and present climatic conditions, plant migration, floods, or diseases. Undoubtedly because of our mutual interests in glacial geology, and in climate and its effects upon plants and animals and on the natural world of Ohio in general, Moseley and I had many discussions and had become well acquainted with each other by 1933.

Moseley was a graduate (1885) of The University of Michigan, an institution for which he had the greatest respect. He was a member of the Michigan Academy of Science, Arts and Letters and apparently attended their annual meetings regularly and presented papers. Early in 1934 I joined the faculty of The University of Michigan, remaining until 1939. During my Michigan sojourn I had a room and house privileges at the home of Dr. Earl O'Roke, his wife Ann, and their daughter Beth. I rather quickly lost the title of "roomer," becoming "one of the family." During the spring of 1934, the day before the annual meetings of the Michigan Academy, Moseley walked into my office, in the Museum of Zoology, a paper bag in his hand, announcing that he was attending the meetings and was looking for a room. I called Mrs. O'Roke, who immediately suggested that I invite him to stay in their third-floor bedroom. In the mornings he had breakfast with the O'Rokes. They quickly realized his earnestness and ability. Dr. O'Roke was a professor of biology at the University, and as a parasitologist, working upon lung worms in deer and leucocytozoon in waterfowl, was also a "field naturalist." The morning after the meetings Moseley appeared at the breakfast table, paper bag in hand, and announced that after breakfast he was leaving Ann Arbor. Thereafter, he was the O'Roke's and my guest annually until 1940.

Undoubtedly Moseley's most-discussed paper at the Michigan Academy meetings was given 18 March 1939. He gave evidence that excessive rainfall occurred during a 45-year period, alternating with a 45-year rain deficiency. His conclusions were based on the width of tree rings; those produced during the excessive rainfall cycle were broad, whereas those produced 45 years later during the cycles of rain deficiency were narrow. He predicted that during the 1970s and nearly every year thereafter, for about a decade, there would be excessive rainfall. These predictions came at a rather unfortunate time, because the extremely low water levels of the Great Lakes during the late 1920s and early 1930s were still fresh in the public's mind. Newspapers had published various theories as to where the water went or who used it. It was seriously suggested that the water was drained out of the Great Lakes into the Mississippi River drainage through the Chicago drainage canal! A reporter for the *New York Times*, present at the meetings, considered it sufficiently interesting, or quaint, to publish Moseley's paper in detail, giving more space to this report than to any other. Interest in the article was quickly forgotten—until the high water levels of the 1970s, when articles appeared in local newspapers in towns along Lake Erie recalling Moseley's predictions of the 1930s and 1940s. As has happened with many of his "quaint" theories, this one has been accepted, especially after additional information and facts have been accumulated during the intervening time.

Between the years 1934 and 1939 I spent innumerable evenings in the bird range of The University of Michigan Museum of Zoology with my good friend, the late Dr. Josselyn Van Tyne, examining and identifying various species of birds of the world. During a conversation, Van Tyne told me that no one knew where the type specimen of *Halcyon lindsayi moseleyi* was located. This taxon was described by Joseph B. Steere in 1890, after he had returned from an expedition to the Philippine Islands. Moseley was a member of that expedition. The type was collected on Negros Island. I visited Moseley at Bowling Green State University the next time that I drove from Ann Arbor to Columbus. After examining the many anomalies in his laboratory, such as albino animals and two-headed calves or ones with five legs, I broached the subject of the present location of the type of the kingfisher that carried the specific name *moseleyi*. He pointed to a number of shelves along the entire side of the laboratory, almost completely filled with shoeboxes, and in

CHAPTER 8 • RECOLLECTIONS OF A CONTEMPORARY NATURALIST

one general direction, indicating that it was in one of the shoeboxes in that general area. Expressing a desire to see it, I asked if he could locate it, whereupon he climbed up a stepladder, removed several shoeboxes, and finally brought one out and stated that the type was in there. Seeing no label or other sign, and noting that the shoebox appeared to be similar to many others, I looked inside and saw the type.

Upon returning to Ann Arbor I related my experiences, whereupon Van Tyne immediately wrote to Moseley requesting that we visit him, which was granted. After Moseley climbed the stepladder, shuffling shoeboxes about, the box containing the type was produced. Then began the inevitable "horse trading" at which Moseley was an expert. Finally an agreement was reached: the type was exchanged for several bird species or mounts and was taken back to Ann Arbor. Van Tyne was a firm believer in preserving a type at all costs. Types in the range of the bird division at the Museum of Zoology in The University of Michigan were kept in special containers and carefully labeled. Van Tyne received much satisfaction in "rescuing" the type from what he considered a possible shoebox firetrap. After viewing the type in its case, Moseley expressed considerable satisfaction.

In 1939 I returned to Ohio, accepting a position with the Franz Theodore Stone Laboratory of The Ohio State University at its year-round field station on Gibraltar and South Bass Islands. Shortly after my arrival I renewed my acquaintance with two successful Sandusky and Port Clinton businessmen, the late Leroy Weier and George Wenger. They were friends since early childhood and ardent duck hunters later. During late autumns my wife, Mary Auten Trautman, and I were invited almost weekly to the Weier cabin beside Middle Harbor. Wenger was usually present. As a biologist interested in vertebrates and in wildfowling, I had much in common with these men. During the many evenings we spent there, they described former habitat conditions in Ottawa County. Almost invariably, during the evening reference was made to Moseley.

Sometime during the period when Moseley taught at the Sandusky High School, between 1889 and 1914, he was Weier and Wenger's teacher. He and his so-called eccentricities profoundly impressed them. They greatly appreciated Moseley's teaching despite their inability to quite understand him. Repeatedly they discussed the man's marked abilities and talents: why should a man so industrious spend his time teaching, when he obviously could have been as highly successful in business and financially as these two later were? To them it did not make sense. Of the many stories that these men told me, three stand out clearly and appear worthy to be repeated.

If a person is satisfactorily married, one cannot understand why another individual also is not married. As friends, Weier and Wenger wanted to do something, usually by suggesting possibilities. As far as anyone knew, Moseley had no interest in any girl except one whose interest in some phase of the natural world caused her to ask questions, thereby arousing the teaching instinct in Moseley. At the high school, another teacher became interested in Moseley, and after employment of devious methods by others, he was persuaded to take her to a concert. Apparently all went well, and both enjoyed the concert. When the concert ended he walked out and went home, apparently forgetting that the teacher had accompanied him.

Perhaps the incident most frequently retold concerned hoarfrost. On a cold January day Weier and Wenger were going to school together, as they usually did. As they crossed the street, they saw a pile of horse manure covered densely with frost. Carefully picking a lump, they took it to Moseley asking him, "what kind of fungus is this?" He replied, "This item is most interesting," and gravely told them to place it on the hot steam radiator which they did. "Now you will learn something," he said. It promptly became warm and began to smell strongly. All morning the odor permeated the classroom. Shortly before the noon recess, Moseley told the boys to examine what was left of their strange object and to report, which they did. After telling them to clean up the mess thoroughly, he proceeded to give a most interesting account of hoarfrost, how it formed and why. Each time the story was retold, I realized what a deep impression this "quaint" method of teaching had upon the boys and what a deep respect they had for him.

Weier and Wenger realized how conservative and "stingy" Moseley was when it came to his eating and other creature comforts. However, he was generous when helping students, usually poor farmboys, whom he considered worthy of being assisted. Also, he was not adverse to spending his own money and time on some scientific project. He was cognizant of the theory of varying and lower Lake Erie water levels in the past, and if this were a fact the ancient channel of the Sandusky River should be evident in Sandusky Bay.

As soon as the ice was sufficiently thick to support their weight, Moseley hired Weier and Wenger to assist him. Both were strong, sturdy high school students, whose jobs were to spud holes in the ice with an iron bar flattened and sharpened on one end. Holes were spudded at right angles to what was assumed to be the river channel. The river channel was ascertained by a greater depth than were its two banks. The former river meandered considerably, resulting in a large number of holes being spudded. Spudding most of a Saturday through ice seven or more inches thick, on a cold day with a high wind, was quite exhausting; however, if the frail-appearing Moseley could stand such unfavorable conditions, pride forced these sturdy boys to attempt to hide their fatigue. Obviously, although they were amused by the driving curiosity of this man, it was evident that he had been a major force in molding their characters, as I have discovered that he was with many other students and associates.

I had become adjusted to Moseley's divergent interests and researches in the natural world; even so, I was not wholly prepared for his knowledge concerning aluminum phosphate causing the milk sickness in humans and "trembles" in other animals. Two of his publications on this subject indicate a knowledge of chemistry that was surprising for a high-school teacher at so early a period (1908-1910). Science and the world in general, especially the natural world, would be a better place if there were more Moseleys.

Milton Bernhard Trautman (1899-1991), a self-taught student of natural history who became an internationally known ornithologist and ichthyologist, authored two books, *The Birds of Buckeye Lake, Ohio* (1940) and *The Fishes of Ohio* (1957, revised 1981). These publications were so meticulously executed that they are considered models in their disciplines. Born 7 September 1899 in Columbus, Ohio, Trautman was a sickly child; and although he attended elementary school, by age 14 his illness prevented him from further formal education. During the next 17 years, despite his illness, he became quite skilled in his father's successful plumbing business and qualified as a master plumber. At age 29, following the removal of a Meckel's diverticulum from his small intestine, his health promptly improved.

Trautman first became excited about fishes at age five, and later developed a passionate interest in birds. Tutored by his parents, and then by museum curators James S. Hine and Edward S. Thomas, and by professional zoologists and ichthyologists Edward L. Wickliff and Raymond C. Osburn, Trautman learned all of these skills from field and library research to writing and publication of the results. From 1926 to 1934, Trautman was employed by the State of Ohio Department of Fish and Game, at first part-time and later full-time. His subsequent appointments were assistant curator of fishes in the Museum of

Zoology at The University of Michigan and assistant director and research biologist for the Michigan Department of Conservation (1934-1939), research biologist at the Franz Theodore Stone Laboratory of The Ohio State University (1939-1955), curator of vertebrates (fishes and birds) in the Ohio State Museum of the Ohio Historical Society, and lecturer in the Department of Zoology and Entomology of The Ohio State University (1955-1991).

At Stone Laboratory, Trautman met Mary Auten. Born 10 February 1898 in Rawson, Hancock County, Ohio, she was a graduate of nearby Bluffton College, a Ph. D. in entomology from The Ohio State University, and an assistant professor of biology at Ashland College. They were married the following year (14 June 1940). She relinquished her college teaching career and research interests in entomology to devote completely her efforts to his research on fishes leading to the completion of both editions of his award-winning book, *The Fishes of Ohio* (1957, 1981). Together, they published an "Annotated list of the birds of Ohio" (1968).

The Trautmans were the first husband and wife team to be inducted into the Ohio Conservation Hall of Fame (1974), and they were the first team to be awarded Honorary Doctor of Science Degrees by The Ohio State University (1978). Earlier Milton was the recipient of an honorary Doctor of Science Degree from The College of Wooster (1951). A very rare darter, *Noturus trautmanii,* is named in his honor following his discovery in 1943 of the fish on Trautman's Riffle in Big Darby Creek, Ohio. The Milton Trautman Nature Center at Maumee State Park on the shore of Lake Erie at the town of Oregon, near Toledo, Ohio, was dedicated 21 May 1993. At age 88 Mary A. Trautman died 8 March 1986, and Milton B. Trautman at age 91 died 31 January 1991. Both are buried in Greenlawn Cemetery, Columbus.

—Adapted from obituaries by Ronald L. Stuckey. *Ohio Journal of Science* 93: 165,166. 1993.

Milton B. Trautman.

(Taken by Edward F. Hutchins; Stuckey Collection)

A massive population of white snakeroot, the plant that causes milk sickness, as discovered through research by Moseley.

(Taken by Ronald L. Stuckey, at edge of woods in Greenlawn Cemetery, Tiffin, Seneca County, Ohio, 15 September 1996; Stuckey Collection)

Scientific Presentations and Publications

CHAPTER NINE

Ronald L. Stuckey

An investigator's contributions and achievements in science can be difficult to analyze and evaluate. Some measures of one's scholarship can be obtained by reviewing the kinds of presentations delivered at meetings of scientific organizations and the scope of papers published in various periodicals. Edwin Lincoln Moseley followed the appropriate pattern. He investigated various diverse aspects of science, reported his findings at scientific meetings and public lectures, and published the results of his efforts in a multitude of archival journals, popular magazines, and local newspapers [see list, pages 123-125].

Examination of Moseley's scholarship record as presently compiled shows that he published four or more papers each in nine disciplines as recognized here: astronomy, botany, geology, health and hygene, medical science, climatology, ornithology, zoology other than ornithology, and a combination of science education and general science [see next page]. Twenty-four publications, the largest number in any one discipline, were published in ornithology. His first known publication, compiled in 1887 while he taught high school in Grand Rapids, Michigan, was a 32-page unannotated catalogue containing the scientific and common names of the birds, mammals, and birds' eggs owned by the Kent Scientific Institute, Grand Rapids,[42] where he was curator. Although he had considerable knowledge of fishes, insects, and other animals, he did not publish specifically on those subjects, except for a few essays in the Sandusky newspapers. Within each discipline, at least one major paper, comprehensive monograph, or book appeared. Furthermore, he pub-

Numbers and Years of Publications for Each Discipline in Books and Archival Periodicals.

Discipline	Publications Total	Publications Major	General Years of Study	Concentrated Years of Study	Discussed in Chapter
Astronomy	4	1	1903-1933		11
Botany	12	2	1895-1938	1889-1899	9
Geology	10	2	1895-1905	1894-1905	9
Health and Hygiene	6	0	1910-1912		—
Medical Science	8	2	1906-1917, 1941	1904-1917	9
Climatology; Meteorology	14	4	1897-1947	1928-1948	10
Ornithology	24	2	1887-1947		9
Science Education and General Science	12	1	1896-1925, 1938		11
Zoology (other than Ornithology)	8	1	1906-1934		9
Totals	98	15			

Note: The titles of these selected "major" publications can be determined by consulting the references listed for Chapters 9, 10, and 11. Those publications chosen for this "major" status within each discipline are identified there with an asterisk at the beginning of the publication's title.

lished papers in each discipline nearly throughout his active life, especially from the 1890s until the 1930s. Certain subjects appear to occupy his interest at certain periods, in approximately 10-year frames. These periods are botany (1889-1899), when he was preparing his "Sandusky flora;" geology (1894-1905), when he was studying the formation of Sandusky Bay and Cedar Point and mapping the preglacial river valleys of that area; and medical science (1904-1917), when he was determining the cause of trembles in animals and milk sickness in human beings. During the 30-year period 1896-1925, he published papers on science education which described his methods and philosophy of teaching by using specific examples drawn from his own personal experiences. These aspects on teaching are discussed in Chapter 11. His concentrated work in meteorology (1935-1948), occupied a 13-year span in the latter part of his life, when he was making detailed studies of tree-ring widths and lake-level records, from which he derived rainfall cycles and made long-range weather forecasts. This topic is detailed in Chapter 10. Moseley's most lengthy and sustained interest was in ornithology; his publications in this subject date from 1887 with the paper on birds and animals in the Kent Scientific Institute[42] to his last publication in 1947 on variations in the bird population in the north-central states.[63]

Presentations at Scientific Meetings

At age 27, Moseley was among the youngest of 59 scientists who joined as Charter members of the newly founded Ohio State Academy of Science following its organizational meeting on 31 December 1891, in Columbus. The Academy was to be the one institution in Ohio to direct its energy and influence in science throughout the state and to secure an honored position among the scientific organizations throughout the country. For Moseley, the Academy was to become his primary scientific organization, the one in which he was most active. Ultimately, he became the last one of its living charter members.

Noted Ohio botanist and conservationist, Paul B. Sears[5] (1891-1990) made reference to Moseley and his affiliation with the Ohio Academy of Science while speaking on "The Future Role of Academies." The topic was Sears' presidential address to the American Association for the Advancement of Science in 1958. Sears, a founding pioneer in natural vegetation mapping and in the interpretation of vegetational history from pollen analysis, discussed the excellent work that state academies were doing for the promising secondary-school pupils. He noted that a substantial number of good scientists owe their initial interest either to family influence or more frequently to an inspiring pre-college teacher. These teachers often attain inspiration from memberships in a state academy. He then further stated:

> We often overlook the fact that in Europe important scientific work, as well as good teaching, is done by teachers in secondary schools. In our own country we have the example of Edwin Lincoln Moseley who, when he taught in the Sandusky Ohio High School years ago, not only sent promising students to good universities but carried out—with the aid of his students—classical studies on the recent geological history of southern Lake Erie.

As a presenter of research papers, Moseley did not become active in the Ohio State Academy of Science until the fourth annual meeting of 27,28 December 1894 in Columbus. There he presented three papers, "Notes on the Bald Eagle," "Attractions for a Scientist in the Vicinity of Sandusky," and "Hygienic Dangers of Modern Civilization," and was elected secretary of the organization. Notice of his paper on the eagle was given in the *Sandusky Weekly Register* (19 January 1895) and the *Erie County Reporter* (24 January 1895), with both papers providing considerable detail about the topic upon which Moseley spoke. Both the *Daily* and *Weekly Sandusky Register* (30 December 1894, 2 January 1895), being especially enthusiastic about his presentation on the "Attractions for a Scientist..." referred to it as a "masterly paper" and printed its entire text. The paper was divided into three components: the geological features, the botanical diversity, and the bird migrations. An abstract was published in the *Third Annual Report of the Academy* (1895).[1]

Moseley's paper generated great interest in the Sandusky area and the members of the Academy decided to hold their fourth annual summer meeting there with Moseley as host and leader. Moseley's report (1895, 1896)[2,3] on that meeting, held in Sandusky July 1895, noted that a large number of individuals attended who thoroughly enjoyed the field trips on which they saw the unusual plants and animals at Cedar Point, the famous Blue Hole at Castalia, and an extensive sand ridge, once a shoreline of an earlier glacial stage of Lake Erie. As secretary of the Academy, Moseley served for nine years (1895-1903) and authored 16 published reports.[4] He was elected president at the annual meeting in Granville, 27 November 1903, and his presidential address the following year at Cleveland was the "Formation of Sandusky Bay and Cedar Point." It was published by the Academy (1905)[24] and in the *Sandusky Register* (20 January 1906). Further discussion of

Moseley's address appears in the geology portion, later in this chapter. Throughout his career, Moseley maintained an interest in the Academy and continued to present papers. An analysis of a list of known titles compiled from the annual programs, reveals that he presented 33 papers, spanning 45 years from 1894 to 1939. On several occasions as many as three papers were delivered at a meeting, with the result that papers were read only 20 different years of the 45-year span. Of the 33 known papers, nine were on botany, eight on zoology, six on geology, and four on medical botany.

The Ohio State Academy of Science was not the first scientific organization that Moseley joined. Soon after moving to Grand Rapids, Michigan, during the summer of 1885, he attended the 34th annual meeting of the American Association for the Advancement of Science (AAAS) in Ann Arbor. He became a member at this meeting, but he did not present a paper until the 45th meeting held 25-27 August 1896 in Buffalo, New York. His presentation there was "A Comparison of the Flora of Erie County, Ohio, with that of Erie County, New York." Moseley, then at age 31, listed his affiliation as the Ohio State Academy of Science, Sandusky, Ohio, rather than the high school. The paper was given in Section G. Botany, where he was part of a program[7] that included some of the foremost botanists of the United States at that time. Among them were Nathaniel Lord Britton, director of the New York Botanical Garden, who also was vice-president of the Association and secretary of the section Botany; Lucius M. Underwood and John K. Small of Columbia University; Frederick C. Newcombe, The University of Michigan; Charles E. Bessey, the University of Nebraska; Daniel T. McDougal, Conway MacMillan, and Francis Ramaley of the University of Minnesota; William A. Kellerman, The Ohio State University; John M. Coulter, University of Chicago; and Liberty H. Bailey, George F. Atkinson, and Willard W. Rowlee of Cornell University. The majority of the papers[7] read concerned topics on vascular-plant morphology and anatomy, physiological processes, and identification and classification. Moseley's paper was innovative and different from all of the other paper presentations. It was a comparison of the numbers of species and their geographical affinities in the flora of Erie county, including Sandusky, where he lived with those of Erie county, including Buffalo, where the meeting was held. The Sandusky area contained 265 more native species than the Buffalo area, and Moseley attributed this difference primarily to variations in climatic conditions at the western and eastern ends of Lake Erie.

Moseley's paper was certainly a pioneer in the realm of phytogeography, a discipline that was becoming organized and being taught in university botanical departments during the 1890s. The most advanced study in plant geography at this time in the United States was being conducted by several botanists of the Botanical Survey of Nebraska organized in 1892. Their work resulted in the classic book, *The Phytogeography of Nebraska* (1898)[9] authored by Roscoe Pound and Frederic E. Clements. Moseley's research effort in this discipline developed independently from the Nebraska botanists.

The abstracts of the papers read at the AAAS meeting in Buffalo were published by the Association in *Science* (1896)[6] and by the Botanical Society of America in the *Botanical Gazette* (1896).[6] Although not identical in wording, abstracts of Moseley's paper appeared in each of these journals. During the following winter, the complete text, except for the scientific names of the plants, was printed in the *Sandusky Weekly Register* (6 February 1897). An abridged version of the text, but with a list of plant names, was published in the *American Naturalist* (1897),[8] an archival journal printed in Philadelphia. Moseley's article was edited by the botanist, Charles E. Bessey, who was a member of the Botanical Survey of Nebraska.

Contributions to Various Disciplines

Botany

Moseley's first scientific endeavors were in botany, which he studied from 1889 to 1899.[10] His contribution to botany emerges in his catalogues of the vascular plants of two of northern Ohio's most diverse floristic areas, the island and Sandusky Bay region of western Lake Erie and the Oak Openings west of Toledo. Upon arrival in Sandusky in 1889, Moseley's first research efforts were directed toward collecting and identifying all the different kinds of vascular plants growing in the Sandusky Bay region, comprising Erie County, Sandusky Bay, and the Marblehead Peninsula in the eastern portion of Ottawa County, and the islands in western Lake Erie. During the first 10-year period of teaching at Sandusky, Moseley took one or more field trips to the large United States islands in Lake Erie and to many sites throughout Erie and Ottawa Counties, as noted from several items published in the *Sandusky Register*. On many of these field trips, he was accompanied by members of his high school botany classes, and engaged the students to make collections of plants on their own for which awards were presented for their efforts. A reward of 50 cents was given to anyone who first called his attention to a plant species native to Erie or Ottawa County, and 25 cents for any foreign plant that had become naturalized in the area. With this effort, by 1892 he had recorded 448 species growing within 10 miles of the high school, and by 1896, 1,086 species in the region, according to the *Sandusky Register* (17 April 1892 and 15 April 1896). Carefully dried and pressed specimens of nearly all the different kinds were represented in the high school museum. The final achievement was his "Sandusky flora. A catalogue of the flowering plants and ferns growing without cultivation, in Erie County, Ohio, and the peninsula and islands of Ottawa County" (1899),[11] published as Special Paper No. 1 of the Ohio State Academy of Science. More than an annotated catalogue of the scientific and common names of the vascular plants, the book contains authoritative information on the origin, distribution, and changes of the flora, as well as the influences of climate, geology, and human history. The botanist at Purdue University, J. C. Arthur (1899),[11] wrote that it "records a piece of careful local exploration worthy of the excellent setting." Moseley's "Sandusky flora" is the foundation on which all future floristic changes in the region are measured. Aside from its careful production and accuracy of plant identifications, it is perhaps the most comprehensive local flora that has ever been published in Ohio. At the time it was printed, Moseley's "flora" contained the names of more species of plants than any other published flora covering an area of comparable size in the United States. Moseley gave credit for valuable suggestions and assistance to two botanists, Charles F. Wheeler (1842-1910) and Erwin F. Smith (1854-1927), both associated with the Michigan Agricultural College in East Lansing. They had published a *Catalogue of the. . .Plants of Michigan* (1881). However, no reference was made to Volney M. Spalding (1849-1918), who was acting professor of botany at The University of Michigan while Moseley was a student there.

After relocating at Bowling Green in 1914, Moseley engaged in a second floristic study, the 130-square mile extensive sand tract on the western extremity of glacial Lake Warren mostly in the western part of Lucas County, a few miles west of Toledo. Although he first visited the Oak Openings in 1897 and 1898, regular visits after 1914 totaling about a hundred were made looking for rare plants, making observations on the abundance of species, and determining the boundary of the region. His "Flora of the Oak Openings west of Toledo" (1928),[12] published as Special Paper No. 20 of the Ohio Academy of Science, is another masterpiece as a

Chapter 9 • Scientific Presentations and Publications

> Ohio State Academy of Science.
>
> SPECIAL PAPERS NO. 1.
>
> # SANDUSKY FLORA.
>
> ## A CATALOGUE
>
> OF THE
>
> ## FLOWERING PLANTS and FERNS
>
> GROWING WITHOUT CULTIVATION, IN ERIE COUNTY, OHIO, AND THE PENINSULA AND ISLANDS OF OTTAWA COUNTY,
>
> By E. L. MOSELEY, A. M.
>
> PUBLISHED BY THE ACADEMY OF SCIENCE,
> MAY, 1899.
>
> PRESS OF CLAPPER PRINTING CO.
> WOOSTER, OHIO.

Title page from Moseley's paper, "Sandusky flora" (1899).

local flora. Louis Campbell, a naturalist of Lucas County, noted that in this pamphlet Moseley had drawn attention to the unique character of the sand country west of Toledo. Campbell considered it to be "one of the greatest contributions to natural science ever to come out of Northwestern Ohio." Moseley's principal reference for his Oak Openings "Flora" was the *Michigan Flora* (1892) by William J. Beal (1833-1924) and Charles F. Wheeler. He also quoted correspondence with Edgar T. Wherry, Senior Chemist at the United States Department of Agriculture, on the chemical composition of the soil. Both of Moseley's publications are extremely valuable for their floristic history, floristic comparisons with other parts of the state and country, and his insights into the "why" and "how" behavior of many of the individual species. Moseley's "Flora of the Oak Openings" has provided the base line data from which N. William Easterly[14,15] and his students at Bowling Green State University have been able to document changes and to report the rare and infrequent species in the flora of this unusual area of northwestern Ohio [see publication note C, page 275].

Throughout his active career Moseley retained his interest in the flora, and occasionally reports appeared in newspapers of rare or unusual species of plants he discovered in the region, among them were the rattlesnake master (1895), the lady's tresses orchid (1924), *Carex aurea* (1925), lance-leaved buckthorn (1926), poison hemlock (1927), and American lotus (1931). His account of some plants believed to have been brought to northern Ohio by Indians (1931)[13] was his last known published contribution to botany. Six plants were named in the paper: *Opuntia humifusa* (common prickly-pear), *Hymenoxys herbacea* (Lakeside daisy), *Nelumbo lutea* (water lotus), *Ceanothus herbaceus* (narrow-leaved New Jersey-tea), *Symphoricarpus albus* (snowberry), and *Gentiana puberulenta* (prairie gentian). The names Moseley used have been updated according to Cooperrider (1995)[16] and other contemporary sources published on the Ohio flora.

Geology

Moseley's investigations into the geology of the local area in the vicinity of Sandusky occupied the second phase of his research accomplishments. These studies were mostly conducted during the years 1894 to 1905. Examination of titles of his papers read at scientific meetings and his publication record, reveals that he made contributions to at least five topics relevant to the local geology. Initially, Moseley marshalled observations and facts demonstrating that the water level in western Lake Erie and Sandusky Bay had risen during the previous centuries. He noted that: (1) large trees had been killed by earlier high lake water levels, (2) stalactites and stalagmites in the caves on South Bass Island were now in water below the present lake water level, (3) valleys eroded by streams entering the Lake or Bay were partly submerged at their outlets, and (4) the species composition of the flora and fauna on the Lake Erie islands was essentially the same as the flora and fauna on the nearby mainland. These facts supported the contention that the land at the western end of Lake Erie had been subsiding because the rebound of the land was greater at Buffalo and eastward following the retreat of the massive weight of ice in the Wisconsinan Glacier that receded from the area about 10,000 years ago. Moseley calculated this rise of water to be at the rate of about 2.14 feet per century. He published these observations and conclusions in the first volume of the *Lakeside Magazine* (1898),[17] a local literary periodical founded and printed at nearby Lakeside, Ohio. The same information, but abridged, appeared in the *National Geographic Magazine* (1902)[18] and the *Ohio Educational Monthly* (1903).[20] Moseley also presented the same topic at the 11th annual meeting of the Michigan Academy of Science held in Ann Arbor, 30 March-1 April 1905, and a summary-abstract was published in the *Report of the Michigan Academy of Science* (1905).[23]

Moseley's early research efforts in geology were strengthened because of his conversation with professional geologists at scientific meetings. In his publications,[20] Moseley noted that he asked questions of G. Frederick Wright (1838-1921) of Oberlin College, and Gore K. Gilbert (1843-1918) and Frank E. Leverett (1859-1943), both of whom were publishing with the United States Geological Survey. These men were actively studying the effects of glaciation in the southern Great Lakes region.

At the annual meeting of the Ohio State Academy of Science in 1900, Moseley presented his first paper concerned with the geology of the Sandusky area. The presentation titled "A Rock Valley Crossing Huron and Erie Counties" has been referred to in this book by Moseley's former students and associates, but the topic is not known to have been published by him. Later accounts concerning this research appeared in the *Erie County Reporter* (1909), the *Sandusky Star-Journal* (1921), and the *Sandusky Daily Register* (1923), the first two having been reprinted by Frohman (1973).[25] With assistance from his students, Moseley toured the area and inquired of farmers as to the depth to bedrock of water wells. The information assembled from the deep wells revealed the course of the ancient buried river valley.

To determine the location and connections of the buried valleys in Sandusky Bay, Moseley began his investigation in January 1901, when the Bay was frozen solid. By using an auger he punched it through the ice and lowered it until it came to rest on the hard clay bottom of the Bay. Following these preliminary efforts, Moseley, during the winter of 1901 and 1902, December through February, along with many of the high school boys traversed the ice-covered Bay and probed the auger into the soft loose mud until it came to the hard clay bottom. By connecting the similar and deepest depths, the pattern of the original streams was mapped. The results were published in the *National Geographic Magazine* (1902).[19] For having high school boys assist him in this original research effort, Moseley received considerable publicity in the newspapers and science education periodicals, for example, the *Sandusky Star-Journal* (20 December 1902), and the *Ohio Educational Monthly* (1903).[20] He noted that nearly a hundred boys helped him to trace the buried channels in Sandusky Bay and to determine the age of the sand ridges on Cedar Point created by the waves of the Lake shifting the sand during severe northeast storms.

One day at the Men's Literary Club in Sandusky during a discussion concerning the city's water supply, a prominent citizen stated that a current of water flowed past the mouths of the city sewers and carried this polluted water toward the intake of the city's water supply. At certain places in the Bay, ice rarely forms or becomes very thick, which Moseley thought might be where water rises from springs below or where strong currents persisted. A study of these currents, he thought, might help answer these questions, in addition to providing clues to the pattern of the deposition of sand brought from the Lake into the Bay. Moseley sought evidence on the water currents in Sandusky Bay by setting adrift 80 bottles between 26 July and 6 December 1902. He presented his study at the annual meeting of the Ohio State Academy of Science, held that December in Columbus. Short notices of this project appeared in the *National Geographic Magazine* (1903),[19] the *Monthly Weather Review* (1903),[21] and the *Annual Report of the Ohio State Academy of Science* (1903).[22] The full text of his presentation was printed in the *Sandusky Weekly Register* (3 December 1902) and later in both the *Daily* and *Weekly Register* (8 June 1903 and 17 June 1903). Moseley's results were short and simple: "I have found no evidence of a persistent current carrying sewage to the waterworks' crib. I have found no evidence of a persistent current anywhere."

Moseley's research on the local geology culminated in his presidential address delivered at the 13th Annual Meeting of the Ohio State Academy of Science held 25,26 November 1904 at Adelbert College, Cleveland, Ohio. Titled, "The Formation of Sandusky Bay and Cedar Point" the *Sandusky Weekly Register* (30 November 1904) referred to the meeting's program "one of exceptional interest. . . . one of the most interesting papers from a local standpoint, was read by the president of the society, E. L. Moseley of Sandusky. . . ." The paper brought together the information Moseley had obtained during the previous 10 years while studying the Bay and the Point. The complete text was published as part of the *13th Annual Report of the Ohio State Academy of Science* (1905). It was also printed in the *Sandusky Daily* and *Weekly Register* (20 January 1906 and 24 January 1906). This work represents Moseley's most comprehensive publication on the geology of the Sandusky region and has become a basic reference source used by geologists and engineers for many projects involving the region through the years. Its importance was so recognized by Charles E. Frohman, Sandusky attorney and historian, that following the devastating Lake Erie storm of 13 and 14 November 1972, he had Moseley's paper reprinted under the title: *Lake Erie: Floods, Lake Levels, Northeast Storms* by the Ohio Historical Society (1973).[24]

Medical Science

During the third frame of Moseley's research career (1904-1917), he conducted the first satisfactory experiments to demonstrate that trembles in animals results from their grazing on a common woodland plant, white snakeroot (*Eupatorium rugosum*, formerly called *E. urticaefolium*), and that the poison enters the milk causing the dreaded disease known as milk sickness in human beings. This mysterious disease, unknown to the Europeans who populated the east coast of North America, was most feared and certainly misunderstood among the pioneer families of midwestern United States. The disease, endemic to the interior of North America, became prevalent after large portions of the forested land were cleared, homes were built, and the livestock were turned into the forests to graze, particularly in late summer and early fall when the grasses in the pastures had withered. In Ohio, as Moseley noted, nearly one-fourth of the early settlers of Madison County died, and in a single year prior to 1850, 43 persons died of milk sickness in the Sandusky-Erie County area of northern Ohio. The true cause of the disease, which still persisted locally when Moseley arrived in Sandusky in 1889, had not been satisfactorily determined in the scientific and medical literature. The physicians of the western country had written hundreds of papers in the medical and popular journals suggesting various causes of milk sickness, among them plants, topographic features, soil conditions, minerals, air of certain localities, heavy metals, water, bacteria, yeast, mushrooms, insects, and others. Among prominent physicians, Dr. Daniel Drake (1785-1852) of Cincinnati, who wrote a lengthy monograph[26] about the disease, attributed its cause to a woodland plant grazed by cattle. Based on much conjecture, he favored the poison ivy plant, and rejected the white snakeroot, because the latter grew in rich soil. Because of his dominance as a medical figure in the Mississippi Valley during the first half of the nineteenth century, Drake's writings were often quoted and his ideas therefore prevailed and probably stifled new suggestions and research approaches for determining the cause of the disease (Niederhofer, 1985).[41]

Beginning about 1904, Moseley visited farmers in the Sandusky area who were convinced that the trembles in farm animals and the milk sickness in people were caused by the woodland plant, white snakeroot. Moseley studied much of the available literature; and in the fall of 1905, with the help of his students, local veterinarians, and physicians, he commenced experiments, in which he and his students, fed leaves and stems of the white snakeroot to cats, dogs, rabbits, and sheep. They kept careful records of what happened to these animals. During the next decade, Moseley read papers on his studies before the Ohio State Academy of Science in 1905, 1909, and 1914, and at a meeting of the Erie County Medical Society in March 1909. His first journal article describing his experimental approaches and results appeared in the Academy's journal, the *Ohio Naturalist* (1906),[27] and later results of his research were described in the *Medical Record* (1909, 1910, 1917),[29,31,35] a weekly journal of medicine and surgery published by William Wood and Company in New York. He also published accounts of milk sickness in *Mulford's Veterinary Bulletin* (1909)[30] of Philadelphia and in the *Ohio Farmer* (1910,[32,33] 15 October, 26 November). Several articles by Moseley on the subject appeared from 1905 to 1917 in the local newspapers, the *Sandusky Star-Journal,* the *Sandusky Register,* and the *Toledo Blade.* Several students and local

CHAPTER 9 • SCIENTIFIC PRESENTATIONS AND PUBLICATIONS

MILK SICKNESS CAUSED BY WHITE SNAKEROOT

By
EDWIN LINCOLN MOSELEY
Professor Emeritus of Biology
State University, Bowling Green, Ohio
Past-President of Ohio Academy of Science

Published jointly by
The Ohio Academy of Science
and
The Author

Presented to Hazel Stockdale by the author, Edwin Lincoln Moseley

BOWLING GREEN, OHIO
1941

Author's signature in Hazel Stockdale's copy of Moseley's book.

(Gift from her nephew Thomas M. Stockdale; Stuckey Collection) physicians helped Moseley with his milk sickness research [see Chapter 17, page 235].

Experiments in feeding animals white snakeroot or preparations made from it were undertaken in 1906 by Albert C. Crawford of the Bureau of Plant Industry, Washington, D.C. His research was conducted because of an outbreak of trembles resulting in the death of about 50 head of cattle near Minooka, Illinois. Working with aqueous extracts from the plants, he reported that the white snakeroot was not the cause of trembles and criticized Moseley's work with the challenge "that it can not be said that Moseley has ever proved *Eupatorium ageratoides* to be a poisonous plant much less the cause of *trembles*" (Crawford, 1908).[28] Except in the state of Ohio, Crawford's statement prevented the country's general acceptance of Moseley's conclusions. For example, Louis H. Pammel[34] of Iowa in his book, *A Manual of Poisonous Plants. . .of North America. . .*, although quoting Moseley's study from the *Ohio Naturalist* (1906), adopted the conclusion of Crawford.

Not until 10 years later, when the studies of Wolf, Curtis, and Kaup (1917-1918, 1918)[36,37] of the North Carolina Agricultural Experiment Station were published, did Moseley's conclusions become accepted on the cause of trembles and milk sickness. These workers wrote (1918, p. 17) that "Moseley's account, beyond doubt, contains the best experimental evidence which had been presented up to that time on the poisonous properties of this weed." Moseley reviewed the situation in his third paper in the *Medical Record* (1917)[35] and in his final study published jointly by him and the Ohio Academy of Science (1941).[40] That the credit for the discovery of the cause of trembles and milk sickness belongs to Moseley was acknowledged further in Chapter 3 [page 21] by Homer B. Williams, who quoted statements from publications by Walter G. Sackett (1919)[38] and Albert Hansen (1927).[39]

During retirement from teaching, Moseley retained his interest in milk sickness and summarized his extensive knowledge of the subject in a 171-page monograph, *Milk Sickness Caused by White Snakeroot* (1941),[40] which discussed the history of the disease, the various theories of how it is caused, the symptoms manifested by those afflicted, and a summary of his own observations and investigations, as well as those of others, since 1917. The following excerpts from letters to Moseley gave praise to the book: "You have carried out a comprehensive research in a very thorough manner, which has characterized all of your scientific contributions, wrote Edward H. Kraus, Dean of the College of Literature, Science, and Arts of The University of Michigan. Another letter contained this message, "It must be a great satisfaction to you to see this study that occupied so many years terminated in such excellent form. You have lived to see your claims accepted. Such is not always the case in the field of Science," stated Frederick A. Wolf, Durham, North Carolina, an author of articles on milk sickness. "Your contribution on Milk Sickness is an extremely valuable one, and if you had never done anything else, your life would surely have been worthwhile," commented Charles C. Dean, botanist and author of the *Flora of Indiana* (1940). Congratulations also came from Wilbur C. Davidson, Dean of the School of Medicine, Duke University, and E. S. McCartney, editor of The University of Michigan Press [see publication note D, page 276].

Zoology

Of all the scientific disciplines to which Moseley contributed, more papers over the longest period were published in zoology, yet no one unique discovery or single contribution seems to emerge in zoology as it does in some of the other disciplines. His greatest zoological interest certainly was in ornithology, the subject of 24 of his 28 known papers on zoology published in journals. Moseley's first paper (1891),[43] containing descriptions of two new species of flycatchers from the Island of Negros, resulted from his field expedition with Joseph B. Steere to the Philippine Islands in 1887-1888. After Moseley settled in northern Ohio, his papers were concerned mostly with bird populations, their size, migrations, fluctuations with change in water levels, and variations influenced by climatic conditions. They are accounts of observations made during field studies.

At meetings of the Ohio State Academy of Science, Moseley presented eight papers on zoological topics. In the first meeting that he participated, held 27,28 December 1894, Moseley gave three papers. One of these was "Notes on the bald eagle," in which he related observations made for nine years on a pair of eagles near Sandusky. A resume of this paper appeared in the *Sandusky Weekly Register* (19 January 1895) and in the *Erie County Reporter* (24 January 1895), with the complete paper being published in the *American Naturalist* (1895)[44] and later in the *Lakeside Magazine* (1898).[45] Of the remaining seven presentations at Ohio Academy of Science meetings, his paper in 1930 on "The heronries of northern Ohio" was the most extensive one researched. It was published as "Blue heron colonies in northern Ohio," in the *Wilson Bulletin* (1936),[59] the archival journal of the Wilson Ornithological Club. Examples of some other short ornithological contributions of noteworthy interest are: "Occasional abundance of certain birds on or near Lake Erie" (1900),[46,47] "Fluctuation of bird life with change in water level" (1930),[55] "Abundance of the golden plover in Ohio in 1930" (1930),[56] and "Shore birds attracted to streams polluted by sewage" (1938).[60]

For 50 years, Moseley maintained records of bird migrations in the Lake Erie area, which he sent to the United States Fish and Wildlife Service, Washington, D.C. The usefulness of certain birds to the farmer was of concern to him. He pleaded for protection of barn owls because of the large numbers of mice they ate (1946).[62] Moseley was largely instrumental in launching a vigorous defense and protection of the bobwhite quail as a song bird also because of its value to the farmer. He published observations (1928, 1929)[51,52,53] showing that where these birds were present in large numbers, potato plants were scarcely infested with potato beetles. In other papers, birds that were rare or new to northern Ohio were reported, among them the white-headed eagle, the gyrfalcon, the Hudsonian curlew, and the Brunnich's murre. Moseley's love of ornithology was shown through his writings, activity on field trips, and genuine interest taken in bird collections made by him and deposited in museums of other investigators. His final contribution to ornithology, written in the golden years of his life, was a twice published paper on "Variations in the bird population" (1946, 1947).[61,63] The study covered Ohio and nearby states with discussions of the effects of climate, wet and dry periods, and local weather conditions on the birds. He further wrote about the decline of northern birds that were formerly often seen in the winter, and southern birds whose range had been extended northward. Another topic concerned the effect of foreign birds on the native species, and how bird life is affected by the activities of human beings. The paper summarizes a lifetime of field observations, correspondence with friends, and a study of the literature. Noteworthy among correspondents were Louis W. Campbell, Charles Goslin (1904-1990), Lynds Jones (1865-1951), Harold F. Mayfield, Milton B. Trautman, and J. Paul Visscher (1895-1950). As a member of the Wilson Ornithological Club, Moseley served as vice-president.

Moseley's zoological publications in archival journals beyond ornithology are only minor by comparison. After joining the American Society of Mammalogists as a charter member upon its founding in 1919, Moseley published four minor notes in its periodical, *Journal of Mammalogy* (1928, 1928, 1930, 1934).[49,50,54,58] Other topics in zoology appeared as short essays or brief notes in the Sandusky newspapers. Among these subjects were prairie rattlesnakes and fox snakes (*Sandusky Star-Journal*, 4 September 1909 and 10 June 1914; *Sandusky Register*, 26 April 1919), 40-year-old eels (*Sandusky Star-Journal*, 23 April 1921), and sea lampreys (*Sandusky Star-Journal*, 5 December 1928). The latter two are unusual occurrences for Lake Erie. Moseley's book *Our Wild Animals* (1927),[48] written for the young student, covered many groups of animals and represents his largest single work in zoology.

References

Note: An asterisk placed at the beginning of certain titles denotes Moseley's major publications in each discipline [see also table, page 100].

Meetings

1. 1895. Edwin L. Moseley. "Attractions for a scientist in the vicinity of Sandusky." [Abstract]. *Third Annual Report Ohio State Academy of Science* 1895: 5.

2. 1895. Edwin L. Moseley. "The Ohio Academy of Science [summer meeting at Sandusky, 2,3 July 1895]." *Ohio Educational Monthly* 44: 408-409.

3. 1896. Edwin L. Moseley. "The Ohio Academy of Science [summer meeting at Sandusky, 2,3 July 1895]." *Fourth Annual Report Ohio State Academy of Science* (1895). 1896: 40-42.

4. 1896-1904. Edwin L. Moseley. "[Reports of meetings by the secretary]." *Fourth through Twelfth Annual Reports Ohio State Academy of Science.*

5. 1958. Paul B. Sears. "The Future Role of Academies." Presentation Manuscript, Sears Papers, Archives. Yale University, New Haven, Connecticut. 5 pp.

Botany

6. 1896. Edwin L. Moseley. "A comparison of the flora of Erie Co., Ohio with that of Erie Co., N.Y. [Abstract]." *Science,* New Series 4: 434; *Botanical Gazette* 22: 224.

7. 1897. Frederic W. Putnam, ed. "Titles of papers read [in botany]," pp. 185-187. In *Proceedings of the American Association for the Advancement of Science, Forty-fifth Meeting*, Buffalo, New York. 270 pp.

8. 1897. Edwin L. Moseley. "Climatic influence of Lake Erie on vegetation." *American Naturalist* 31: 60-63. (Review notice by C. E. Bessey. *American Naturalist* 31: 61,62. 1897).

9. 1898. Roscoe Pound and Frederic E. Clements. *The Phytogeography of Nebraska. I. General Survey.* Jacob North & Co., Lincoln, Nebraska. xxi, 329 pp., 4 maps. (2nd ed., 1900. Botanical Seminar, University of Nebraska, Lincoln. 442 pp., 4 maps; reprinted, 1977. Arno Press, New York).

10. 1899. Edwin L. Moseley. "Sandusky flora." *Lakeside Magazine* 5(3): 7-13.

*11. 1899. Edwin L. Moseley. "Sandusky flora. A catalogue of the flowering plants and ferns growing without cultivation, in Erie County, Ohio, and the peninsula and islands of Ottawa County." *Ohio State Academy of Science, Special Papers*, No. 1. 167 pp. (Review by J. C. Arthur. *Botanical Gazette* 28: 139,140).

*12. 1928. Edwin L. Moseley. "Flora of the Oak Openings west of Toledo." *Proceedings of the Ohio Academy of Science* 8: 79-134. *Special Papers*, No. 20.

13. 1931. Edwin L. Moseley. "Some plants that were probably brought to northern Ohio from the West by Indians." *Papers of the Michigan Academy Science, Arts and Letters* (1930) 13: 169-172.

14. 1979. Nathan William Easterly. "Rare and infrequent plant species in the Oak Openings of northwestern Ohio." *Ohio Journal of Science* 79: 51-58.

15. 1984. Nathan William Easterly. "Some rare and infrequent flora of the Oak Openings: Addenda to Professor Moseley's findings." *Northwestern Ohio Quarterly* 56(1): 18-20. Winter.

16. 1995. Tom S. Cooperrider. 1995. *The Dicotyledoneae of Ohio. Part 2. Linaceae through Campanulaceae.* Ohio State University Press, Columbus. xxi, 656 pp.

Geology

*17. 1898. Edwin L. Moseley. "Lake Erie enlarging. The Islands separated from the mainland in recent times." *Lakeside Magazine* 1(9): 14-20.

18. 1902. Edwin L. Moseley. "Submerged valleys in Sandusky Bay." *National Geographic Magazine* 13: 398-403.

CHAPTER 9 • SCIENTIFIC PRESENTATIONS AND PUBLICATIONS

19. 1903. Edwin L. Moseley. "Testing the currents in Lake Erie." *National Geographic Magazine* 14: 41,42.

20. 1903. Edwin L. Moseley. "[Mapping the channels of Sandusky Bay] Original work in high schools." *Ohio Educational Monthly* 52: 367-374; see also *Sandusky Daily-Star*, 20 December, p. 5. 1902.

21. 1903. Edwin L. Moseley. "Currents in Sandusky Bay." *Monthly Weather Review* 31: 236.

22. 1903. Edwin L. Moseley. "The currents in Sandusky Bay." *Eleventh Annual Report Ohio State Academy of Science* 1902: 21-26.

23. 1905. Edwin L. Moseley. "Change of level at the west end of Lake Erie." [Abstract]. *Seventh Annual Report Michigan Academy of Science* 1905: 38,39.

*24. 1905. Edwin L. Moseley. "Formation of Sandusky Bay and Cedar Point." *Thirteenth Annual Report of the Ohio State Academy of Science* (1904). 1905: 179-238. (reprinted, 1973. *Lake Erie: Floods, Lake Levels, Northeast Storms: The Formation of Sandusky Bay and Cedar Point.* The Ohio Historical Society, Columbus. ii, 64 pp.).

25. 1971. Charles E. Frohman. Item 80. "Professor Moseley," [3 pp.] In *Sandusky's 3rd Dimension*. The Ohio Historical Society, Columbus. [84 pp.].

Medical Science

26. 1841. Daniel Drake. "A memoir on the disease called by the people *Trembles*, and the sick stomach or *milk-sickness*; as they have occurred in the counties of Fayette, Madison, Clark, and Green[e] in the State of Ohio." *Western Journal of Medical Science* 3: 161-226. March. (reprinted, Maxwell, 1841. 57 pp.).

*27. 1906. Edwin L. Moseley. "The cause of trembles in cattle, sheep and horses and of milk-sickness in people." *Ohio Naturalist* 6: 463-470, 477-483.

28. 1908. Albert C. Crawford. "The supposed relationship of white snakeroot to milksickness, or *trembles*." United States Department of Agriculture, Bureau of Plant Industry, Washington, D.C. *Bulletin* 121: 5-20. *Miscellaneous Papers* (see pages 12-15).

29. 1909. Edwin L. Moseley. "The cause of trembles and milk sickness." *Medical Record* 75: 839-844. (reprinted, William Wood & Co., pp. 1-20).

30. 1909. Edwin L. Moseley. "[On the cause of trembles and milk sickness]." *Mulford's Veterinary Bulletin,* Philadelphia. [Efforts to locate this item have failed].

31. 1910. Edwin L. Moseley. "Antidote for aluminum phosphate, the poison that causes milk sickness." *Medical Record* 77: 620-622. (reprinted, William Wood & Co., pp. 1-6).

32. 1910. Edwin L. Moseley. "White snakeroot, the cause of trembles and milksickness." *Ohio Farmer* 126: 320. 15 October.

33. 1910. Edwin L. Moseley. "Milksickness—trembles." *Ohio Farmer* 126: 476. 26 November.

34. 1911. Louis Pammel. *A Manual of Poisonous Plants: Chiefly of Eastern North America, with Brief Notes on Economic and Medicinal Plants, and Numerous Illustrations.* The Torch Press, Cedar Rapids, Iowa. viii, 977 pp. (pages 771,772).

35. 1917. Edwin L. Moseley. "Milk sickness, or trembles, caused by resin of white snakeroot." *Medical Record* 92: 428.

36. 1917-1918. F. A. Wolf, R. S. Curtis, and B. F. Kaup. "Studies on trembles or milk sickness and white snakeroot." *Journal of the American Veterinarian Medical Association* 52: 820-827.

37. 1918. F. A. Wolf, R. S. Curtis, and B. F. Kaup. "A monograph on trembles or milksickness and white snakeroot." *North Carolina Agricultural Experiment Station, Raleigh. Technical Bulletin* 15: 1-74. (pages 10,16,17).

38. 1919. Walter G. Sackett. "The connection of milksickness with the poisonous qualities of white snakeroot (*Eupatorium urticaefolium*)." *Journal of Infectious Diseases* 24: 231-259.

39. 1927. Albert A. Hansen. "Beware of milk sickness. Poison lurks in Ohio woodland pastures." *Ohio Farmer* 160(11): 9, 25. 10 September.

*40. 1941. Edwin L. Moseley. *Milk Sickness Caused by White Snakeroot*. Ohio Academy of Science and the Author. 171 pp. (Review notice by G. W. B[laydes]. *Ohio Journal of Science* 43: 266. 1943; "Prof. Moseley's latest book, *Milk Sickness*, wins praise;" from an unidentified newspaper clipping, Archives, Bowling Green State University).

41. 1985. Relda E. Niederhofer. "The milk sickness: Drake on medical interpretation." *Journal of the American Medical Association* 254: 2123-2125.

Zoology

42. 1887. Edwin L. Moseley. *Lists of the Birds, Mammals, Birds' Eggs, and Desiderata of Michigan Birds in the Museum of the Kent Scientific Institute, Grand Rapids, Mich[igan]*. Grand Rapids, Michigan. 32 pp., 1 pl.

43. 1891. Edwin L. Moseley. "Descriptions of two new species of flycatchers from the Island of Negros, Philippines." *The Ibis,* Sixth Series 3(9): 46,47, pl. II.

44. 1895. Edwin L. Moseley. "The white headed eagle in northern Ohio." *American Naturalist* 29: 168-170.

45. 1898. Edwin L. Moseley. "The white headed eagle in northern Ohio." *Lakeside Magazine* 4(2): 36. (reprinted by Eleanor Durr. 1984. Heritage Notes. "Eagles—as observed by Professor Moseley." *Peninsular News*, 26 April).

46. 1900. Edwin L. Moseley. "Occasional abundance of certain birds on or near Lake Erie." *Lakeside Magazine* 6(4): 29,30.

47. 1900. Edwin L. Moseley. "Occasional abundance of certain birds on or near Lake Erie." *Eighth Annual Report Ohio State Academy of Science* 1899: 12-15; also *Proceedings*.

*48. 1927. Edwin L. Moseley. *Our Wild Animals*. D. Appleton & Co., New York. 310 pp.

49. 1928. Edwin L. Moseley. "Red bat as a mother." *Journal of Mammalogy* 9(3): 248,249.

50. 1928. Edwin L. Moseley. "The number of young red bats in one litter." *Journal of Mammalogy* 9(3): 249.

51. 1928. Edwin L. Moseley. "Bob-white and the scarcity of potato beetles." *Wilson Bulletin* 40(3): 149-151.

*52. 1928. Edwin L. Moseley. "Bob-white useful to the potato grower." *Potato Association of America Proceedings Fifteenth Annual Meeting*, Dec. 1928. pp. 259-262.

53. 1929. Edwin L. Moseley. "Bob-white and scarcity of potato beetles." *School Science and Mathematics* 29: 196-198.

54. 1930. Edwin L. Moseley. "Feeding a short-tailed shrew." *Journal of Mammalogy* 11(2): 22,225.

55. 1930. Edwin L. Moseley. "Fluctuation of bird life with change in water level." *Wilson Bulletin* 42(3): 191-193.

56. 1930. Edwin L. Moseley. "Abundance of the golden plover in Ohio in 1930." *Wilson Bulletin* 42(4): 292,293.

57. 1931. Edwin L. Moseley. "The heronries of northern Ohio." *Ohio Journal of Science* 31(4): 270. [Abstract].

58. 1934. Edwin L. Moseley. "Increase of badgers in northwestern Ohio." *Journal of Mammalogy* 15(2): 156-158.

59. 1936. Edwin L. Moseley. "Blue heron colonies in northern Ohio." *Wilson Bulletin* 48(1): 3-11.

60. 1938. Edwin L. Moseley. "Shore birds attracted to streams polluted by sewage." *Wilson Bulletin* 50(3): 204,205.

*61. 1946. Edwin L. Moseley. "Variations in the bird population of Ohio and nearby states." *Ohio Journal of Science* 46: 308-322.

62. 1946. Edwin L. Moseley. "Useful farm bird, the barn owl." *Ohio Conservation Bulletin* 10(7): 30.

63. 1947. Edwin L. Moseley. "Variations in the bird population of the north-central states due to climatic and other changes." *The Auk* 64(1): 15-35, pl. 4.

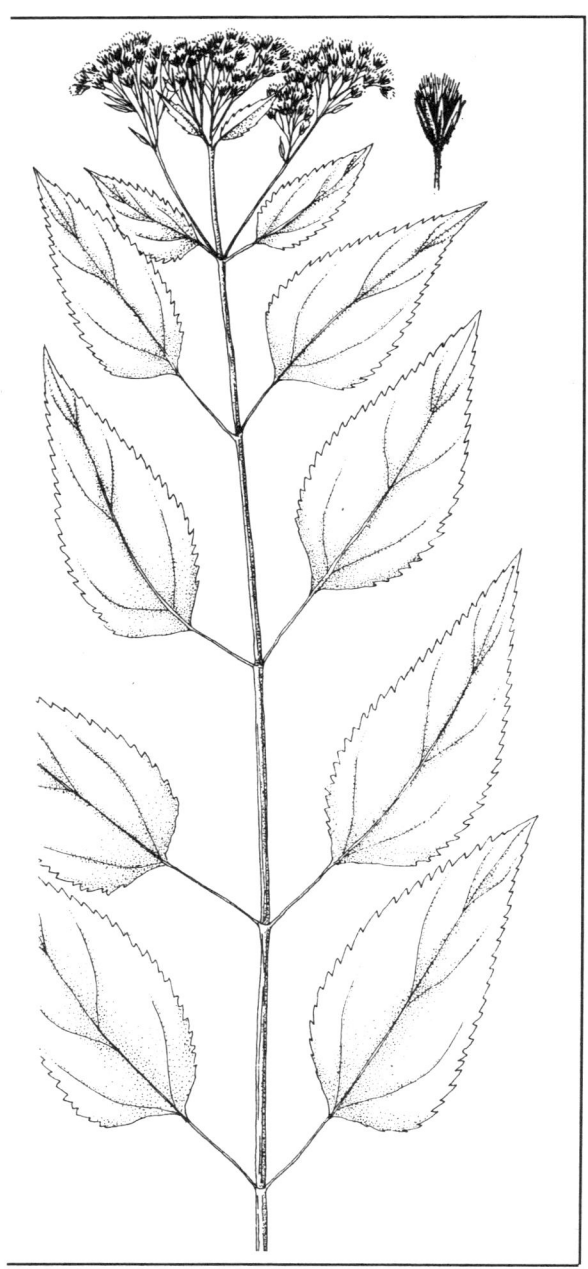

***Eupatorium rugosum*,* the white snakeroot plant.**

(T. Richard Fisher, 1988. *Part 3. Asteraceae of Ohio.* The Ohio State University Press, Columbus. p. 34)

CHAPTER 9 • SCIENTIFIC PRESENTATIONS AND PUBLICATIONS

Membership in Professional Scientific Organizations and Summation of Publications in Periodicals

A. **Activities in Organizations and Publication Summation**

American Association for the Advancement of Science (New York City)
Member, 1885; Fellow, 1902; Papers Read at Meetings, one in 1896;
Fifty Year Member, 1937, one of 37 who was a member for 50 or more years.

	Numbers of Publications
Published Papers:	
Science, 1896, 1901	2

American Society of Mammalogists (Baltimore)
Charter Member, 1919
Published Papers:
Journal of Mammalogy, 1928(2), 1930, 1934 — 4

Central Association of Science and Mathematics Teachers (Chicago)
Papers Read at Meetings, one in 1923
Published Papers:
School Science, 1902 — 1
School Science and Mathematics, 1912, 1924, 1929, 1938 — 4

Chicago Academy of Sciences (Chicago)
Elected Honorary Life Member, 1945

Field Naturalists Association (Toledo)
Charter Member, 1932; Honorary Member
Published Papers:
Toledo Naturalists Association, Annual Bulletin (Toledo, Ohio), 1939, 1947; 2 reprinted articles, 1946, 1947 — 2

Michigan Academy of Science (Lansing); name changed to **Michigan Academy of Science, Arts, and Letters (Ann Arbor)**
Member, 1905; Chairman for the Botanical Section, 1934-1935
Papers Read at Meetings, five during the years 1905, 1930, 1935

CHAPTER 9 • SCIENTIFIC PRESENTATIONS AND PUBLICATIONS

      (Chairman), 1939, 1943
      Published Papers:
         Annual Reports, 1905   1
         Papers of the Michigan Academy of Science, Arts,
            and Letters 1931, 1940, 1941   3

The Ohio State Academy of Science (Columbus); 1913 name changed to
The Ohio Academy of Science
    Charter Member, 1891, Secretary, 1895-1903; President, 1904;
    Elected Honorary Life Member, 1943
    Papers Read at Meetings, 33 papers read during the years
        from 1894 through 1939
        Published Papers:
           Annual Report, 1895-1905   10
           Ohio Journal of Science, 1931, 1939, 1946   3
           Ohio Naturalist, 1906   2
           Special Papers, 1899, 1928, 1941   3
           Annual Report, Reports of Meetings by
              the Secretary, 1896-1904   16

Wilson Ornithological Club (Sioux City)
    Member, 1925; Vice-President, 1932-1933
        Published Papers:
           Wilson Bulletin 1928(2), 1930(2), 1936(3), 1938   8

B. **Publication Summation by Topics in Periodicals not Affiliated with Professional Organizations; or if affiliated, then Moseley not known to be a member**

Astronomy; Meteorology
        Popular Astronomy (Northfield, Minnesota), 1904, 1944   2
        Journal of the Royal Astronomical Society of Canada (Toronto), 1941   1
        Monthly Weather Review (Washington, D.C.), 1903   1
        American Fruit Grower (Cleveland), 1945   1
        Scientific American (New York City), 1931   1

Botany
        Botanical Gazette (Crawfordsville, Indiana), 1896   1
        American Naturalist (Philadelphia), 1897   1

Geology
National Geographic Magazine (Washington, D.C.), 1902, 1903 (2)   3

Medical Science
Medical Record (New York), 1909, 1910, 1917   3
Mulford's Veterinary Bulletin (Philadelphia), [not located], 1909   1

Ornithology
The Ibis (London), 1891   1
Bird Lore (New York), 1912, 1914   2
The Auk (Lancaster, PA), 1943, 1947   2
American Naturalist (Philadelphia) 1897   1

Science Education
Elementary School Journal (Chicago), 1925   1
American Schoolmaster (Ypsilanti, Michigan), 1925   1
Ohio Educational Monthly (Columbus), 1896, 1903 (2), 1917, 1921   5
Bee Gee News (Bowling Green, Ohio), 1921, 1925   2

C. Publication Summation in Popular and Literary Periodicals
Cappers Farmer (Topeka, Kansas), 1947 (2)   2
Ohio Conservation Bulletin (Columbus), 1946   1
Country Gentleman (Philadelphia), 1943   1
Lakeside Magazine (Lakeside, Ohio), 1898 (2), 1899, 1900   4
Ohio Farmer (Cleveland), 1910 (3), 1911 (4), 1912   8

D. Newspapers (cited most frequently)
Cleveland Plain Dealer
Daily Sentinel-Tribune (Bowling Green, Ohio)
Erie County Reporter
Sandusky Daily Register
Sandusky Daily-Star
Sandusky Register
Sandusky Star-Journal
Toledo Blade

Moseley studying the annual rings in a cross-section of a bur oak stump.

The stump, from Allen County, Indiana, is 47 inches x 52 inches x 30 inches high and has 283 annual rings.

(Taken by O. E. Ehrhart, Antwerp, Paulding County, Ohio, 2 May 1939. Published in the *Ohio Journal of Science* 39:225, pl. I. 1939; Stuckey Collection)

Forecasting Long-Range Weather Conditions

CHAPTER TEN

Ronald L. Stuckey

Moseley stimulated much interest locally and nationally by making forecasts based on detailed studies of tree-ring widths, Great Lakes water-level depths, Ohio River floods, and actual meteorological rainfall records. His first public announcement of these long-range weather forecasts was made 30 March 1937 at his retirement party, after 51 years of teaching science in two high schools and at the college level on the Bowling Green State University campus. Moseley's stated predictions were printed in the local Bowling Green newspaper, the *Daily Sentinel-Tribune* (31 March 1937, p. 1) and in the *Sandusky Star-Journal* (3 April 1937, p. 1), but in no other periodicals so far seen. There Moseley[4] made the following rainfall predictions:

> Within the next 40 years there will be no drought comparable in duration and severity with that which recently ended. As in the past, there will be dry years and wet years, but more wet ones than in the past 40 years. Probably, as in the past, many of the next 40 years will not show notable departures from the normal precipitation.
>
> It is not unlikely that there will be two or three dry years within the next five. With this exception there will probably be no long periods of either unusually low or unusually high rainfall before 1949.
>
> I believe that the middle of the century, beginning, perhaps with 1949, will have unusually heavy rainfall. For a period of some 15 years following 1948, and probably for a considerably longer period, there will be only a few dry years, the rainfall greatly exceeding that of recent years.

Chapter 10 • Forecasting Long-Range Weather Conditions

• • •

Lake Erie is already showing a great rise in level. I think none of you will ever see it so low again as it was in 1934. The south shore of the lake from Cleveland to Toledo will experience unusually high water about 1950 and many times after that within the next quarter of the century. The same is true of Milwaukee, Chicago, and all of the southern border of Lake Michigan. Owners of cottages or other property which is so little elevated above the lake level that a rise of the water of two or three feet above the near level of the past 30 years will cause inundation should be prepared for it.

While many people along the lakes and many along streams will be inconvenienced by the increased precipitation, millions of people whose welfare depends on the success of their crops will derive very great benefit.

The Bowling Green newspaper, the *Daily Sentinel-Tribune*, also carried an addition to his prediction, believed to have been written by his former student and friend Ivan E. Lake, a reporter for the paper. Lake[5] explained the history and rationale of Moseley's research, which he noted as having been ongoing for many years. He further wrote that Moseley was familiar with the research of Charles G. Abbot (1872-1973), an astrophysicist of the Smithsonian Institution, Washington, D.C. who had published many papers, on the relationship between sunspots and the weather. Abbot (1933)[3] stated: "The principal departures from normal climates which comprise weather are due primarily to a group of periodic variations of the sun's radiation rather than to terrestrial complexities." These disturbances of the sun, known as sunspots, are associated with important modifications of the weather. These sunspots occur in cycles, which in turn cause weather patterns also to cycle at intervals of 23 and 46 years, or their multiples. Because of these correlations, weather can be forecasted for many years into the future. This information intrigued Moseley to the extent that he wanted to investigate how these sunspot cycles influenced the amounts of rainfall and general weather conditions in Ohio and midwestern United States. He wrote a general article about these vagaries of weather two months later in the campus newspaper (Moseley, 1937).[6]

Actual measurements and reports of rainfall amounts for each year were not available back far enough in the historical record, and Moseley had to look for other sources of either less accurate or correlative data. In his study of the formation of the Cedar Point Peninsula, referred to in the previous chapter, Moseley (1905)[1] discovered that the parallel seven ridges provided an approach for measurement. These ridges were formed during times of high water by the great northeast storms that shifted the sand to make the ridges. These ridges could be dated by determining the ages of the trees on them. Their ages would approximately equal the time of the wet periods, and the number of years between them would approximate the length of the complete cycle, which when measured resulted in the following years that were wet ones, 1429, 1504, 1594, 1684, 1724, 1859, and 1878. The time interval between most of the years is about 90 or 91 years, except for one ridge, the year 1724, which Moseley was able to explain years later when he had more information. It was evident to Moseley that the wet and dry periods alternate at about 46 years duration for each period.

Moseley (1940)[10] sought information from other sources. Upon examination of the water-level depths for Lake Erie, dating from 1860, he noted high water levels from 1860-1890 and low levels from then until 1937. Annual rainfall amounts in Cincinnati, Marietta, Pittsburgh, Rochester, and Sandusky showed similar records with wet years from 1857 to 1890 and dry years from then until 1937. The earliest known occurrences of floods along the Ohio River were between 1762 and 1832, during which time a total of seven were recorded at Pittsburgh. Each one of them was followed by a great flood about 90 or 91 years later, the water in some of them attaining about the same height as in the corresponding earlier floods. The annual growth rings of trees also proved to be an important source of data, for they ultimately allowed Moseley to determine a long history of rainfall conditions, as far back as 1429.

In the above mentioned newspaper article by Ivan Lake (1937)[5] explaining how Moseley became involved in weather predictions, he made reference to Professor Andrew E. Douglass (1867-1962) of the University of Arizona, Tucson, as did Josephine True (1945)[17] in her biographical sketch of Moseley. Douglass, an astronomer and director of the Steward Observatory at the University of Arizona, is credited with founding the science of dendrochronology, the recording and studying of past events that can be interpreted from the study of growth rings in trees (Thybony, 1987).[26] The definitive publication by Douglass, "Climatic cycles and tree-growth: A study of the annual rings in trees in relation to climate and solar activity" (1919)[2] provided the details of how to study the tree sections and their rings, and how to interpret their characteristics for determining their relationship to rainfall and solar phenomena. Moseley certainly was familiar with and probably studied in detail Douglass' publication. Two additional volumes were published by Douglass (1928, 1936),[2] the latter concentrating on a study of cycles.

Since 1928, according to various reports, Moseley had studied the tree-ring widths and patterns in more than 300 tree stumps by 1937, and some reports have stated that he had examined over 500 of them by the time of his death in 1948. From these tree stumps, obtained from various states in the Mississippi valley and the Great Lakes region, Moseley measured the width of growth rings and determined those years with wide rings representing wet years and those with narrow rings representing dry years. From the literature, he studied the recorded water levels of the Great Lakes and the accounts of the floods along the Ohio River. The actual records of rainfall were obtained for many localities throughout the region. By correlating the data from these four basic sources, Moseley developed the theory that the amount of rainfall in most areas of the interior of the North American continent repeats itself in cycles of 90.4 years, or four times the period of the magnetic sunspot cycle. His publications on what may be learned from stumps (1938),[7] the dating tree rings (1939),[8] and the Ohio River floods (1939)[9] provided the initial rationale and supporting data for these studies. On 17 March 1939, at a meeting in Ann Arbor of the Michigan Academy of Arts, Sciences, and Letters, he explained the ninety-year precipitation cycle, and made long-range predictions of rainfall in midwestern United States for nearly the next half century, or until 1975. His predictions were generally that a drought would begin in the year 1943 which would become severe in the latter part of 1946 until late 1947; then beginning in 1948 above average rainfall would occur until 1957, followed by a two-year drought with more abundant rainfall in 1959 and 1960; the early 1960s would have less than average precipitation, and from then on until about 1975 nearly every year would be a wet one. These predictions, quoted from Moseley, are given in the portion of this chapter by Moran Tudury and evaluated by me.

Moseley's rainfall predictions made at the Michigan Academy Meeting and published a year later in the Academy's *Papers* (1940)[10] attracted considerable attention from the popular media. Summaries of his predictions were noted in newspapers throughout the country, including his full prediction in an extensive editorial article in the *New York Times* (19 March 1939). For nearly the next 10 years, or until his death, Moseley focused his research attention on the rainfall forecasts, his journal publications discussing sunspots and tree rings (1941),[11] the solar influence on variations in rainfall (1942),[12] precipitation prospects for 1943-1947 (1944),[14] the recurrence of floods and droughts after intervals of about 90.4 years (1944),[15] tree stumps as weather indicators (1945),[16] and his long-range weather forecasts for the Midwest (1947).[21,22] Moseley's novel research continued to attract the attention of the media, as reporters wrote numerous articles in the newspapers on the success and failure of his predictions. For the most part, based on these newspaper accounts, his predictions held true through the years.

In August 1943, when Moseley was awarded an honorary degree of Doctor of Humane Letters by Bowling Green State University, he took the opportunity to state predictions with reference to future water levels of Lake Erie from 1944 to 1976, as reported anonymously in the *Sandusky Register* (10 August 1943), but based on a news release from Bowling Green State University by Paul W. Jones[13] which quoted Moseley, as follows:

1944 — the lake level will be below that of 1943 but above the average of the last 50 years.

1945 — further decline until late in the year.

1946 — high water early in the year, but a drop in the level the latter half.

1947 — lowest level since 1936.

1948-60 — higher average than during any previous long period on record. In 1954-58 the lake probably will not be quite so high as in 1948-53.

1961-65 — decline.

1966-76 — average level about the same as the high average expected in 1948-60.

At no time in either 1948-60 or 1966-76 is the water expected to remain long at a level so much as a foot higher than its present level.

Those individuals familiar with the fluctuations in the water level of Lake Erie know that during the summers since 1943 Lake Erie reached low water levels in 1948, 1958, and 1964. By allowing for a short period of time for the lack of rainfall to be reflected in the lake-level readings, these years correspond with the low rainfall periods predicted by Moseley. In contrast, Lake Erie reached high water levels in 1952, 1973, and 1985, the latter year the highest ever to that time in recorded history, and these years correspond with the high rainfall periods predicted by Moseley.

Moseley's last printed article on long-range rainfall forecasts was one he wrote especially for the *International News Special Service*. The copy seen appeared in the *Cleveland Plain Dealer* (4 January 1948, p. 15-A). Among his predictions were these for Ohio, as quoted here:[23]

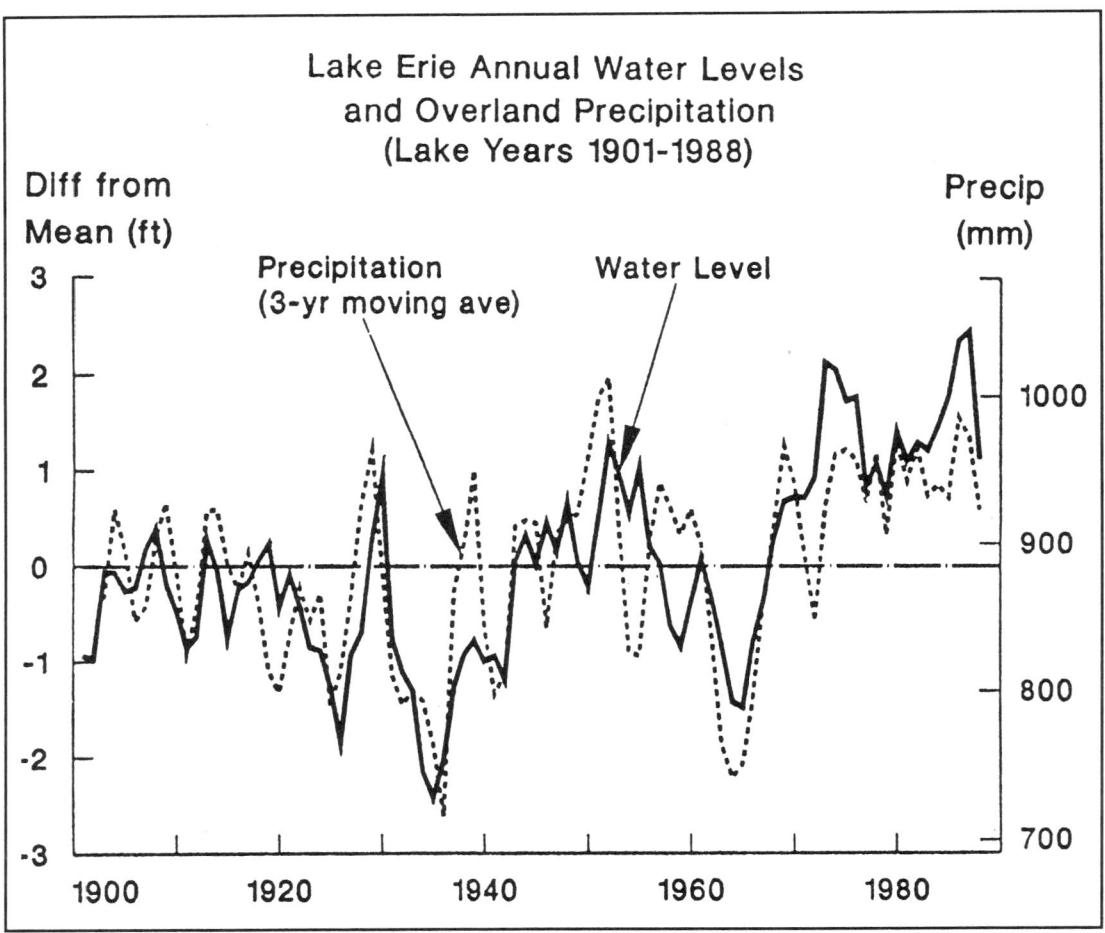

Graphs comparing the water levels and rainfall amounts by year in Lake Erie.

(Lake Erie shorelines. *Ohio Coastal Resources Management Project* 2(1): 2. 1989, June)

...Ohio...will probably get more than the usual amount of rain during most of 1948 and the first part of 1949. June and July of 1948 may be exceptions. A shortage of rain is probable from May to August 1950, and in parts of the [wider] area until the end of 1950.

Earlier in the article, Moseley discussed his evidence for periods of droughts, based on tree stumps having very narrow growth rings corresponding with specific past years. These years were 1494, 1584 and 1585, followed by other pairs of years at intervals of 90 and 91 years. These were the years 1675 and 1676; 1766 and 1767; 1856 and 1857. Continuing the subject of droughts Moseley[23] wrote, "In this series, the latest is that of 1946 and 1947. Another will occur in 2037." Ivan Lake (1948),[24] in his obituary of Moseley in the Bowling Green newspaper, reported that Moseley, "had foreseen the general drought conditions which had come in 1946-47 [and] he recently predicted that the year 2037 will be a dry one." Other newspaper writers, Paul W. Jones (1946, 1947)[19,20] and Don Strouse (1946),[18] also confirmed Moseley's predictions of a dry period during the summer and fall of 1946.

Moseley (1939, 1940[9,10]) published two lists of years: one for those trees which had wide rings, and one for those trees which had narrow rings. This list was reprinted by Frohman (1973)[25] and provides a means by which one can use Moseley's data to continue to make predictions of wet and/or dry years. Moseley's own published predictions extended to the mid-1970s, but beyond that time for the next 20 years it was virtually impossible for him to make predictions because of the absence of tree-ring records forming the 90-91 interval sequence. From the table, it can be noted that a sequence of years with narrow tree rings for the years 1636, 1726, 1816, and 1907 would lead to the prediction that the year 1997 should have been a dry year in midwestern United States. The years 2000 and 2001 should be dry as predicted from Moseley's tree-ring list of years.

In articles[21,23] published during the last year and a half of his life, Moseley gave credit to Ralph E. DeLury (1881-1956), an astronomer of the Dominion Observatory, Ottawa, Canada, for information that the motions of the moon affect the abundance of sunspots at about every 90 years. Moseley, quoting DeLury,[21] wrote: "the amount of influence... [the moon] exerts depends on its position as well as direction. The blending of two periods of the moon with respect to rotation of its major axis and its orbital plane, gives a pulsation in about 9 years, 10 times which is 90 years." DeLury's information gave support to the rainfall cycle of 90.4 years as determined by Moseley.

Years When a Majority of the Trees in the Region Extending from Southern Michigan to Tennessee Formed Wide or Narrow Rings

Wide					Narrow			
	1852	1761	1671	1936	1845	1755	1665
	1850	1760	1669	1934	1843	1753	1663
1939(?)	1849	1759	1668	1931-2	1841	1751	1660
1938	1848	1758		1930	1839	1748-9	1658
1937	1847	1756		1925	1834	1743-4	1652-3
1928	1837	1747	1657	1911	1821	1730	1640
1927	1836			1910	1820	1729(?)	1639(?)
1922	1832	1741		1907	1816	1726	1636
				1901	1811	1721	1630
	1887	1797	1707	1900	1810	1720	1629(?)
	1886	1796	1706	1898-9	1808-9	1718	1628
	1885	1795	1705	1895	1804	1714	1624
	1884	1794	1704	1894	1802-3	1712-3	1622-3
	1883	1793	1703	1891	1801	1711	1620
	1881	1791		1890	1799-0	1709-0	1618-9
	1878	1788	1697(?)	1874	1784	1693	1603
	1877	1787	1696	1871	1781	1691	1600
	1876	1786	1695	1870	1780	1690	1599
	1869	1779(?)	1688	1868	1778	1687	1597
	1859	1769	1678	1867	1777	1686	1596(?)
	1858	1768	1677	1864	1774	1683	1592
				1857	1767	1676	1585
				1856	1766	1675	1584

The table shows that each wet year was followed after an interval of 90 or 91 years by another wet year, likewise each dry year by a dry year. If the precipitation cycle were as long as ninety and one-half years, the 91-year interval would appear as often as the 90-year interval, but it does not. If the cycle were just ninety and one-third years, then after three such intervals the difference between dates would be 271 years, as it usually is, but in some cases it is 272 years, which implies that the cycle is a little more than ninety and one-third years.

By using records of rainfall prior to 1848 many attempts have been made to correlate months of excessive or deficient rain with months between 90 and 91 years later. The best correlations were found by using the months ninety years and five months later, the next best by using an interval of ninety years and four months. This result is in good agreement with the table of dates of wet and dry years shown by the width of tree rings. Both methods lead to the conclusion that the length of the cycle is not far from 90.4 years.

Moseley's table of years when trees had wide or narrow growth rings.

(*Ohio Journal of Science* 39: 224. 1939)

In articles about Moseley's scientific contributions, uninformed writers since his death usually credit him with originating the idea of using data from the tree rings and correlating it with rainfall conditions. To the contrary, Moseley was not the originator of this idea or procedure. Clues from two of his contemporary writers, Lake (1937)[5] and True (1945),[17] who mention Moseley's familiarity with the solar studies of Abbot and of the interpretation of tree-ring data from Douglass, provide evidence that Moseley adopted their contributions to his own studies. What he did was to incorporate rainfall data interpreted from his own tree-ring studies in midwestern United States and to correlate those data with rainfall information or inferences from other sources. By using these various data sources, Moseley discovered that the rainfall pattern repeated itself in cycles of 90.4 years, or four times the period of the magnetic sunspot cycle. From this pattern Moseley then could predict future weather situations in various parts of the Midwest. His predictions were based on the new and innovative features of his research, which in turn brought fame and national recognition not only to him personally, but also to Bowling Green State University, who released this information to the popular press of newspapers and magazines.

References

1. 1905. Edwin L. Moseley. "Formation of Sandusky Bay and Cedar Point." *Thirteenth Annual Report of the Ohio State Academy of Science* (1904). 1905: 179-238. (reprinted, 1973. *Lake Erie: Floods, Lake Levels, Northeast Storms: The Formation of Sandusky Bay and Cedar Point.* The Ohio Historical Society, Columbus. ii, 64 pp.).

2. 1919. Andrew E. Douglass. "Climatic cycles and tree-growth. A study of the annual rings of trees in relation to climate and solar activity." *Publication No. 289. Carnegie Institution of Washington*, Washington, D.C. 127 pp.; 1928. II, vii, 166 pp; 1936. III, vii, 171 pp.

3. 1933. Charles G. Abbot. "Sunspots and weather." *Smithsonian Miscellaneous Collections* 87(18): 1-10.

4. 1937. [Edwin L. Moseley]. "Prof. Moseley predicts forty-six years of wet weather ahead." *Daily Sentinel-Tribune,* Bowling Green, 31 March, pp. 1,2; also *Sandusky Star-Journal,* 3 April 1937, p. 1.

Chapter 10 • Forecasting Long-Range Weather Conditions

5. 1937. [Ivan E. Lake]. "Prof. Moseley predicts forty-six years of wet weather ahead." *Daily Sentinel-Tribune*, Bowling Green, 31 March, pp. 1,2; also *Sandusky Star-Journal*, 3 April 1937, p. 1.

6. 1937. Edwin L. Moseley. "Moseley writes on vagaries of weather." *Bee Gee News* 21(38): 1,4. 30 June.

*7. 1938. Edwin L. Moseley. "What may be learned from stumps?" *School Science and Mathematics* 38: 528-533.

8. 1939. Edwin L. Moseley. "The dating tree rings." *Toledo Naturalists Association, Annual Bulletin.* pp. 30-32.

*9. 1939. Edwin L. Moseley. "Long time forecasts of Ohio River floods." *Ohio Journal of Science* 39: 220-231.

*10. 1940. Edwin L. Moseley. "The ninety-year precipitation cycle." *Papers of the Michigan Academy Science, Arts, and Letters* (1939) 25: 491-496.

*11. 1941. Edwin L. Moseley. "Sun-spots and tree rings." *Journal of the Royal Astronomical Society of Canada* 35: 376-392.

12. 1942. Edwin L. Moseley. "Solar influence on variations in rainfall in the interior of the United States." *Popular Astronomy* 50: 419-422.

13. 1943. [Paul W. Jones]. "Prof. Moseley says south shore of Lake Erie will have high water again in 1946." *Sandusky Register*, 10 August, p. 1. (Based on news release, BGSU, 7 August 1943 by Paul W. Jones).

14. 1944. Edwin L. Moseley. "Precipitation prospects, 1943-47, for Ohio and near-by states." *Papers of the Michigan Academy of Science, Arts, and Letters* (1943) 29: 23-29.

15. 1944. Edwin L. Moseley. "Recurrence of floods and droughts after intervals of about 90.4 years." *Popular Astronomy* 52: 284-287.

16. 1945. Edwin L. Moseley. "Tree stumps as weather indicators." *American Fruit Grower* 65: 36,37.

17. 1945. Josephine True. "Edwin Lincoln Moseley: The biography of an educator." *Nature Magazine* 38: 37-39.

18. 1946. Don Strouse. "Tree rings reveal this section [central Ohio] is in for drought." *Columbus Citizen*, 20 October, p. 38.

19. 1946. Paul W. Jones. "Diet, droughts keep retired Bee Gee scientist happy as long-range predictions materialize. Dr. Moseley at 81 continues study of tree rings." *Toledo Times*, 20 October, p. 23.

20. 1947. [Paul W. Jones]. "Heavy spring rains reverse Dr. Moseley, Local scientist states meager records of 1857 weather are responsible." *Daily Sentinel-Tribune*, Bowling Green, 22 May, p. 1. (Based on news release, BGSU, 20 October 1946 by Paul W. Jones).

21. 1947. Edwin L. Moseley. "What will the weather be? Here's a limited forecast for 1947 based on the records made in a few states 90.4 years ago." *Capper's Farmer* 58 (February): 16.

22. 1947. Edwin L. Moseley. "Long-time weather forecast. The 90.4-year cycle applied to old records forms the basis for long-range predictions." *Capper's Farmer* 58 (March): 36.

23. 1948. Edwin L. Moseley. "Ohio's tree-ring authority predicts record 1950 drought." *Cleveland Plain Dealer*, 4 January, p. 15-A.

24. 1948. [Ivan E. Lake]. "[Long range weather forecasts, predicts drought in 2037]." In "Dr. E. L. Moseley's life one of great achievements. . ." *Daily Sentinel-Tribune*, Bowling Green, 7 June, p. 2.

25. 1973. Charles E. Frohman. "Predicting lake levels." *Inland Seas* 29: 182-185.

26. 1987. Scott Thybony. "Dead trees tell tales. By analyzing the growth rings, scientists can now predict drought and plot the effects of pollution." *National Wildlife* 25(5): 40.

CHAPTER 10 • FORECASTING LONG-RANGE WEATHER CONDITIONS

Long-Range Weather Man: A Description by Moran Tudury [1943]

Moran Tudury, a writer for the farm magazine, Country Gentleman *(1943), provided many examples of Professor Moseley's long-range rainfall forecasts, as told by him at that time in the 1940s. Tudury's essay contains examples of these weather predictions, providing an historic record of Moseley's techniques, thinking, and specific forecasts.*

Professor Edwin Lincoln Moseley is perhaps unlike any other person in America or in this world. The room of his scholarly retreat is filled with row after row of tree stumps, sections of wood cut from stumps, some ancient as the bones of Columbus, and all tagged, boxed, and carefully indexed. The 78-year-old scholar who sits in the midst of this indoor forest, quietly pursuing his studies, likewise is unlike the majority of academicians. For although he studies the past, it is simply for the purpose of foreseeing the future: the seasons to come which will bring weather dry, wet, hot, and cold, a subject ever uppermost in the minds of farming people.

Moseley is sometimes picturesquely called, by newspapermen, the "Reader of the Rings." And if ever a weatherman deliberately climbed out on a limb, and stuck his neck out into the bargain, Moseley is that one. For he does not predict the weather for tomorrow, but for next year and all the years following to 1974. Two interesting features exist concerning his predictions. First, according to reputable witnesses, his forecasts are usually accurate. Second, he reads the weather-to-come not by the stars, not by instruments, not by guess and by gosh, but from tree rings. . . .From his researches, and a comparison of the widths of the tree rings, plus a careful check with existing weather records of the past, Moseley has reached this conclusion: Regional rainfall occurs in cycles of 90.4 years, which is to say that every 90.4 years, weather begins to repeat itself.

Moseley's long-range weather forecasts have been unusually accurate, according to President Frank J. Prout, of Bowling Green University. Failure has resulted only when the data have been insufficient. Moseley predicted the end of the 1930-1936 drought. Paul W. Jones, head of the University's News Bureau, says, "He is believed to be the only scientist who predicted the drought in New York State in the summer of 1939. In August that year the *New York Times* commented editorially on the success of his forecasts. He predicted the heavy rains of this spring [1943] in an address in 1939 before the Ohio Academy of Science, which recently made him an honorary member.

• • •

Moseley is a fascinating source of folk superstitions concerning homely weather signs:.

"Red sky at night, sailor's delight; red sky in the morning, sailors take warning," for example, he does not wholeheartedly endorse, although it has some foundation in fact. Many of these old sayings, he tells you, are only true if various elements are present; many are wholly untrustworthy. "Rain before seven; clear before eleven," is only accurate if the rainfall begins about sunrise, Moseley says. The time-honored local prophet who could tell you that it was going to rain merely by consulting goosebones, simply smiles. The late "Caterpillar Bill" Sheats, of Washington, New Jersey, was a widely known homely forecaster.

"The fact that a possum or a muskrat grows a thick fur does not indicate the coming of a hard winter," Moseley says. "No animal or bird possesses any mysterious 'weather sense', any more than man. And this is also true of the ground hog. For 57 years, spring and fall, I have observed bird migration and reported my findings to the United States Biological Survey. Time and again I have seen the too-early return north of bird flights which encountered severe cold."

"Indians, being of much the same brand, no doubt, as Skookum Joe, contrary to belief, were no better prophets," says Moseley. Each fall, it appears, Skookum Joe could predict whether the winter would be heavy or mild. Finally pressed by town citizens for an explanation of his powers, Joe made this simple yet revealing answer: "Easy to tell. Me watch white man's woodpile."

"Rheumatics are able to predict imminent weather change," Moseley admits. "And cattle begin to head for home when a great storm approaches. Atmospheric pressure is probably the answer in both cases."

Short-range weather prediction, for a week in advance, which would be a boon to a farmer with hay to get in the barn, is something which Moseley expects soon to become an actuality. "Right now the United States Weather Bureau might be predicting four or five days ahead but for the war," he says. "As soon as such information is no longer useful to America's enemies, the Bureau will probably begin releasing it."

And now, hold on to your hat; Moseley really takes you on a sweeping breathless trip into the future. Here is his forecast for 31 years to come. It applies to the populous area that extends from Missouri and Iowa to Pennsylvania and New York State, he says.

> This is an area for which we have more early data regarding rainfall than we have for the states situated farther west or north or south. Much of the forecast will also apply beyond these limits, to southern Minnesota, eastern Kansas, parts of the Gulf States, and parts of Virginia and New England that are not near the coast.

Chapter 10 • Forecasting Long-Range Weather Conditions

As in the past, we may expect wet and dry seasons. The dry ones will be less numerous than they were in the 45-year period from 1891 to 1935. Average precipitation will be greater than it was then, and much greater than it was during the 20 years beginning with 1917.

After the middle of 1943 the precipitation for nearly five years may not average above normal; in fact a drought may be expected in many states from the latter part of 1946 until late in 1947. In 1948 and 1949 much more rain than usual will fall; after that about the normal amount may be expected most of the time until 1957, except for a dry period in the latter part of 1954.

Late in 1957 and throughout most of 1958, a drought will affect a large area. Abundant rain will fall again in 1959 and the first part of 1960. In several states farther west than New York and Pennsylvania the rainfall will average below normal during a period of more than four years beginning in the fall of 1960, especially in the first half of this period.

After 1964 precipitation will exceed the normal nearly every year for more than a decade.

So there you are. The next time you get caught in the rain without an umbrella, don't say that the professor didn't warn you!

—Modified and edited by RLS from Moran Tudury. 1943. "Long-range weatherman. An Ohio scientist with a remarkable record of accuracy, gives *C.G.* readers a forecast of dry and wet periods in years ahead." *Country Gentleman.* 113 (11): 12, 38, 40. November.

Moran Tudury, an associate editor and staff writer for the farm magazine, *Country Gentlemen*, came to Bowling Green where he interviewed Moseley on 19 and 20 September 1943. The magazine editor, Robert H. Reed, sent him to Bowling Green to obtain information about Moseley's long-range weather forecasts as reported earlier in the *New York Times*.

Evaluation of Moseley's Rainfall Predictions

Moseley's long-term rainfall forecasts, quoted by Tudury on the opposite page, correspond quite favorably with the annual average precipitation records taken at Toledo, Ohio, as published in the "Ohio section climatological data" by the *United States Department of Commerce, Weather Bureau* (1936-1980) [see chart, page 143]. The annual average rainfall is a little over 31 inches there, which occurred for the years 1940 and 1957.

Moseley's prediction that the number of dry years would be fewer between 1891 and 1935 than during the next 45-year period, can be corroborated by the annual average rainfall amounts at Toledo. During the 45-year period from 1891 through 1935, 21 years had precipitation levels below average, which are dry years, while the next 45-year period, from 1936 through 1980, had 16 dry years. As Moseley predicted, these years were mostly normal to wet ones. Expressed as a percentage, 53% of the years were wet from 1891 to 1935, while 64% were wet from 1936 to 1980.

By examining the Toledo area rainfall record more closely for the mid-to-late 1940s, it can be stated that during 1943, precipitation in Ohio was not evenly distributed. "Rainfall was far too much in March, May, and July; but from August on beyond the end of the year there was far too little," according to the Weather Bureau's Report. During the first four days of January, a flood occurred on the Ohio River caused by rains late in December 1942. The crest at Cincinnati was 8.8 feet above flood stage. Precipitation was much below normal in January, and nearly one-third less than normal in February. In March, more than half of the precipitation came between the 15th and 20th, creating considerable flooding in the Ohio River downstream from Pomeroy. Persistent wet weather continued for the next four months, with July being the wettest since 1915. Dry weather prevailed during the autumn months, with rainfall less than half normal in November and even drier in December, the driest in 18 years.

A prolonged summer and autumn drought was the major precipitation feature in Ohio for 1944. January of that year was the sixth consecutive month with a serious deficiency in precipitation, which continued to remain below normal in February. Heavy rains occurred from March through the first half of June, but drought conditions followed, becoming severe in July and continued in that condition until the end of November. In December precipitation was above normal, and snowfall was average, not exceeded in any winter month since January 1918.

The winter of 1944-1945 was the period of the deep snow in northern Ohio. This memorable event occurred during my first grade year in school, and many days were missed because of these weather conditions. With the snow already available from December, a heavy snowfall occurred in January 1945, the greatest amount for that month since 1926. Highway traffic was curtailed from the drifting snow. During February, this unusually heavy snow remained in northern Ohio until the middle of the month, but melted from Columbus southward a week earlier. In March rainfall was exceptionally heavy and the Ohio River flooded from Marietta to Cincinnati, reaching the highest stages known except in 1913 and 1937. Wet weather prevailed until July, and by August, it was the driest for that month since 1910. This drought continued until 20 September, when ample rains occurred near the end of 1945. The locality in Ohio having the least amount of average precipitation, 31.58 inches, was at Bowling Green.

Rainfall in Ohio was ample during the first half of 1946, with May and June being the wettest months. Rainfall was light for the remainder of the year, with September being unfavorably dry and no general rain falling until 11 October. Snowfall was the least on record for any November. Paul W. Jones, Director of the News Bureau at Bowling Green State University, wrote in the *Toledo Times* (20 October 1946, p. 23), that although it rained day after day in May and early June in 1946, skeptics wondered if Moseley would be correct in his prediction. By 20 June, however, the rains became curtailed and only 3.37 inches were recorded at Toledo for July, August, and September. The drought that Moseley successfully had predicted was occurring, and it was to remain dry until the autumn of 1946. Wet weather, however, prevailed during the first six months of 1947, and continued at about normal for the remainder of the year. Jones discussed this prediction failure on the front page of the *Daily Sentinel-Tribune* (22 May 1947) with the statement from Moseley that the records available to him for 1857 were insufficient. His forecast of more than usual rainfall for the spring of 1947 in Illinois and Iowa were confirmed by him. They were based on more ample records. Abundant rainfall occurred in 1948, and was exceeded by only 1937 and 1945 in the past 20 years. In April the Ohio River flooded with many places reading its highest stages known since 1937. Precipitation was near normal during 1949.

Comparison of Moseley's rainfall predictions to the recorded annual average amount of precipitation for 1936-1980 at Toledo, Ohio. Moisture Condition: D= Dry (below 30.5 inches), N= Normal (30.5 to 31.5 inches), W= Wet (above 31.5 inches).

Year	Inches	Moisture Condition		Year	Inches	Moisture Condition	
		Moseley	Recorded			Moseley	Recorded
1936	30		D	1958	28	D	D
1937	36		W	1959	37	W	W
1938	30		D	1960	27	W-D	D
1939	30		D	1961	28	D	D
1940	31	W	N	1962	26	D	D
1941	25	D	D	1963	22	D	D
1942	33	W	W	1964	24	D	D
1943	32	W-D	W	1965	41	W	W
1944	29	N-D	D	1966	32	W	W
1945	32	D-W	W	1967	32	W	W
1946	24	N-D	D	1968	33	W	W
1947	35	D	W	1969	36	W	W
1948	35	W	W	1970	38	W	W
1949	34	W	W	1971	23	W	D
1950	48	N	W	1972	38	W	W
1951	36	N	W	1973	33	W	W
1952	26	N	D	1974	29	W	D
1953	32	N	W	1975	39	W	W
1954	32	N-D	W	1976	29	W	D
1955	32	N	W	1977	39	W	W
1956	34	N	W	1978	32	W	W
1957	31	N-D	N	1979	36	W	W
				1980	32	W	W

As predicted by Moseley, a dry period occurred late in 1957 and throughout 1958, except in the months of July and August. The year 1959 was wet, and from late 1960 through 1964, precipitation was below normal. Beginning in 1965 and for every year through 1975, each one was wet with above average rainfall amounts, except in 1971 and 1974 which were below average in amounts of precipitation.

A comprehensive weather forecast for 40- or more years requires a huge base of knowledge derived from many sources. The historic precipitation records and the patterns of growth rings in trees were the major sources of data to Moseley. With his intelligent and analytical mind, he could make a long-range prediction that proved remarkably accurate through that time period.

NEW-WORLD SCIENCE SERIES
Edited by John W. Ritchie

TREES, STARS AND BIRDS

A Book of Outdoor Science

by

EDWIN LINCOLN MOSELEY, A.M.

*Head of the Science Department
State Normal College of
Northwestern Ohio*

*ILLUSTRATED IN COLORS
from paintings by Louis Agassiz Fuertes
and with photographs and drawings*

Yonkers-on-Hudson, New York
WORLD BOOK COMPANY
1919

Title page from Moseley's book, *Trees, Stars and Birds* (1919).

Books and Science Education

Ronald L. Stuckey

CHAPTER ELEVEN

Perhaps Moseley's greatest achievement was his teaching of science at the high school and college levels to more than six thousand students, yet this very important intangible contribution is the most difficult to discuss and document. A pioneer in outdoor science teaching, Moseley's main objectives were for his students to make careful, critical, original observations of natural phenomenon, and to ask questions, seek logical answers, and create independent thinking. His teaching philosophy became crystallized very early in his career, and in his first paper on science education, published in the *Ohio Educational Monthly* (1896),[1] he discussed four chief causes of failure in high school science teaching: (1) "The pupils study *about* things instead of studying the things." (2) "The habit of learning by rote . . . most of us deplore and yet much of the teaching in our schools at the present time appeals to the memory more than the understanding." (3) The use of books is "an exaggerated notion . . . in all studies." (4) An "undue regard [exists] for logical order in teaching." Moseley's paper (1902)[2] describing original work done by high school students was presented in a series of papers sponsored by the Michigan School Masters' Club as part of the Michigan Academy of Sciences meeting, 29 April 1902. He reported how high school boys helped him during winter time to locate the buried valleys of streams in the bottom of Sandusky Bay.

Moseley wrote of his own experiences in the teaching of science, and the titles of subsequent papers provide the messages that he wanted to impart to science educators elsewhere. These titles were: "Original work in high schools" (1903),[3] "Seeing and understanding" (1921),[8] "A plea for more outdoor science teaching" (1924),[9] and "Some suggestions for outdoor science teaching" (1925).[10] From this last paper, he gave a number of suggestions, from which a few examples follow:

> (1) look at more than one group of objects; (2) make comparisons of features between closely related species; (3) ask a great variety of questions; (4) provide opportunities for students to ask questions; (5) spell names of organisms; (6) talk in a low tone and then, when speaking louder, prompt attention should come from all of those present; (7) review names of organisms to be learned or retained at end of session; (8) take proper collecting equipment if making specimens to retain permanently.

Three General Science Books

Moseley published three books on topics in general science. His greatest contribution to this subject was his book, *Trees, Stars and Birds: A Book of Outdoor Science*,[5] which became very popular as a textbook in the junior high and high schools. First published in 1919, it was reprinted at least five times during the next eight years, with a revised edition in 1935. The book covered three fields of nature that not only reflected Moseley's three most knowledgeable phases of natural phenomenon, but it also represented those fields that have a perennial interest for the human mind. It helped bring to teachers, who lacked special training in outdoor science, the wide knowledge and teaching experience of the author. Published as one of several books in the New-World Science Series by the World Book Company, located at Yonkers-on-Hudson, New York, the text was most compatible with the company's motto, "the application of the world's knowledge to the world's needs," which certainly represented one of Moseley's objectives. The book's mission was succinctly stated by its author in the preface:

> This book is designed to encourage students to observe and think. It may also furnish some information about trees, birds, and heavenly bodies which will enhance the pleasure of living wherever these things can be seen. The language is simple enough for students in the sixth or seventh grade, the facts important enough for more mature students.
>
> • • •
>
> The student who is well started in nature study is likely to continue his outdoor observations, as opportunity affords, throughout his life. He will get a better

NEW-WORLD SCIENCE SERIES
Edited by John W. Ritchie

TREES, STARS *and* BIRDS
A BOOK OF OUTDOOR SCIENCE

By EDWIN LINCOLN MOSELEY
Head of the Science Department, State Normal College of Northwestern Ohio

THE usefulness of nature study in the schools has been seriously limited by the lack of a suitable textbook. It is to meet this need that *Trees, Stars, and Birds* is issued. The author is one of the most successful teachers of outdoor science in this country. He believes in field excursions, and his text is designed to help teachers and pupils in the inquiries that they will make for themselves.

The text deals with three phases of outdoor science that have a perennial interest, and it will make the benefit of the author's long and successful experience available to younger teachers.

The first section deals with trees, and the discussion of maples is typical: the student is reminded that he has eaten maple sugar; there is an interesting account of its production; the fact is brought out that the sugar is really made in the leaves. The stars and planets that all should know are told about simply and clearly. The birds commonly met with are considered, and their habits of feeding and nesting are described. Pertinent questions are scattered throughout each section.

The book is illustrated with 167 photographs, 69 drawings, 9 star maps, and with 16 color plates of 58 birds, from paintings by Louis Agassiz Fuertes.

It is well adapted for use in junior high schools, yet the presentation is simple enough for pupils in the sixth grade.

Cloth. viii + 404 + xvi pages. Price $1.80.

WORLD BOOK COMPANY
YONKERS-ON-HUDSON, NEW YORK
2126 PRAIRIE AVENUE, CHICAGO

Advertisement for Moseley's Book, *Trees, Stars and Birds* (1919).

(Gift of William R. Burk; Stuckey Collection)

start by using this book in school for two or more consecutive years than by going over all of it in one year.

Trees, Stars, and Birds received favorable reviews. Ornithologist John T. Nichols (1919)[6] noted that it would fill a need "as a textbook of nature study in the schools for which it has evidently been planned with care. Trees, Stars, and Birds are perhaps the three classes of natural objects about us most consistently through life, and some knowledge of them cannot fail to broaden the viewpoint and be a source of constant pleasure." With reference to the portion on birds, he wrote that the subject matter was "throughout well chosen and authoritative," the many text-figures had much merit, and the 16 colored plates of 58 species of birds were a valuable asset.

A review by Carroll L. Fenton (1921)[7] of the Walker Museum at the University of Chicago added several additional noteworthy remarks:

> The style is interesting and the facts, while not new, are exactly those which most people do not know. The numerous quotations from poets serve to link the natural science of the book with the literature of the world, and they do it far better than could any long formal essay on the relation of poets and nature.
>
> The section of the book devoted to trees is almost a complete popular manual for their study. There is an excellent discussion of the structure of the limbs, trunk, and roots of various typical tree groups, and of the proper ways in which to care for trees, both old and young. The second part of the book, headed "Stars," not only treats of stars, but the planets, satellites, and nebulae. It, like the rest of the book, is non-technical, but is at the same time accurate and specific.
>
> The third section...on birds...should be enlarged...by discussions of some of the general facts and problems of ornithology, and then published as a separate book...it would be accepted with enthusiasm by people all over the country who find the ordinary beginner's bird manual too conventional and stereotyped to arouse either their own enthusiasm or that of their children. The interesting discussions of the various families, the excellent half-tones, and the sixteen pages of colored plates by Louis Agassiz Fuertes make this section one of the finest popular treatments of the birds of North America that has appeared in some years.

The *Sandusky Register* (24 January 1919) carried an article about the publication of Moseley's book, *Trees, Stars, and Birds*. The anonymous writer noted that the book "should be valuable in all schools, . . .the topics. . .[being] those of most general interest....The book can also be used to advantage by such organizations such as the Campfire Girls and the Woodcraft League." The writer noted that the publication had been delayed by war conditions, which may explain why Moseley's first book has been cited as *Nature Study*, a textbook for Junior High and Grammar Schools, published by the World Book Company in 1917 (Van Tassel, 1917).[4] So far as is known, no knowledge of this book exists, which then suggests that by waiting two years, Moseley would have expanded the book and given it the more attractive descriptive title, *Trees, Stars, and Birds*.

Moseley's second book, *Our Wild Animals* (1927)[11] published by D. Appleton and Company, New York, was written to supply accurate information about most of the wild mammals common to North America. The preface tells for whom the book was written:

> Primarily, the volume is intended as an interesting science reader, but it has a deeper purpose in that it presents scientifically accurate facts about most of our wild animals in a form that children in the intermediate grades can read, understand, and enjoy,...particularly...for use in fifth and sixth grades.
>
> When one or two chapters have been given to pupils for reading, they have invariably asked for more. They take an intense interest in the observations recorded in the book and are usually quite ready to tell of their own experiences with and conclusions about animals. To encourage class discussion of what pupils have observed of wild animals,...thought-provoking questions [are] included in the text of each chapter. Properly presented, the material encourages the pupil to observe carefully and to draw sound conclusions from his observations.
>
> Much of the information in the book is based on the personal observation of the author; other material has been obtained from accepted authorities on North American mammals, several of whom have read a part or all of the manuscript. The text is supplemented by authentic illustrations.

Charles M. Turton (1927),[12] a high school science teacher, noted in his review that Moseley's text was "one of the most fascinating and interesting books [he had] read for years." The anonymous reviewer writing in the *Sandusky Register* (4 September 1927) emphasized the entertainment quality of the book. He stated it was:

> ...painstaking, instructive, and thoroughly interesting....Written...in a scientific as well as interesting manner, [it] will make good family reading, and is said to have an especial appeal for those who love the wild life. Exacting but not too technical style is used....The author illustrates the habits of the animals he

Chapter 11 • Books and Science Education

OUR WILD ANIMALS

BY

EDWIN LINCOLN MOSELEY

HEAD OF THE SCIENCE DEPARTMENT
IN THE STATE NORMAL COLLEGE
OF NORTHWESTERN OHIO; AUTHOR
OF "TREES, STARS AND BIRDS"

ILLUSTRATED

NEW YORK
D. APPLETON AND C[O]

OTHER WORLDS

BY

EDWIN LINCOLN MOSELEY, A.M.

HEAD OF THE DEPARTMENT OF BIOLOGY
OHIO STATE NORMAL COLLEGE

D. APPLETON AND COMPANY
NEW YORK :: 1933 :: LONDON

Title pages of Moseley's books, *Our Wild Animals* (1927) and *Other Worlds* (1933).

discusses by anecdotes rather than by ordinary descriptions. Interspersed among the 300 pages. . .are many fine engravings.

Moseley's acknowledgments to those individuals who assisted him with the *Animals'* book is extensive. Many of them, whose names are given in the book, supplied information, comments, and criticisms. The manuscript was read by 16 zoologists or writers of nature, and used by nine teachers of city, village, and rural schools for suitability of certain grade levels. More than 100 teachers, who had studied at the Bowling Green State Normal College, read parts of the manuscript and made modifications of it for Moseley.

In 1933, Moseley's book, *Other Worlds*[14] appeared, also published by D. Appleton and Company, New York. The preface brought forth Moseley's sense of humor, as well as notation about the subject information and for whom the book was intended, as follows:

> The knowledge possessed by uniformed persons about the heavenly bodies is not much greater than that of a dog which barks at the moon or of an infant who reaches for it. None of them can tell by merely looking at the moon or the stars whether they are farther away than the nearest woods, or whether they are larger than a football. Yet every normal child at some period in its life is curious to know what the stars are. Older persons, if they are not wholly absorbed in business, are like children in wanting to learn something about other worlds.

> This book is not a systematic treatise on astronomy, but it attempts to present to the busy reader some facts which have been ascertained by careful research about a few of the best known of the heavenly bodies. How some of these facts have been ascertained the author has endeavored to make clear. The explanation of others would require more time and more knowledge of mathematics, mechanics, optics, and other branches of science than the average reader has at his command.

Other Worlds received an anonymous review notice in the *Sandusky Star-Journal* (12 December 1933), stating that the book had been expanded from an article that Moseley had written in the November 1931 issue of *Scientific American*.[13] This paper, "Are there creatures like ourselves in other worlds?," after receiving favorable comments, editor Watson Davis of D. Appleton Publishing Company invited Moseley to expand the paper into this full-length book. Among the topics discussed were meteors, comets, the moon, and the planets. Compared to other scientific disciplines in which Moseley published his research, very little was written about astronomy. Most of his contributions were printed in the local Sandusky newspapers on the subjects of meteors, Halley's Comet, meteorites, and star showers from 1903 to 1926.

The factual information in Moseley's books should be as useful today as it was in his time. The topics covered the components of the natural world that have a lasting interest for the human mind. His books also provided assistance to those teachers who lacked special training in outdoor science. These books brought to their attention the wide knowledge and outdoor teaching experience of the author. Understanding the environment allows for the satisfaction of the fundamental instinct of human beings. Their desire to learn about and come into with the natural world must not be neglected in the instruction of young people. Moseley's books were intended to and certainly did help satisfy that need for the human race.

Field Trip and Classroom Incidents

Many stories about incidents on field trips and in the classroom have been generated about Moseley. Some of these are recorded in earlier chapters. Ivan E. Lake,[16] a former student of Moseley, and writer for the *Daily Sentinel-Tribune*, Bowling Green's local newspaper, printed during April 1937, four anecdotal stories. They were supplied by other students, whose names remained anonymous.

Though Moseley's humorous nature seldom was in evidence before the general public, he had a keen sense of humor and enjoyed a good joke, whether on himself or at the expense of others. His classes frequently took field trips as soon as the weather became suitable, and while on these trips many enjoyable incidents often occurred, as follows:

> Years ago before Ridge Street east of the cemetery was improved the class took a field trip along the open ditch. Little log branches had been built across the ditch, and the class stopped at one of them when an interesting zoological specimen was observed.
>
> Clem Premo and myself brushed aside the vines and bushes at the edge of the bridge and sat down to listen to the lecture. Prof. Moseley talked for a while and then stopped abruptly as he looked at us and asked, "Mr. Premo, are you and Mr. Lake immune from poison ivy?"

We echoed that we did not know and the professor grinned widely as he replied, "Well you'll soon find out. You're sitting in it!"

On another field trip on the University campus, the class came across a mint plant which had been the subject for study in the classroom the previous day. Moseley asked the class to identify this one now observed outside on the campus. The incident continued as follows:

> After much hesitancy, I ventured an answer and upon being asked the reason for such identification and to name the differences between the two, I did so, although I'll confess I wasn't sure that I had them properly identified in my own mind.
>
> The professor cleared up my doubts when he said that I had the characteristics of the plants mixed up and that I had therefore wrongly identified the plant which we were viewing. I had the sinking feeling that comes to a student who knows that the grade of "F" went down against my name that day, but aside from that I gave it no further thought that day. But not Professor Moseley, [as] apparently he had some doubts, too.
>
> The next day as the class assembled in the classroom, he led us immediately to the 'herbarium,' where he had on file thousands of pressed botanical specimens. There before the group, he called attention to the fact that on the previous day while on the field trip . . . a difference of opinion about the identity of a plant, . . . [which we called by two different scientific names]. Then he grinned broadly, as he said [that I] was right. This incident . . . shows more than ever the fairness of Professor Moseley in dealing with his students and his good natural attitude toward those whom he was teaching. He was ready to admit publicly that he was wrong.

Whenever possible Moseley enjoyed using live specimens to illustrate his lessons in the teaching of biology. Some students, bored by scientific subjects, sometimes had difficulty in staying awake in class, especially in the springtime. On the day before the following described incident, two students had dozed away while the professor was lecturing. The story continues as follows:

> On the following day a stray cat, showing much abuse and being a particularly homely orange, black and white spotted fellow, followed Morris Bistline through the corridors and into the biology room a few minutes before recitation was to start.

A most pleased smile was inspired on Prof. Moseley's face as he espied the cat in the room, and he said, "Look at the pretty animal."

The cat was placed on the desk and the class was asked to examine it carefully before the professor, discarding the assigned lesson for the day, decided to read from a chapter on "Cats" in a new book which he was writing at that time. After about 20 minutes of reading, the professor noted that not only had the cat curled up contentedly asleep on the desk, but the two students who had slept the day before were again nodding their heads.

Prof. Moseley saw the funny side of the picture and chuckled as he looked over the class saying, "Yesterday, two of our number fell asleep and today, I see, the latest addition to the class is also asleep. Will someone awaken our friends so that we may continue?"

The two students were brought rudely out of their slumbers and the cat, apparently realizing the breach of etiquette, arose, stretched and yawned before sitting at attention to look over the class.

"Now that we are all awake again, we shall resume," Prof. Moseley stated good naturedly as he returned to reading his copy to the group.

No sooner had he started doing so, however, than the cat again curled up on the desk and fell asleep, practically stopping the show, for Prof. Moseley joined the class in one of the best laughs of the year. It was one of the few times that I ever heard him laugh audibly.

The fourth anecdote pertains to those professors that have grudges against athletes and make their courses particularly tough for that clientele of students. The particular story related here refutes the idea that Moseley held this sort of grudge. On this particular occasion the final examination in zoology class was to come on Friday before the close of the semester. The three students involved were members of the varsity basketball squad, which was making a three-day trip to eastern Ohio and was to be gone all day Friday. The incident follows in the words of the students:

We feared the consequences because we too had heard that the professor would make it more difficult for us because of the fact that we missed a class for athletic purposes. We were to make up our exam on Monday afternoon.

When we returned Monday morning we inquired of fellow classmen as to the degree of difficulty of the exam and heard it was terrific. I'll admit that I couldn't have answered half the questions and I was a "B" student.

You can imagine how hard we crammed during the morning, realizing that we wouldn't get the same exam questions and fearing that the ones we would get would be even more difficult.

With fear in our hearts we reported for the exam and were summoned by Prof. Moseley in widely scattered parts of the room. Then turning to the blackboard he wrote the following on the board:

"1. — Cats
2. — Cats and Dogs
3. — Bees"

Placing the chalk in the tray he turned to us quietly and said, "Write all you know about those subjects. For question No. 2 you can outline the differences between cats and dogs. When you have finished you may place your "bluebooks" on the desk here." Then he left the room and never returned while we were answering questions. Bluebooks are small tablets in which students write exam answers.

Our supply of information about those three subjects was almost unlimited. In fact, we could almost have written a book about those three items from ordinary observations, without study. As it was we each filled about 4 bluebooks, on the questions before we had finished. We learned later that Prof. Moseley had already turned in our grades and paid practically no attention to our exam. We always wondered if he was chuckling to himself as he left the room that day. You can never tell me that he had a grudge against athletes.

Unusual incidents or noteworthy events on Moseley's field trips or in his classroom continue to live on in Sandusky and on the Bowling Green campus. Many of these situations, as related by those who knew him or were experienced by those who took his courses, are recorded many times in this book, particularly in Chapters 3, 4, 5, 6, and 8. While by now most of Moseley's students are gone, it is the children of these students that find interest in knowing these stories that have been told by their parents. For that reason in itself, preservation is worthwhile of these past stories of *School Americana*.

CHAPTER 11 • BOOKS AND SCIENCE EDUCATION

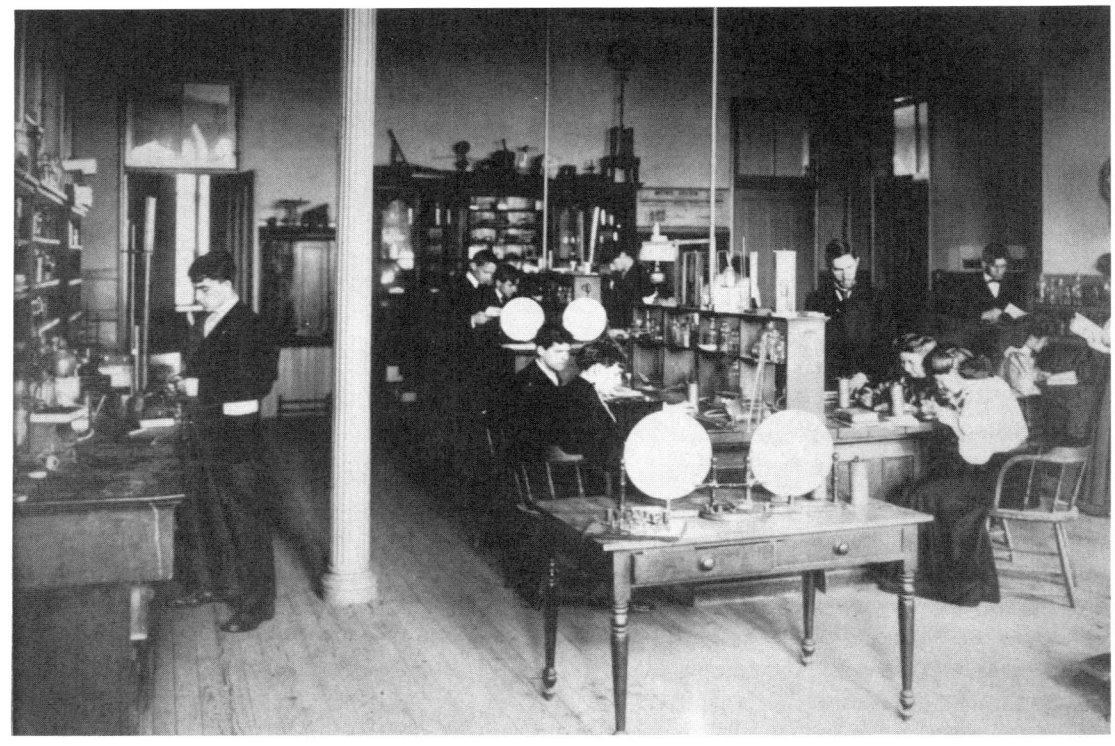

The chemistry and physics laboratory in the Sandusky High School as it appeared in 1907.

l. to r., Bartel Reinheimer, Fred Groch, Kenneth Kugel, Glen Cullen, Clair Ditchey, Frank Wangler, **Professor Moseley**, Marguerite Molitor, Lenora Schoepfle, Eugene Ruth, Florence Chaney, and Elsa Pusch.

(Wilbert Ohlemacher, in his *Sandusky Register* article, 31 January 1982, p. A-4; Sandusky Library Archives)

Evaluation As A Teacher

Perhaps the most appropriate evaluation of Moseley as a teacher of science should come from those who knew him for long periods of time in the classroom at the schools where he taught. Dr. Clare S. Martin (1959),[17] first chairman of the Chemistry Department at Bowling Green State University, wrote that Moseley was "not a specialist in any branch of science, . . . but belonged to that vanishing class of scientists we call *naturalists*." He continued:

> An individualist in matters of habit and personal appearance, Mr. Moseley fitted almost perfectly into the local community's conception of a college professor. Town and campus relished many anecdotes that sprang up about him. When someone inquired how any man, no matter how learned, could teach so many college subjects, the answer was likely to be that it was, after all, quite simple. He taught only one lesson each day but taught it in five different subjects. There was just enough truth in this to make it funny. Mr. Moseley was more interested in persuading students to reason and think clearly than he was in piling up information. That he succeeded in this far beyond most teachers is well attested.

> In a new Normal College addicted to lesson plans and the latest methodology, Mr. Moseley's classroom tactics were likely to outrage his colleagues. His opening gambit might be: "Miss Brown, tell what you know about . . . (usually some large topic)." If the student, appalled by the enormity of the question, floundered and rambled, he passed the question on to others without comment. Sometimes he summed up these contributions with the remark, "Nothing's been said yet." His occasional, "I don't think you know much about (the topic discussed)" was especially devastating. A member of the Board of Trustees once remarked to a new instructor, "If while you are here you do as much good and as little harm as Mr. Moseley, you'll do well."

Two presidents of Bowling Green State University, Homer B. Williams (from 1912-1937) and Frank J. Prout (from 1939-1951) are among that clientele. Their evaluations of and tributes to Moseley are communicated in Chapters 3 and 4, respectively. Succinctly, Williams (1937)[15] said: "Professor Moseley is the best example of exact and thorough scholarship in his field that I have ever known in any type of school. I would say it has been the open sesame to his pedagogical greatness." Similarly, Prout (1959)[18] stated: "Mr. Moseley's greatness as a teacher lay in his emphasis on always searching for the reason of things." As a truly devoted teacher, Moseley received overwhelming loyalty from his students.

CHAPTER 11 • BOOKS AND SCIENCE EDUCATION

References

1. 1896. Edwin L. Moseley. "Science." pp. 416-418. In "Do the public schools give a reasonable mastery of the subjects studied?" *Ohio Educational Monthly* 45: 410-420.

2. 1902. Edwin L. Moseley. Original work for the high school teacher. *School Science* 2: 188; full article published in *Sandusky Daily-Star*, 20 December, p. 20.

3. 1903. Edwin L. Moseley. "Original work in high schools." *Ohio Educational Monthly* 52: 367-374.

4. 1917. Charles S. Van Tassel, ed. 1917. "Edwin Lincoln Moseley," pp. 269,270. In *The Ohio Blue Book, or Who's Who in the Buckeye State: A Cyclopedia of Biography of Men and Women in Ohio*. Charles Summer Van Tassel, Toledo, Ohio. 479 pp.

*5. 1919. Edwin L. Moseley. *Trees, Stars, and Birds: A Book of Outdoor Science*. World Book Co., Yonkers-on-Hudson, New York. 404 pp. (reprinted, 1921, 1922, 1924, 1925, 1927; Revised Edition, 1935. 418 pp.).

6. 1919. John T. Nichols. [Review of *Trees, Stars, and Birds*]. *Bird Lore* 21: 117.

7. 1921. Carroll L. Fenton. [Review of *Trees, Stars, and Birds*]. *American Midland Naturalist* 7: 159,160.

8. 1921. Edwin L. Moseley. "Seeing and understanding." *Ohio Educational Monthly* 70: 46-48.

9. 1924. Edwin L. Moseley. "A plea for more outdoor science teaching." *School Science and Mathematics* 24: 151-155.

10. 1925. Edwin L. Moseley. "Some suggestions for outdoor science teaching." *Elementary School Journal* 26: 58-66.

11. 1927. Edwin L. Moseley. *Our Wild Animals*. D. Appleton & Co., New York. 310 pp.

12. 1927. Charles M. Turton. [Review of *Our Wild Animals*]. *School Science and Mathematics* 27: 770.

13. 1931. Edwin L. Moseley. "Are there creatures like ourselves in other worlds?" *Scientific American* 145: 308-310.

*14. 1933. Edwin L. Moseley. *Other Worlds.* D. Appleton & Co., New York. xi, 231 pp.

15. 1937. Homer B. Williams. "Dr. Williams lauds Moseley: Teacher, author, scientist honored this week." *Bee Gee News* 21 (26): 1, 2, 4. 31 March.

16. 1937. Ivan E. Lake. "Anecdotes from Moseley classes." *Daily Sentinel-Tribune*, Bowling Green, [on poison ivy], 1 April, p. 5; [on falling asleep in the classroom], 3 April, p. 5; [on proper identification of two mint plants], 5 April, p. 5; [on giving final exams to absentee athletes], 6 April, p. 8.

17. 1959. Clare S. Martin. "The physical sciences: Chemistry, geology, physics; fifty years has wrought great changes. . ." *Bowling Green State University Magazine* 4 (2): 11,12. May.

18. 1959. Frank J. Prout. "The inquiring mind of Mr. Moseley." *Bowling Green State University Magazine* 4 (4): 16-20. November.

Ivan E. "Doc" Lake (1901-1967), author of "Anecdotes from Moseley classes," received the name "Doc" upon becoming trainer of the football team for the high school in Bowling Green, Ohio.[24,25] His primary interests, however, centered at the University, having entered as a student in 1919, graduated in 1923, and befriended Professor Edwin Lincoln Moseley. Most of his life, Lake was with the *Daily Sentinel-Tribune*, Bowling Green's newspaper, at various times serving as a writer, telegraph editor, sports editor, and managing editor from 1923 to 1953, when he left to take a position as a reporter for the *San Diego Union*. While a student, Lake wrote news stories and for many years later, without pay, was the University's publicity director. He wrote articles about the life and research work of Moseley,[19,20,21] in addition to his obituary for the *Daily Sentinel-Tribune*.[22]

Among the many activities associated with Bowling Green State University, Lake[23,24] was a member of the first football team to win a game, and he was awarded 14 varsity letters for cheerleading and one for tennis, a total of 15, more than any other non-athlete in the history of the school. He helped organize the campus *Bee Gee News* and served as its sports editor and later alumni editor; created the name "Falcons" for the University sports teams, and "Bobcats" for the high school teams; initiated in 1922 the University's first Homecoming and supervised all of the activities; organized the first male quartet on campus; was a member of the first debate team; was one of the founders of the Five Brothers Fraternity,

Chapter 11 • Books and Science Education

and helped organize the Interfraternity Club, the only one of its kind in the nation at the time; served as the alumni editor of the first college yearbook, *The Key*, and became secretary and later president of the University Alumni Association, and promoted the first alumni news publication. In 1964, Ivan Lake was honored by the University alumni with its first Distinguished Alumni Service Award, and named as its first member of the Hall of Fame.

Born 24 March 1901 in North Baltimore, Wood County, Ohio, to Walter L. and Maude L. (Householder) Lake, young Ivan Lake two years later moved with his family to Bowling Green, Ohio. On 9 October 1934, he married Miss Vernetta Kreves. Following a massive cerebral hemorrhage on 15 October 1967, Ivan Lake died 26 October 1967 in Grossmont District Hospital, La Mesa, California. He was survived by his wife and sons Dennis, Jerry, and Larry.

References for Biographical Sketch

19. 1937. [Ivan E. Lake]. "Prof. Moseley predicts forty-six years wet weather ahead." *Daily Sentinel-Tribune*, Bowling Green, 31 March, pp. 1,2.

20. 1937. [Ivan E. Lake]. "Prof. E. L. Moseley wins plaudits of his admirers at a birthday dinner." *Daily Sentinel-Tribune*, Bowling Green, 31 March, p. 4. (Also *Sandusky [Daily] Register*, 4 April, p. 11).

21. 1937. [Ivan E. Lake]. "Biographical sketch of Prof. Edwin L. Moseley." *Daily Sentinel-Tribune*, Bowling Green, 31 March, p. 5.

22. 1948. [Ivan E. Lake]. "Dr. Moseley, eminent B.G.U. scientist, dies....;" "Dr. E. L. Moseley's life one of great achievements. . . ." *Daily Sentinel-Tribune*, Bowling Green, 7 June, p. 1; p. 2.

23. 1967. James R. Overman. *The History of Bowling Green State University*. Bowling Green University Press, Bowling Green, Ohio. 234 pp.

24. 1967. Anonymous. "Ivan (Doc) Lake, 66, dies; served on *Sentinel-Tribune*." *Daily Sentinel-Tribune*, Bowling Green, 26 October, p. 2.

25. 1967. Anonymous. "Ivan E. Lake, 'Mr. B-G' dies." *Bee Gee News* 52(24): 1, 27 October.

Moseley's teaching certificate, issued 31 August 1889.

(Sandusky Library Archives)

CHAPTER 11 • BOOKS AND SCIENCE EDUCATION

On the Bowling Green State Normal College Campus.

Science Building (Moseley Hall), about 1940.

(Archives, BGSU)

Biology classroom, Science Building (Moseley Hall).

(Archives, BGSU)

Photographs at right: Upper left: Williams Hall, ladies dormatory (post card); Upper right: Leora I. Shuey (1922) at entrance of Elementary School Building (Hanna Hall); Middle left: classmates of Miss Shuey (1922); Lower left: alumnus, Alice L. (Shuey) Baldosser with husband Ralph and daughter Leanna Mae (1946) at walkway to Science Building (Moseley Hall); Lower right, l. to r.: sisters, Alyce and Grace Myers (1924), the latter a BGNC student and life-long friend of the Shuey sisters. All four women were teachers. Grace Myers married Jesse Miller; Leora Shuey married Guy Stuckey, parents of Ronald L. Stuckey.

CHAPTER 11 • BOOKS AND SCIENCE EDUCATION

(All photographs taken on the campus at Bowling Green; Stuckey Collection)

Display room in the Moseley museum in the northeast corner on the third floor of the Sandusky High School building.

(Wilbert Ohlemacher, in his *Sandusky Register* article,
6 December 1981, p. A-4; Sandusky Library Archives)

The High School Museum

CHAPTER TWELVE

Relda E. Niederhofer

In 1891, with specimens from his own collections as well as many donations, Edwin Lincoln Moseley established the first natural history museum in a single room of the Sandusky High School. For nearly 40 years, his exhibits were on display to the general public during annual open houses. The number of items increased through the years to an amazing 17,000 specimens before 1938. Moseley organized what became known as the finest high school museum in the state of Ohio.

Collections in natural history for the museum were first obtained in 1887 when Moseley was a part of the Joseph Beal Steere Scientific Expedition to the Philippines. Steere had been Moseley's professor in zoology at The University of Michigan. Twelve months of the expedition were spent in the Philippine Islands working from two to six weeks on each of the 15 larger islands. Moseley was one of a party of five collectors, working with natives to obtain both vertebrates and invertebrates.[1]

When Moseley returned from the expedition, he accepted a teaching position in the Sandusky High School. During his first summer vacation of 1890 he toured Europe with the president of the school board, Charles Graefe, M.D., visiting nearly all of the large natural history museums in Europe, and did not return until about a month after the beginning of fall classes. In his absence, George D. Sones, a student at The University of Michigan, substituted until 29 September 1890.² Moseley met with the Board of Education Saturday 18 October 1890 to describe his vast collection of natural history specimens to the members, and to explain his project for creating a museum. The Board granted permission for the museum and commissioned the construction of four large cases to hold the specimens.³ The former superintendent's room in the Central Building, the present Adams Junior High School, was made available for the museum. For the next three months Moseley worked diligently preparing specimens for the grand opening on 1 January 1891.⁴

Grand Opening

A reporter from the *Sandusky Register*, who interviewed Moseley the day after the opening, described his observations of the museum, "On either side of the room are large glass cases containing birds, not real birds, of course, but mounted specimens...."⁵ One of the showcases contained about 140 species of foreign birds. One particular prize possession was a bird's nest just a little larger than a hummingbird. Moseley told the reporter the nest would bring 25 dollars a pound in Hong Kong, where it is used with pigeon's eggs to make pudding. The reporter noted that, "somewhere he had tasted bird's nest pudding, but it could not have been the genuine Chinese article."⁵ Another showcase housed the exhibit of 180 species of the American birds.⁵ Included were warblers, swallows, sparrows, finches, hawks, bald eagle, etc., "in fact almost everything and in all sizes from a hummingbird to a swan."⁵

The reporter noted the marine invertebrates occupied another showcase in the center of the room, in which were displayed 450 of shells and 25 kinds of coral. The pearly nautilus (*Nautilus pompilius*) and tent olive (*Oliva porphyria*) were among the rare shells, as well as many of the more numerous cowries, cones, olives, and strombs. The shells ranged in size from the tiny, beautiful vallonia *Vallonia pulchella*), about the size of a pin's head to the horned helmet (*Cassis cornuta*) the size of a man's head.

Another exhibit observed by the reporter included foreign coins, European photographs, and Chinese and Japanese curios to illustrate the Oriental culture. A model of a five-story pagoda, Chinese chop sticks, opium pipes, books, idols, and a printing block all helped inform the public about their unusual customs. Even a three-inch cast of a young lady's foot was displayed to illustrate the ancient custom of wrapping the feet to keep them small and prevent proper growth.

Geological specimens of gypsum from Grand Rapids, Michigan, calcite, marble, pipestone, and jade were arranged in another case. The reporter pointed out that jade was used by the Chinese for ornamental purposes. The case also included specimens of American and foreign woods. The reporter concluded his article indicating the museum was, "...a valuable acquisition and will be highly appreciated by the students."[5]

Relocation of Museum

The museum was moved to other locations in the Central Building several times as the need for space changed. From its beginning in the superintendent's former office, the museum was moved into a room in the northeast part of the building vacated by the ladies library.[8] In 1894, the Monroe Elementary School was built to remove the primary grades from the Central Building.[9] This move enabled the high school to expand into the third floor, where Moseley's museum and laboratory were relocated in 1898. The museum occupied just one of the six rooms on the third floor. The specimens that could not be displayed in showcases were stored in boxes. In preparation for an open house Moseley would have students set up displays on tables in other classrooms. In 1906[10] he needed five rooms for an open house and by 1911[15] he had expanded into seven rooms. The museum remained on the third floor until December 1932,[22] when crowded conditions caused by the increased enrollment, compelled the school board to store the specimens in the attic to make space for another classroom.[23] After 42 years, the last open house in Sandusky was held on Sunday, 4 December 1932. Moseley had tried to find 2,500-3,000 sq. ft. of space in a fire-proof building for the museum as early as 1924,[17] when he suggested the Soldiers' Memorial Building be used. The museum specimens remained in the attic storage for six years until 2 July 1938, when eight trucks and a trailer moved the 17,000 specimens to Bowling Green State University.[24]

1905 Description of Museum

In 1905, Moseley, writing for the Sandusky High School news magazine, *The Fram*, indicated that the museum contained ten thousand specimens. Many of the items were from the professor's private collection. "Some specimens of rock, shells, bone, and fossils were in the building long before 1890."[9] The Board of Education purchased a few collections of rocks and woods of Ohio, a Philippine exhibit and

Indian relics. The teachers and pupils of Sandusky High School collected and identified 600 local species of flowering plants in addition to a number of grasses and sedges to augment an existing small herbarium.[7] During the summer of 1906, Moseley secured specimens on a trip to southern Europe and northern Africa.[12] In 1907, he received 30 species of birds from the American Museum of Natural History in New York City, all but three were species new to his collection.[13] A number of items were obtained by exchanging specimens with other museums. In 1892, he received several excellent specimens of minerals and 33 species of hummingbirds from London in exchange for a number of species from his museum.[6] Hundreds of specimens were donated in the 15 years since the museum opened in 1891.[9] One of the largest was full-sized birch bark canoe made by the Chippewa Indians. There was a saw, not for cutting lumber, but from a sawfish, which had measured 22 feet long and 1,500 pounds when caught off the Florida coast.

Ornithology was one of Moseley's specialities, so it was not surprising that birds were among the most numerous items on display. He had rare birds, such as the prairie chicken, extinct in Ohio by 1905, and the passenger pigeon quite rare then. Now both birds are extinct in the United States. An excellent specimen of the snowy owl, protected by a glass shade, had been caught in Sandusky on its migration from the far north in search of food. Of the several varieties of pheasant, the copper pheasant from Japan was one of the most beautiful birds. Its plumage had a look of bright copper in reflected light. The rare lyre bird was named because its tail resembled the Apollo's lyre. Moseley's comment about the lyre bird was, "One of the habits of the cock is to form small round hillocks, which he constantly visits during the day, mounting upon them and displaying his tail by erecting it over his head, drooping his wings, scratching and pecking at the soil and uttering various cries."[9]

Open House Attendance

Attendance to the museum open houses varied from seven visitors on 4 March 1900 to 840 on 18 March 1906.[11] While Moseley was teaching in Sandusky, his museum drew large crowds averaging 300 per Sunday in 1905 to over 800 per Sunday in 1914. After leaving Sandusky in 1914 to teach in the Bowling Green State Normal School, he had less time to prepare for the open houses. His newspaper publicity dwindled to an occasional article until 1927 when it appears that he established a campaign to spark interest in the museum. (Some of his articles would have put P. T. Barnum to shame in advertising for the famous Ringling Brothers and Barnum and Bailey Circus.) The articles in the newspaper would indicate which special item would be featured for an open house. One week the African plover from the Nile Valley was selected to be publicized Thursday, 22 March 1928,[20] then Saturday, 24 March 1928[21] the hummingbird collection was featured. In a 16 January 1927,[18] letter to the editor of the *Sandusky Register*, Moseley requested information from the citizens of Sandusky regarding the origin of the human skeleton at the museum. The macabre incident ended on 30 January 1927[19] with a reply published in the *Sandusky Register* from Charles E. Stroud, a local dentist, that, "*Johnny Bones* is not a native of this city, nor was *he* ever." Stroud indicated the skeleton was purchased probably by the local board of education in 1874 from some anatomical laboratory for the reputed sum of $60.

In 1914, Moseley asked the high school teachers to request their pupils to research and write essays on "Why More People Do Not Visit the High School Museum?" Six of those essays were published in the newspaper indicating a variety of reasons ascertained by the pupils: inability to read English (the early German immigrants resisted learning English to the extent that the first few grades were taught in German), lack of proper dress, inability to climb the stairs to the third floor museum, indifference, too busy to come on Sunday afternoon, and not widely advertised. Moseley observed in 1914 that of the nearly 20,000 Sandusky population the annual average of 2,000 attended the open houses. In retrospect certainly other factors must have had an influence on the attendance, such as the automobile. More people traveled out of the city on Sunday to visit relatives in near areas or to watch ball games in Cleveland. Certainly the depression of the early 1930s took its toll on attendance at the museum. Moseley was concerned that he was not reaching as many people in the city as he should. He strongly believed, . . .the purpose of the museum is not so much to amuse as to instruct.[16]

Large Concretion Unusual Museum Artifact

The boulder or concretion in Washington Park at the north side of Adams Junior High School, the former Sandusky High School, was preserved by the efforts of Norbert Lange and his teacher Edwin L. Moseley.[25,26,27] Strange muffin-shaped boulders, such as this one, were formed in sedimentary rock some 400 million years ago during the Devonian Period. Much of what is now northern Ohio was then covered by water forming a shallow sea. Into this sea, streams carried sediments which sank to the bottom. This bottom mud solidified into layers to form the shale of today. The concretions were forming at the same time when particles sank into the mud around which crystals developed by chemical action. Carbonates began to engulf them as they grew in size.[28]

In the fall of 1910 the Hinde and Dauch Paper Company began construction of a paper mill along the shore of the Sandusky Bay. Jobs were scarce after Norbert Lange graduated from high school in 1910, so he took a position as a time keeper and general errand boy on the construction site. During the excavation with hand shovels the workmen uncovered a large boulder, which young Lange recognized as a huge concretion. He persuaded the workmen to save the rock until he could contact Professor Moseley by phone. After school Moseley came to the site with a little hand satchel to carry the concretion back to the High School. Much to his surprise the concretion measured nearly 16 feet in circumference.

Moseley made plans immediately to have the concretion moved to the High School grounds. A spur railroad track was located close by so Moseley persuaded Mr. Bender, the local railroad agent to bring in a wrecking train with a crane to lift the concretion from the Bay onto a flat car. It was transported about three quarters of a mile to the foot of Jackson Street where it was loaded onto a low, flat-bottomed dray drawn by horses furnished by George Feick, Sr. The horses pulled the load along Jackson Street for about a block when the five o'clock whistles blew, which was quitting time. The men unhitched the team of horses from the dray and went home. The concretion was left sitting on the dray in the middle of the street all night. In the morning Moseley noticed that the concretion had dried and split from top to bottom into two giant pieces. Moseley then had it hauled to Hinkey's blacksmith shop on East Market Street, where an iron band was fitted around the middle of the concretion. In the meantime a concrete base was prepared in Washington Park just outside of the entrance to the museum of Sandusky High School. The horse drawn dray finally moved it to that location, which Moseley had selected.[25]

About 75 years later, in 1985, the underside of the concretion began to split under the band that Moseley had fastened around its middle. For a short time a fence was constructed around the concretion to prevent anyone from being injured if it fell apart. Geologists were consulted to find the best way to save the concretion. They explained that with the freezing and thawing that occurs during the winter in Sandusky, this breaking apart is what happens to concretions. The best solution was undertaken by the Erie County Historical Society in 1990 to remove the concrete base on which it rested and bury the broken half of the concretion in the ground. Now only the half above ground is visible.

Moseley's large concretion in Washington Park at the north entrance of the former Sandusky High School.

(Taken about 1981 by Dennis Horan, Firelands College; Sandusky Library Archives)

A Trip Through Moseley's Museum

If one could turn the clock back to 1914 and take a trip through Moseley's museum, one of the first items a visitor saw was a large block of limestone, showing glacial grooves, that was inside the building of the lower hall.[11] The first item visible at the top of the stairs was the insect collection. Many beautiful butterflies and moths from South America were also exhibited in addition to a stag beetle from Cuba, which had an enormous pair of claws. The fossil collection shared the same room, which displayed a giant fish skeleton of *Macropetalichthys sullivantii*, the most complete, as well as the best in the world.[14]

In the next room were the ethnological collections showing the culture of the Philippine, Hawaiian, Indian, Chinese, and Japanese peoples. Each culture had many items used by these groups for travel, farming, protection, cooking, and clothing.

One of the most outstanding sections of the Museum was the herbarium. Only a representative number of herbarium sheets were displayed on student desks of the 1,100 pressed and mounted plants obtained in Erie County, the Erie Islands, and the Marblehead Peninsula. Many of these were collected by Moseley's students.

Walking between the cases of stuffed specimens of brown bear, lynx, wild cat, beaver, fruit bat, baboon, several kinds of monkey, pelican, fox, eagle, cranes, flamingos, opossum, raccoon, and peacock reminded the visitor of what it must be like to walk in a jungle looking around on all sides for wild animals. Just ahead on the top of one of the showcases was a male African lion perched there as if to spring on someone below.[14]

In the bird room, nearly 500 mounted birds were displayed throughout. They were collected from such places as Africa, India, Australia, New Guinea, the Himalayas, the Philippines and all over Europe.[29] The colors of the nearly fifty kinds of hummingbirds were magnificent. One particular ruby-throated hummingbird had a lustrous green back and the male sparkled like a gem when the light struck it at the proper angle. If viewed in other light it had no brilliance.

The shells of the some 5,000 specimens of mollusca were one of the most complete in the country. The giant clam (*Tridacna*) was about one-half foot across, but one of the professor's student assistants indicated that kind of shell grew to gigantic proportions of over 41 inches in breadth. These marine shells were a menace to bathers. The shell might close on a foot and trap the bather under water.

Living creatures were also displayed in the Museum. On the counter in one of the laboratories, the living tenants were housed in aquariums and suitable maximum security containers. The fox snake was Moseley's teaching aid, to show visitors how to recognize this helpful snake, so as to prevent its destruction by frightened farmers. Other live crayfish and freshwater species of fish were shown to visitors, who otherwise would not see them unless they went on field trips with him. The horned toad, not native to Ohio, certainly attracted much attention to his container as he burrowed in the sand to hide.

Finally the visitor walked past the striking collection of 1,000 minerals. The gypsum rocks were considered the best collection in a high school museum. In addition, precious ores of gold, silver and diamond, amber, agate and beautiful quartz crystals were also displayed.[11] The stalactites and the stalagmites from the limestone caves in the area were fascinating.[14]

Walking down the stairs, the visitor realized the impact of having just spent three hours of a Sunday afternoon observing and learning from a remarkable collection in a natural history museum. The seven rooms that were toured had as many of the 17,000 specimens as Moseley could assemble for this viewing. As he so aptly put it, to see all of the items would require, "All of the desks in all of the rooms in all of the public and parochial school buildings in Sandusky would not suffice to exhibit the specimens in the Museum without putting more than one kind on a desk."[15]

References

1. 1890. Joseph B. Steere. "Introduction," pp. 1-4. In *A list of the birds and mammals collected by the Steere Expedition to the Philippines*. The University of Michigan, Ann Arbor. 30 pp.

2. 1890. Anonymous. "[Returns from trip abroad]." *Sandusky Daily Register*, 29 September, p. 4.

Chapter 12 • High School Museum

3. 1890. Anonymous. "[Board of Education provides a room for museum]." *Sandusky Daily Register*, 18 October, p. 1.

4. 1890. Anonymous. "[Engaged in assembling museum for exhibit]." *Sandusky Daily Register*, 6 December, p. 4.

5. 1891. Anonymous. "An interesting exhibit," *Sandusky Daily Register*, 2 January, p. 4.

6. 1892. Anonymous. "[Humming birds obtained from a London museum]." *Sandusky Daily Register*, 15 January, p. 4.

7. 1893. Anonymous. "Our museum," pp. 128-131. In *Annual Report. The Board of Education of the City of Sandusky, Ohio for the School Year Ending August 31, 1893*. I. F. Mack & Bro., Sandusky, Ohio. 340 pp.

8. 1896. Anonymous. "[Room change for museum]." *Sandusky Daily Register*, 28 March, p. 8.

9. 1905. Edwin L. Moseley. "Growth of the high school museum," *The Fram*, Sandusky High School, 4(7): 3-6. May.

10. 1906. Anonymous. "A nice fat boa con–." *Sandusky Star-Journal*, 30 January, p.2.

11. 1906. Anonymous. "Big crowds at museum." *Sandusky Daily Register*, 8 April, p.4.

12. 1906. Anonymous. "Adds to museum." *Sandusky Star-Journal*, 6 September, p. 5.

13. 1907. Anonymous. "Ornithological treasures." *Sandusky Daily Register*, 4 March, p. 3.

14. 1910. Lee W. Sexton. "The high school museum." *The Fram*, Sandusky High School. 9(6): 8-10, April.

15. 1911. Edwin L. Moseley. "Interesting exhibits at our high school museum." *Sandusky Daily Register*, 10 March, p. 4.

16. 1914. Anonymous. "Records show surprising increase in high school museum attendance." *Sandusky Daily Register*, 10 May, p. 4.

17. 1924. Anonymous. "Nearly 17,000 specimens in Sandusky High School museum." *Sandusky Register*, 27 April, Section 2, p. 1.

18. 1927. Anonymous. "Prof. Moseley seeks to learn where skeleton at museum came from." *Sandusky Register*, 16 January, p. 8.

19. 1927. Paul B. Mason. "[18]77 rattles skeleton." *Sandusky Register*, 30 January, p. 3.

20. 1928. Edwin L. Moseley. "Local museum to exhibit specimen of crocodile bird." *Sandusky Register*, 22 March, p. 5.

21. 1928. Anonymous. "Hummingbird collection is high [school] museum feature." *Sandusky Register*, 24 March, p. 3.

22. 1932. Anonymous. "High school museum may be moved from Sandusky." *Sandusky Star-Journal*, 3 December, p. 3.

23. 1933. Anonymous. "Attic houses valuable museum." *Sandusky Register*, 6 August, p. 8.

24. 1938. Anonymous. "Prof. Moseley's museum moved to [Bowling Green State] University." *Sandusky Star-Journal*, 2 July, p. 1.

25. Without Date. Norbert A. Lange, letter to Joseph P. Welter. Sandusky Library Archives, Sandusky, Ohio. 1 p.

26. 1939. Albert Gililland. "Much hard work used to obtain noted local curio." *Sandusky Daily News*, 6 February, p. 1.

27. 1978. Karl Kurtz. "The Elderlies: Sandusky's pet rock [16-foot concretion]." *Sandusky Register*, 18 February, p. A-4.

28. 1981. John A. Blakeman. "Geological wonders withstand time: *Rock of Ages*." *Erie Shores Magazine*, p. 2. March. (Copy in file labeled "Parks" at Sandusky Library Archives, Sandusky, Ohio).

29. 1984. Patti Skinner. "Stuffed exotic birds highlight showcases." *BG News*, 18 April, p. 3.

CHAPTER 12 • HIGH SCHOOL MUSEUM

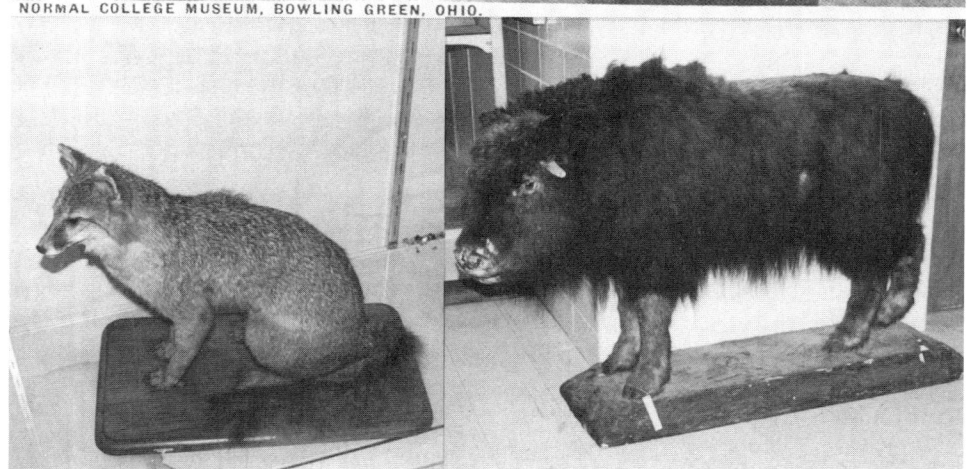

Birds and mammals displayed in Moseley's museum at BGSU.

Above: post card view of museum specimens; Below: mammals.

(Mammals photographs taken 1996 by Relda E. Niederhofer; Niederhofer Collection)

WRITINGS & LEGACY

SECTION III

Faculty of 1912, Sandusky High School.

Back Row: l. to r., F. J. Prout, Bessie Taylor, Mabel Cogill, Elsie Denham, Charlotte Field, Berta Jackson, Louise Colton, Jennie Lewis, Mr. Neeb.

Front Row: W. A. Brown, C. E. Fleming, R. E. Offenhauer (principal), H. B. Williams (superintendent), **Edwin L. Moseley**, W. A. Richardson.

(Sandusky Library Archives)

PROFESSOR EDWIN LINCOLN MOSELEY
BIOLOGY DEPARTMENT
STATE UNIVERSITY
BOWLING GREEN, OHIO

July 15, 1936.

Raymond C. Osburn, Director
Franz Theodore Stone Laboratory,
Gibraltar Island, Lake Erie,

Dear Professor Osburn:

Your letter of July 13 received this morning. I am planning to come this week Friday and will probably arrive at Put-in-Bay about 7:30 P.M. on Steamer Chippewa from Sandusky. Should I come by a different route I will telephone. (over)

I am very glad to have an opportunity to make this trip.

Yours truly,
E. L. Moseley.

Selected Letters From Correspondence

CHAPTER THIRTEEN

Edwin L. Moseley

Seven of Edwin Lincoln Moseley's personal letters are reprinted here to create the content of this chapter. These letters are ones he sent to former students, colleagues, or friends. The letters contain information about his scientific research projects, a request for some help relating to certain investigative efforts, or advice he was providing to his recipients. He also makes comments relative to the then current events. These letters undoubtedly represent a very small sampling from his extensive correspondence. These few letters are ones we encountered in the course of investigating Moseley's life, or they emerged during our other related or unrelated research efforts. In the Center for Archival Collections at Bowling Green State University, Moseley's personal correspondence dates from 1922 until his death in 1948. These letters have not been studied for use in this book project. Additional explanatory notes about each letter or some topic within its contents are provided in appropriate footnotes.

Sandusky, Ohio

December 11, 1902

My Dear Miss Pratt:[1]

Your letter was indeed welcome. I had been wondering at your going without my knowing when. I think no other pupil of mine has ever been associated with me so long as you were for it was my good fortune to have you for a near neighbor for several years as a teacher. I will remember too when you entered the high school. You had not been there long, I think, before all the teachers were impressed with your amiable disposition and pleasing manner. It is not strange

179

that I should have missed you and wondered why you had not said "good bye." I wonder when I shall see you again.

Am glad you are enjoying N.Y. I am anticipating a visit to Washington the Holiday vacation.

Many of the teachers here saw Walker Whiteside as Shylock in *The Merchant of Venice* recently.

You will, no doubt, be interested to know that the November number of the *National Geographic Magazine* contained an article on "Submerged Valleys in Sandusky Bay."[2] It has attracted a great deal of attention in this region, having been reviewed or noticed in editorials by Cleveland, Toledo, and Detroit papers, and I am told also Pittsburgh & Chicago. So far as I have seen they seem to accept my conclusions and to appreciate their importance to navigation and other interests along the lakes.

You will perhaps be more interested to hear about the bottles set adrift. The one you set adrift was found near No. 10 culvert east of the stand-pipe. I enclose an article on the subject.[3] I have heard from several [individuals]since it was published.

Give my regards to your mother and Ada.

I expected to answer your letter long ago or even to write before I heard from you if I had known where to get your address. [The Ohio State] Academy of Science meeting has taken my spare time.[4]

Your friend,

E. L. Moseley

[Bowling Green, Ohio]

February 11, 1929

Dear Stella,[5]

It was a pleasure to meet you and the others at your home Friday evening, and learn not only of your wishes about the birds your father had collected and preserved so well, but also of his regard for me. Of the many rewards for long service in teaching, few, if any, are more satisfying than appreciation. That same evening Mrs. Yunck told me of her frequent use of the facts she learned in my classes at the high school, and that her friend, Mrs. McCrystal, had had a similar experience.

I think you will be interested to know that, when I was living on Vine Street, I often wished that I had an opportunity in some auditorium to interest the working men of the factories and shops in Sandusky in some of my scientific discoveries, such as those described in my "Formation of Sandusky Bay and Cedar Point,"[6] and in discoveries of others about the stars or the earth. The particularly interesting thing in this connection for you is that whenever I visualized such an occasion, your father was in my mind as typical of the men whom I thought I could interest in scientific subjects. It may have been because among my near neighbors who were employed in the city's industrial establishments he was the one I knew best, or the one who most frequently consulted me about scientific problems.

I am sending you a copy of the Ohio Academy Proceedings referred to above, also of some of my other publications, which I hope you will find useful.

Yours Truly,

E. L. Moseley

Bowling Green State College

Bowling Green, Ohio

H. B. Williams, President

July 10, 1936

Professor R. C. Osburn, Director

Franz Theodore Stone Laboratory

Gibraltar Island

Lake Erie

Dear Prof. Osburn:[7]

I have spent a good deal of time this summer in going over my notes on heronries of Ohio, for the U.S. Biol. Survey. I have never been on West Sister Island, where I have heard there are hundreds of nests of Black-crowned Nig[ht] Herons. If you can make it possible for me to visit that island without interfering with the work of your laboratory, I would highly appreciate the opportunity. I am teaching forenoons, Mon. to Sat. Twice I have been able to get away Fri.

P.M., for the weekend, by having afternoon trips for my classes that justified one in excusing them Saturday. This I probably could do again if a Sunday trip to West Sister Island is not easily arranged for.

I could come next week-end, (July 18-19), or the following weekend or, perhaps, even the week after that, but would like to know in advance what date to plan it for.

Yours truly,

E. L. Moseley

Professor Edwin Lincoln Moseley

Biology Department

State University

Bowling Green, Ohio

July 15, 1936

Professor R. C. Osburn, Director

Franz Theodore Stone Laboratory

Gibraltar Island

Lake Erie

Dear Professor Osburn:[7]

Your letter of July 13 received this morning. I am planning to come this week Friday and will probably arrive at Put-in-Bay about 7:30 P.M. on Steamer *Chippewa* from Sandusky. Should I come by a different route I will telephone.

If no one has made a careful estimate of the numbers of heron nests on West Sister Island, perhaps you could organize a group of students who would like to divide up the territory occupied by nests and make an approximate, if not exact, count.

I am very glad to have an opportunity to make this trip.[8]

Yours truly,

E. L. Moseley

CHAPTER 13 • SELECTED LETTERS FROM CORRESPONDENCE

[Envelope addressed to]: Mr. & Mrs. Robert Van Gundy

Holloway farm,

Whitehouse, Lucas County, Ohio]

B.G. June 7, '44

Dear Friends:[9]

Dr. Wehr,[10] who took me to Seymour's[11] the middle of May (after stopping some time to look for birds near Maumee) thinks he can take me to your place Friday evening this week. He cannot start until five oclock. We may eat lunch in the Oak Openings; plans are not mature yet. It may be after sunset when we get to the farm. I hope you did not get a frost last night.

I wonder if you and Seymour were able to get in all the corn you wanted to plant before this month, as well as various things in your gardens, where I would like to spend some time.

I presume your radio is working as well as when I was there last. I spent considerable time yesterday listening to the news and commentators and king and president. Let us hope that your farms and gardens make a substantial contribution to the war effort.[12]

E. L. M.

February 20, 1945

Dear LeRoy:[13]

Your project of providing a windbreak for shooting grounds, along with food and protection for various other birds and at the same time a thing of beauty that may be seen from afar, is a worthy one and will be still more so if the aim is to convert in time the whole marsh into a sanctuary for waterfowl and other birds.

Success will hinge upon a well made plan. The selection of the species of trees and shrubs best suited for these purposes, is very important and needs careful consideration. I have already thought of quite a list and should have gone to the University Library this morning for further information about them, but the walks are so slippery that I did not venture to go so far. I have had no classes there since 1936.

I shall need to take parts of several days to obtain needed information. Besides our extensive literature relating to the subject we have in the Biol. Dept. two botanists whom I expect to consult on points about which I am not so well versed. One, Dr. Otis, is author of *Trees of Michigan* Pub. by the Univ. of Mich. in 1915 and carefully revised about 18 years later.[14] It has had a large sale not only in Mich. but in other states also.

I receive many letters asking for information or advice and make no charge when the answers take only an hour or two of my time. Your project is very interesting to me, but I would feel justified in devoting more time to it if there were a prospect of some remuneration. The amount I would leave for you to decide after you get my report and can form some idea of its value to you.

Your old teacher,

Edwin L. Moseley

P.S. You would be interested in a biography of me in the Jan. 1945 Nature magazine[15] which may probably be found in your Carnegie Library.[16]

Nov. 6, 1947

Dear Mrs. Drewsen:[17]

After a long search I found quarters where I think I can be comfortable and have room for 3 or 4 other University people - faculty or students. I have been busy finding and installing furniture and have not yet moved in. It is conveniently located but rather near a railroad and also to route 6.

It was indeed good of you to give me all of those interesting curios. If you have friends who also have such things which they are willing to part with and let them go where they will interest numerous other people, please tell them about our museum here.[18]

I appreciate also your kind offer to help me to get to places I would like to visit. A letter of Nov. 3 from Mrs. Ruth Hills of Kelley's Island tells me to help myself to specimens, fossils, etc. which were collected by her late husband Norman E. Hills![19]

The peculiar spindle-shaped specimen which at first I took to be ivory and the geography professor here thought was highly compressed volcanic ash proves to be a soft limestone of geologic age yet to be determined. Instead of being a tomahawk, it is an Indian war club. These had a very flexible rawhide handle which was made to cover the stone while wet and clasp to very tightly when it became dry. Its shape may have been done partly by erosion, but people (Indians) had much to do with the polishing and grooving and boring.

Yours truly,

E. L. Moseley

Notes

1. Miss Ione R. Pratt was a student of Moseley's in the Sandusky High School. The letter was seen by RLS in the Moseley file at the Sandusky Library, 23 September 1974.

2. Edwin L. Moseley. 1902. "Submerged valleys in Sandusky Bay." *National Geographic Magazine* 13: 398-403.

3. [Edwin L. Moseley]. 1903. "How the currents act in the Bay of Sandusky." *Sandusky Daily Register*, 1 December, p. 5.

4. The twelfth annual meeting of the Ohio State Academy of Science for 1902 met at The Ohio State University, 28,29 November. Moseley, as secretary of the Academy, had those responsibilities, in addition to which he presented three papers: "Additions and corrections to the Sandusky flora," "Currents in Sandusky Bay," and "The Meteor of September 15th." (*Eleventh Annual Report of the Ohio State Academy of Science* 1902: 26. 1903).

5. Moseley wrote this letter to Stella M. Horn (d. 1973), a teacher in the Sandusky public school system for many years, having retired from that profession in 1943. The letter was seen by RLS in the Moseley file at the Sandusky Library, 23 September 1974.

6. Edwin L. Moseley. 1905. "Formation of Sandusky Bay and Cedar Point." *Thirteenth Annual Report of the Ohio State Academy of Science* (1904). 1905: 179-238. (reprinted 1973. *Lake Erie: Floods, Lake Levels, Northeast Storms: The Formation of Sandusky Bay and Cedar Point*. The Ohio Historical Society, Columbus. ii, 64 pp.).

7. Raymond C. Osburn (1872-1955), professor of Zoology and 25 years as Chairman of the Department of Zoology at The Ohio State University (1917-1942), also served concurrently as the third director of the Franz Theodore Stone Laboratory (1919-1936), Put-in-Bay, Ohio. This letter and the next one are preserved in the Raymond C. Osburn Papers, RG 40/31/1, Stone Laboratory, 1936; Archives, OSU.

8. An account of Moseley's trip to West Sister Island is told by Clarence Clark [see Chapter 5, page 44] who was a graduate student at that time at the Stone Laboratory. He was the student that Director Osburn arranged to accompany Moseley to the Island for the research investigation.

9. Moseley's friends were Mr. and Mrs. Robert Van Gundy, parents of Seymour D. Van Gundy (b. 1931), who wrote a tribute to Moseley [see Chapter 17, page 228]. Mrs. Van Gundy was a Holloway, and they lived on 40 acres of the original Holloway homestead, about a mile from Monclova, Lucas County, Ohio. The senior Van Gundy, an electrician, worked for the Toledo Edison Company in Toledo. Mrs. Van Gundy, a school teacher, had Moseley as one of her professors at Bowling Green State Normal College. While there, she became acquainted with Moseley who later came to visit at the farm. Moseley, a vegetarian, was especially interested in the products of their extensive fruit and vegetable gardens, which nearly every rural northwestern Ohio family cultivated during the years of World War II in the early 1940s.

   Moseley's letter is a gift to RLS, 3 November 1979, from Guy L. Denny, who obtained it when he lived in the Toledo area. Information for this note and the next two come from a letter of 28 March 1997 to RLS from Seymour D. Van Gundy (Stuckey collection).

10. The identity of Dr. Wehr has not been learned, but Moseley, who did not have an automobile, gives the gentleman credit for driving him to the Van Gundy's.

11. Seymour's refers to the farm of Seymour Holloway, brother of Mrs. Robert Van Gundy and uncle of her 13-year-old son, Seymour D. Van Gundy. Mr. Holloway, a naturalist, was heir to the Holloway Farm of about 250 acres, where his children now reside. Both Mr. Holloway and Mrs. Van Gundy wanted young Seymour to follow their footsteps, and encouraged Moseley to spend time with the boy.

12. Moseley's reference to listening to the radio brings to mind that these were the days when radio, a relatively new means of communication, brought the news of World War II into the living rooms of the American people. In the 1940s, George VI (1895-1952) was the King of England and Franklin Delano Roosevelt (1882-1945) was the president of the United States. These years are considered the "Golden Age of Radio," and also are referred to as "The War Years" in radio. Emerging in the 1940's were the

CHAPTER 13 • SELECTED LETTERS FROM CORRESPONDENCE

radio network news commentators, who gave their opinions on world events in a 15 minute-time span that put an explanation point on the happenings of the day. The most important news commentators at this time were Hans von Kaltenborn (1878-1965), Lowell Thomas (1892-1981), Elmer Davis (1890-1958), Raymond Gram Swing (1887-1968), Edward R. Murrow (1908-1965), Gabriel Heatter (1890-1972), Fulton Lewis, Jr. (1903-1966), and Walter Winchell (1897-1972), according to Irving E. Fang (*Those Radio Commentators*, Iowa State University Press, Ames. 1977, p. 14). Who might have been Moseley's favorite news commentator is not known.

13. This letter appears to be about Middle Harbor marsh, Ottawa County, which at one time was owned by J. LeRoy Weier (1888-1971), formerly one of Moseley's students in the Sandusky High School. Weier, who lived in Sandusky, was a good friend of Milton B. Trautman [see Chapter 8, page 91]. The letter, originally in the Library of Norbert A. Lang, Sandusky, was seen by RLS, 23 September 1974, in the Moseley file at the Sandusky Library.

14. Charles Herbert Otis. 1913. *Michigan Trees: A handbook of the native and most important introduced species.* University of Michigan Botanical Garden and Arboretum. Published by the Regents, Ann Arbor. 246 pp. A second edition was also issued by the Regents as a *University Bulletin* (New Series) 14(16): xxxii, 1-246. 1913. The book was also recopyrighted in 1915 and 1931, and reprinted by the Regents of the University of Michigan, Ann Arbor. 247 pp. & 362 pp., respectively.

15. Josephine True. 1945. "Edwin Lincoln Moseley: The biography of an educator." *Nature Magazine* 38: 37-39 [see Chapter 1, page 3].

16. The Carnegie Library, opened in July 1901, is the original name of the public library in Sandusky, which was financed from funds from Andrew Carnegie.

17. Moseley's letter is addressed to Mrs. Ellen Drewson, Box 661, Sandusky, Ohio. No additional information has been learned about her.

18. "Our museum here" refers to the Moseley museum which had been developed in the Sandusky High School and moved to Bowling Green State University in 1938 [see Chapter 12, page 165].

19. Norman E. Hills was the author of a book about Kelleys Island, titled, *A History of Kelley's Island, Ohio.* Published by the author, Toledo, Ohio. 155 pp.

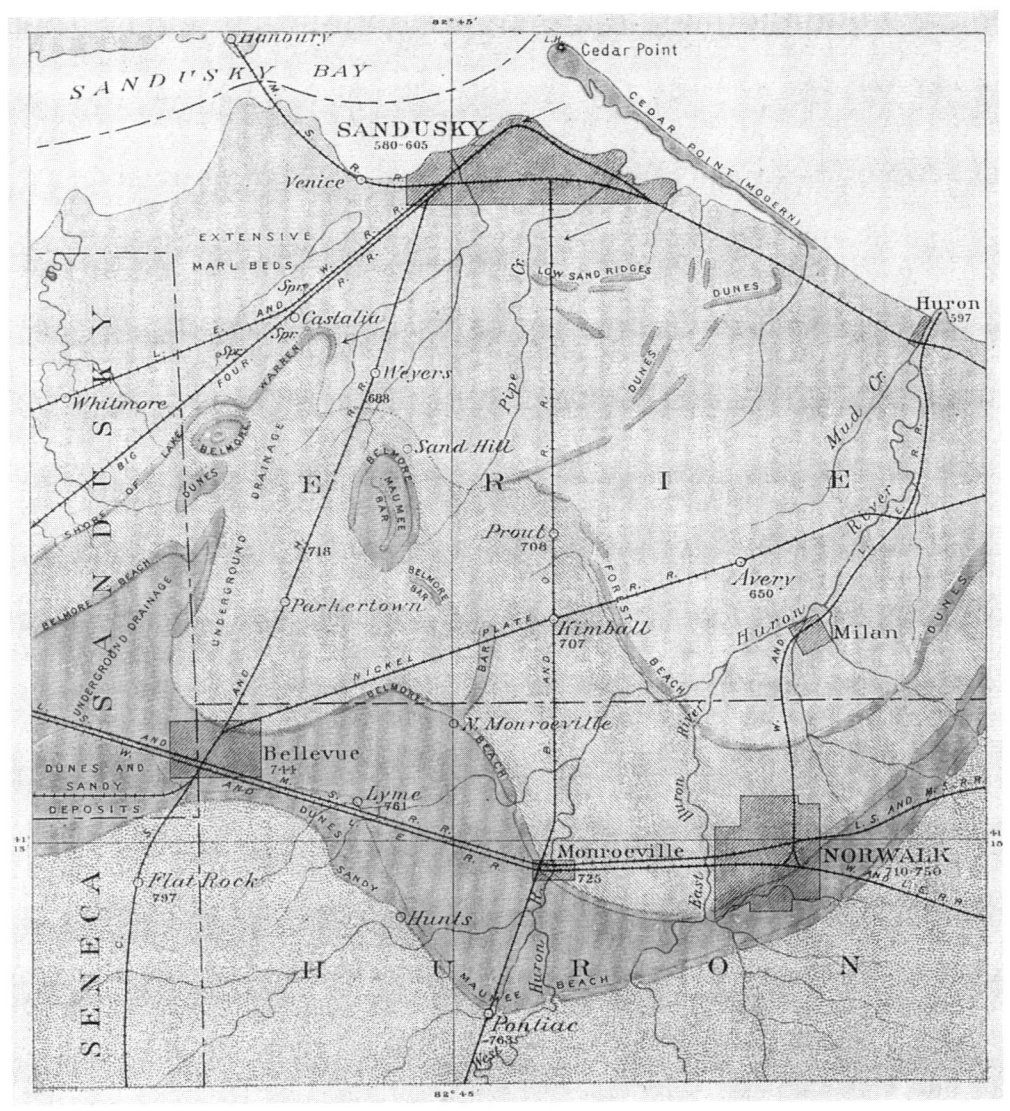

Map of glacial lake beach ridges near Sandusky, Ohio, as drawn in 1901 by Frank Leverett (1902, pl. xxii, opp. p. 730).

(Frank Leverett. 1902. "Glacial formations and drainage features of the Erie and Ohio basins". *United States Geological Survey, Monograph*, No. 41. 802 pp.)

Sandusky's Scientific and Economic Advantages

Edwin L. Moseley

Professor Moseley had a sincere appreciation for the Sandusky area, and had researched a totality of its natural resources and environment during the 25 years that he lived there. One of his missions was to inform the school students and community members about the history and occurrence of the natural wonders in their area. He accomplished this mission through his teaching of science in the Sandusky High School, the opening of his museum to the students and the local citizens, and by writing informative essays for the local newspaper.

This chapter, in three parts, is comprised of information modified and edited by RLS from three of Moseley's essays that were printed in the Sandusky Register. *Part I is his paper, "Attractions for a scientist in the vicinity of Sandusky" (1895),[1] read at the annual meeting of the Ohio State Academy of Science in 1894. To this account has been added more topics in the sections on botany and zoology, which were selected from later articles by him in the* Sandusky Register. *Part II contains four selected places of interest taken from his field trip guide to "Points of interest around Sandusky, and interesting bits of their history" (1914).[5] Part III is the topic of natural resources for economic benefit; and is an abridged version of his essay, "Nature played big part in making Sandusky one of the garden spots of the world" (1922).[6] This contribution, largely on geological formation and glacial lake history of the Sandusky area, was written by Moseley for the Centennial Edition of the* Sandusky Register. *All of the component parts that comprise the entire text of this chapter are derived totally from Moseley's essays in the* Sandusky Register. *None of the information, so far as known, has been published in any books or archival journals, except a short abstract of the "Attractions" paper which appeared in the* Third Annual Report *of the Ohio State Academy of Science (1895)[1] and two paragraphs quoted from his publication of the "Formation of Sandusky Bay and Cedar Point" (1905).[4]*

Chapter 14 • Sandusky's Scientific and Economic Advantages

Attractions for a Scientist[1]

It would be an imposition to take the time of the Ohio Academy of Science with an exhaustive enumeration of Sandusky's advantages as a place for scientific study and field excursions. Merely mentioning a few of them will be sufficient to induce members who have not already been there to avail themselves of the first opportunity to come.

Geology

To the geologist Erie County offers several attractions which other counties do not possess. That supremely beautiful spring, known locally as the Castalia Blue Hole,[9] which Dr. Edward Orton,[10] before this Academy a year ago, characterized it as the noblest spring in Ohio. Of the spring he said, if we were to see the classic fountain in Greece from which our Castalia takes its name, it would probably bear the comparison very favorably. The spring is located but six miles from Sandusky and connected with it by two railroads, as well as good carriage and bicycle roads. The glacial grooves[11] that have made Kelleys Island famous throughout the scientific world are easy of access by steamer. On the other Islands, on the Marblehead Peninsula, and in the city of Sandusky itself, are to be seen grooves,[12] scratches and polished surfaces that make this whole region one of peculiar interest to the student of the glacial period. Here, too, may be seen the sandy ridges which formed the shore of Lake Erie when it stood at a higher level and covered the region now occupied by fertile farms. On the highest part of the Peninsula that bounds Sandusky Bay on the north may be seen wave-worn ledges of limestone that remind one of the present rocky shores of the Islands.[1]

A period at which Lake Erie was at a lower level than at present has left its record in the stalactites which now extend below the water in Perry's Cave on Put-in-Bay Island [South Bass], as well as in the deep rocky channel excavated by the Huron River. When waters flowed farther than at present before reaching the level of the Lake, or perhaps, the river into which it flowed, the rocky bed of the Huron was below the present level of the Lake for several miles back from its mouth. This same river at points between Milan and Monroeville, easily accessible by electric car from Sandusky, offers fine examples of erosion of the Huron shale, transportation of huge boulders by ice, and such a number and variety of large calcareous concretions as few localities in the country afford. The finest specimens of celestine in most of the American museums have come from Green Island. Fluorite is on Rattlesnake Island, and Gypsum on the north side of Sandusky Bay. Sandstone of fine quality is quarried in the eastern part of Erie County, and limestone occurs in great abundance on Kelleys and other Islands, on the Marblehead Peninsula, and in and about the city of Sandusky. From these quarries have come a fair share of the specimens of *Onochodus, Macropetalicthys,* and some other kinds of fossil fishes that all the cabinets of the world contain, while invertebrate remains may be located in nearly every fragment of the rock.[1]

Botany

To the botanist the vicinity of Sandusky affords as much of interest as to the geologist. No where else in the United States, so far as learned, were there at the time of settlement, so many wild flowers growing on an area of only three hundred square miles as in the region near Sandusky.[13] Here are to be located not only plants characteristic of the lake shore[14] and marshes also but,...many which are in few if any other localities in the State....[15] The number of species in the flora of Erie County is equal to that of many counties of twice the size, and it is doubtful if another town in the State from which localities representing such a diversity of soil and climate with the accompanying diversity of plants can be reached so easily and cheaply as from Sandusky.[1]

Our manuscript list of the plants of Erie County, Sandusky Bay, the Islands of Ottawa County and the Marblehead Peninsula as far west as Port Clinton, includes now 1,086 species and varieties of phanerogams and vascular cryptogams. Nearly all of these are represented by specimens in the Sandusky High School herbarium....In order to make the list more nearly complete before publication and have it represent the combined knowledge of the people living in the different townships within this area, I have decided to offer 50 cents to each person that will call my attention for the first time to any native species in Erie County or the portion of Ottawa County referred to above, and 25 cents for any foreign species that has become naturalized. That quite a number of plants grow wild in this region which have not yet been noticed is made probable by the fact that about two hundred of those on the list were not discovered until 1895, also by the fact that many species are known to grow in Lorain County and Cuyahoga County which have not yet been included in our manuscript list.[1]

Some idea of the richness of the flora of Erie County and the eastern part of Ottawa County may be inferred from the number of species and varieties of certain genera or families which have been collected in this small area between 1892 and 1896. [Specimens are preserved in the herbarium at Bowling Green State University.] Of wild asters there are twenty-four species and varieties, of goldenrods nineteen, sunflowers twelve, gentians five, buttercups ten, violets fourteen, milkweeds ten, knotweeds twenty-three, willows seventeen, orchids nineteen, mint family forty, grass family one hundred and three, ferns twenty-six. This richness of the flora of the region about Sandusky is due partly to the variation in soil and rock and partly to topographic features such as prairies, lake beaches and marshes, rocky shores, sand ridges, and steep river banks. It is due also to the mild climate, the summers here reckoning between killing frosts, lasting 192 days on an average, as compared with 138 days at Buffalo, 152 at Bowling Green, and 181 at Columbus.[3]

Zoology

Zoologically considered, the Sandusky area has also some advantages. Among the public generally it has gained almost as wide a reputation for its fresh fish as among geologists for their fossil remains. Though the main part of the city, on account of the scarcity of trees, Sandusky has fewer birds than Cleveland and other cities. Cedar Point[16] seems to form a link in the chain by which land birds cross the Lake, the stream of migration being divided by the unbroken expanse of water to the east, so that birds of ordinary powers of flight must go to the east end of the Lake or cross by the chain of Islands that extends north from Sandusky towards the Canadian mainland. Water birds abound in many different kinds at one season or another. Swans, geese, about 25 kinds of ducks, cormorants, loons, many species of sandpipers and snipes, several each of plovers, herons, rails, terns and gulls, as well as many other kinds of water birds may be seen at one time or another about Sandusky Bay or in the connected marshes.[1]

The bald eagle in northern Ohio nests at Kelleys Island, Put-in-Bay, on the Marblehead Peninsula, and at various other points in northern Ohio. One pair of eagles which have an eyrie near a country post office in the vicinity of Sandusky have occupied their nest for years. Some have been recognized by old fishermen as having been 60 years in one nest, and others 40 to 50 years. On the Islands the eagles are decreasing in numbers, but on the Marblehead Peninsula they are increasing. Some 60 have been counted on the West Harbor and some 30 more on the East Harbor near the Peninsula.[2]

Eagle Island in western Sandusky Bay 75 years ago was comprised of approximately 58 acres of land. Today not much more than an acre of it is left. The Island got its name because it was the nesting place for large numbers of these birds. Once an old hunter and trapper told that it was worth a fellow's life to enter upon the Island after the young had left the nest, unless he had a club.[2]

As late as 1890 as many as 75 eagles were fed at a time by fishermen handling fish at East Harbor, near Lakeside. The eagle's food is 90 percent fish, and that is the reason you will always find the bird near water. On Kelleys Island some years ago, four nests were there, but now only one. The reason for the decrease is not known.[7]

Several kinds of snakes not common in every county add to the attractions for the naturalist, among them are the rattle snake on the Marblehead Peninsula and some of the Islands, the fox snake on the Islands and the mainland, and the pretty and fascinating blowing viper on Cedar Point. The marshes are rich in dragon flies and June flies, the latter more often called May flies, have sometimes piled up their bodies under the electric lights on a single evening so high as to supply the entomologists of the world for a century. Aquatic molluscs are of course well represented.[1]

A few thousand years ago huge beasts[8] similar to elephants roamed over the region where Erie and Ottawa Counties are now located, as well as other parts of North America. A grinder, or molar tooth, of one of these animals was found in a bog near the Baltimore and Ohio railroad, seven miles south of Sandusky by A. H. Prout, uncle of superintendent Frank J. Prout, and is now at the Sandusky High School. Some bones of another individual of the same species were found about the same distance from Sandusky near the south end of Columbus Avenue. The tusk of another was located projecting from the mud along the bank of Mills Creek, five or six miles from Sandusky. This specimen aroused so much interest that the finder for some time after charged a fee for seeing it. No animal just like these whose bones and teeth are referred to above have lived in historic times so far as is known, but some were still living after prehistoric man appeared upon the earth. Naturalists have bestowed upon them the name mastodon, which means that their teeth have large projections shaped like nipples.[8]

• • •

Selected Places of Interest[5]

Castalia Prairie

Passing the grounds of the Castalia Sporting Club from east to west, comes the Castalia Prairie[17]. It stretches north and west from the village of Castalia, an area too wet for trees until artificially drained. Before issuing from the spring the water had been flowing a long distance through soluble limestone. Spreading over this Prairie, it deposited much of the material it had dissolved, thereby forming marl and tufa[18]. These deposits are also created by the plant *Chara*, which grows abundantly in the water. It takes from the water, while it lives, much carbonate of lime and, after it dies, becomes encrusted with the same substance, forming the marl and tufa. The great cement mills at Castalia and Bay Bridge mix this material with a smaller quantity of clay and heat it in furnaces to make portland cement. For making good cement most limestone contains too large a percentage of magnesium. The magnesium compounds in the spring water, being more soluble than the calcium carbonate, were not deposited so readily but carried on into Sandusky Bay, leaving behind the material needed for making cement. Much of the Prairie has tufa at the surface so that it cannot be plowed but is used for pasture. Many rare plants grow upon it. Here may be seen and heard the Bartamian sandpiper, dickcissel and other birds which do not inhabit woods.

Blue Hole Springs

The blue hole was 43 feet deep before the recent cave-in. After it clears, it will be interesting to see if the depth has changed. Probably no spring in this part of the world surpasses it in beauty.

At the pond[19] in the village of Castalia, is another large spring near the pump, and a few yards farther west in the pond, the water bubbles from still another spring. The four or five springs in this pond together send out 25,000 gallons a minute or five times as much as issues from the Blue Hole. South of the stream which issues from this pond, half way up the hill, south and west of the village is the west end of the Wagner quarry. In a small pasture just west of this quarry are the Rockwell Springs, about seven in number, each like the Blue Hole in miniature and together pouring out a larger volume of water. From these Springs and those at Castalia, about two million barrels issue each day. Where does it all come from? At the grounds of the Rockwell Springs Club in adjacent Sandusky County can be seen another use of the spring water. It is unnecessary to put a screen across the stream to prevent the trout going up as far as the springs, for the lack of oxygen in the water turns them back.

• • •

Shorelines of Glacial Lakes

The road between Castalia and Clyde is built on a ridge of gravel and sand, which gently slopes toward the north. This road is on the shore of Lake Warren, a glacial lake which, some 10,000 years ago, covered the land to the north and stretched east into the western part of New York state. Its northern border was ice, which then covered the lower part of the St. Lawrence valley. South of Castalia is a road built on another old lake beach, which extends toward Sandusky. This ridge slopes gently to the north and, in places, also in the opposite direction. Consisting of sand and gravel, it is about 65 feet higher than the shore of Lake Warren and about 165 feet higher than Lake Erie. It is the Belmore beach, or the shore of Lake Whittlesey, whose outlet was across Michigan, via the Grand River valley, then past Chicago into the Illinois and Mississippi Rivers. In the west part of Bellevue or the southeastern part of Norwalk, may be seen a still higher and older beach, the shore of Lake Maumee, whose outlet at Fort Wayne led into the Wabash and Mississippi Rivers.

Sink Holes South of Castalia

Several miles south of Castalia is an area of sink holes. These are so numerous that many days would be required to visit them. The country from Castalia to Bellevue and many miles farther south is drained by subterranean channels in the limestone, there being no permanent surface streams. During the floods of 1913 these channels could not carry all the water so that low parts of Bellevue and of certain fields north of it were covered with water which issued from openings where, at other times, water enters. This water must have entered the ground farther south, where the surface is higher.

Chapter 14 • Sandusky's Scientific and Economic Advantages

Sink holes also occur south of Castalia, within a mile or two, and some very interesting fields where the solution of limestone under the upper layers has allowed these to settle, so that, in some instances, several acres of sunken land can be seen, without surface outlet, but faced by cliffs of rock, still in its original position. One of these fields lies on the southwest side of the road which extends southeast from Castalia to Maple Avenue near a bend in the road. Here the rock has settled and is covered with ferns and abundant wildflowers, the blue ash and other trees, the nighthawks, and, perchance, a woodchuck.

Natural Resources for Economic Benefit[6]

The legislature, the Chamber of Commerce, the railroads, and other corporations have contributed to the growth of Sandusky, but no man-made institution can make a city without the aid of natural resources. Cities do not develop in tropical deserts or arctic tundras, nor in barren places even in temperate regions. The part of North America lying north of the 51st parallel is as large as the United States, containing two thousand times as much land as Erie, Lorain, and Cuyahoga counties together, yet there are more than half as many people living in these three counties on the south shore of Lake Erie as in all that vast expanse lying north of the 51st parallel.

• • •

What has made Sandusky one of the garden spots of the earth? It was not created as it now is, but attained its present condition by the slow process of evolution. Many millions of years passed before any Indians were in the world, as were any deer, or fur bearing animals, or any birds. Where Sandusky is now, a shallow sea occurred, and in this sea lived myriads of polyps whose skeletons were coral, numerous brachiopods with shells that resemble clam shells, cephalopods and gastropods with coiled shells and several kinds of fish, some of them very much larger than the largest living in Lake Erie now.

For thousands of generations these creatures lived and died, leaving their hard parts to be ground up by the waves and distributed by currents, or to be imbedded whole in the calcareous mud thus formed. These sediments deposited upon the sea bottoms in time became hard rock. Thus was formed the Sandusky limestone upon which the city, to some extent, has been built. Beneath this limestone are stratified rocks of earlier age, which were also laid down as sediment on the floor of a shallow sea. In these older rocks, too, we find the remains of an abundant animal life, but less complex than in the rock at the surface. The deposition of the sediment that formed these rocks required an inconceivably long time, millions and millions of years, probably more than a million centuries.

Sometime after the formation of the rock upon which rest the foundations of Sandusky, a movement of the earth's crust lifted it above sea level and it may never have been covered by the sea during all the long ages that have since elapsed. But first the sea was not far away or may have continued to cover all of Erie County, and into it the rivers emptied their water, laden with sediment which contained much clay as well as material derived from the wearing away of the limestone. Out of such stuff was formed the Ohio shale which outcrops along the Huron River between Milan and Monroeville and at various places along Lake Erie from the vicinity of Rye Beach to Cleveland and Buffalo. When this shale had been lifted above the water level the waves washed up sand along the shore and this, in time, consolidated into the sandstone called Berea grit, that outcrops at Berlin Heights and in many places to the east. Both this sandstone and the shale may have covered the Sandusky limestone at one time in Sandusky, itself, as they still cover it farther east. If so, they were worn away long ago.

Later, in the region farther south, extensive marshes developed in which grew ferns, some of them much larger than any found now outside of the tropics, giant club mosses and calamites which resembled our horsetails and scouring rushes, but were as tall as apple trees. At that time no fruit trees existed anywhere, nor any trees at all like those we have now, neither was there grass nor any flowering herb nor vine nor bush, nor any bees nor butterflies. Out of the remains of the ferns and rushes and other plants that grew in those ancient marshes nature formed the coal which we now burn in our furnaces and from which, after millions of years, we are getting back the warmth and light of the sun's radiance which enabled those plants to grow.

After the Carboniferous, or Age of Coal, the land we call Ohio remained above sea level and so no more limestone, sandstone, shale, or coal was formed. But in other parts of the country where shallow seas still covered the land, rock formation went on for millions of years longer. Other kinds of plants flourished in the marshes and on land. After a time plants developed a more complex means of reproducing themselves than any which the Carboniferous plants possessed. They developed flowers which have within them organs that cannot be seen without careful study with a microscope. From the earlier kinds of insects, bees and other insects developed that visited the flowers in search of nectar. By carrying this nectar from one flower to another, pollination and fertilization occurred resulting in seeds that would grow into flowering plants with strong supporting vascular tissue.

• • •

The glacial period, which occurred next, may have lasted for a million years — a short time when compared with the ages that intervened between the forming of the Sandusky limestone and the beginning of the Ice Age. . . .The ice that covered northern and western Ohio to a depth of several hundred feet, after several advances and retreats, melted away from this region about 10,000 years ago.

The glacial waters were too cold to support life, but the glacier itself was active, as present glaciers are, and carried along great quantities of fragments broken off from the rock over which it slowly moved. Ground down by rubbing, one against another, or on the bedrock, these fragments formed boulders, gravel, and clay. Some of this material, the glaciers brought from Canada even as far as the region northeast of Lake Huron, other parts were moved only a short distance.

The huge spherical concretion now in Washington Park near the high school building [now Adams Junior High School] was moved by the glacier to the western part of Sandusky, probably from a spot not very far northeast of Rye Beach. Here similar concretions may still be seen partly embedded in the shale where they had formed millions of years ago before the shale had solidified. Some of them, like the one in the park, have tops flattened and scratched by the glacier passing over them.

In some places the glacier, by means of hard boulders frozen at the bottom, as it pressed these with great force upon the bedrock, cut deep grooves. Most kinds of rock were friable enough to be broken by such treatment, but the very massive rock of Sandusky, Johnson's Island, Marblehead, and Kelleys Island retains polished grooves and flutings of such large size that they might well be ranked among the wonders of the world. The direction of most of these grooves is nearly parallel with the long axis of Lake Erie.

The valley now occupied by this lake altered the motion of the lower part of the ice so that it moved more nearly west than south. The glacier cut some new valleys where the rock was weak or enlarged those already existing, such valleys as that now occupied by Sandusky Bay, and the valleys where the harbors between Lakeside and Catawba now are, likewise where a marsh and low ground separate the main part of Kelleys Island from the high northern part, and a shallow valley south of the Lake Shore Electric railway west of the slate cut. All of these valleys are approximately parallel with the glacial grooves.

For a good while after the glacial ice had disappeared from this region, the land was deeply covered with water, for the Niagara River with its fall did not exist and had no outlet for the water toward the east. The water from the rain and the melting ice formed a lake [Lake Maumee] that overflowed into tributaries of the Mississippi. The first point of outlet for this lake was where Fort Wayne, Indiana, is now, from which the glacial waters flowed to Huntington on the Wabash River.

The water over Sandusky was then some two hundred feet deep and the shore of the lake was fifteen miles to the south where the standpipe has been built in the City of Norwalk. After the glacier had melted back farther to the north, an outlet was formed south of the ice across Michigan, whence the water followed across the present site of Chicago to the Illinois River. If Sandusky had been built before that, its tall standpipe and the spire of St. Mary's church would have projected out of the water. The shore of the lake [Lake Whittlesey] at this stage was where the main street of Norwalk is now.

When the glacier had retreated still farther, the lake extended farther north so that the water could exit around the Saginaw Thumb and thence past Grand Rapids and Chicago to the Illinois and Mississippi Rivers. The water was lowered by this new outlet so that over the land where Columbus Avenue and Monroe Street now intersect, it was then only seventy-six feet deep. The south shore of the lake [Lake Warren] at this stage was just where a well-paved road now extends from Clyde nearly to Castalia.

The beaches that were formed at the margin of the glacial lake at these three stages may still be traced through much of northern Ohio and in many places have long been used for roads because they are well drained. Euclid Avenue in Cleveland, like the Clyde-Castalia Road, follows the lowest one. All three beaches show plainly in that city and they are close together in Berlin Heights. Farther west where the land rises more gradually toward the south they are miles apart.[20]

The surface of the land was altered also in other ways by the water that covered it during the melting of the ice. Fine silt, picked up by the waves along shore, was carried out to the deeper water, where, settling gradually, it filled up the hollows and left the surface level in excellent condition for the growth of wild vegetation to be followed later by fertile farms.

The glacier and the waters that followed it did much to alter the surface of the earth in northern Ohio. . . .The most beautiful scenery in northern Ohio, excepting the Islands in the Lake, is due to erosion by streams still at work, such as the Huron River, Vermilion River, and all the important streams that enter the Lake farther east. Between Sandusky and Toledo the land bordering the Lake is low for many miles back and with no ravines or deep valleys, but rather has shallow water marshes and swamps.

One of the sources of wealth in the vicinity of Sandusky is the marl and tufa of the Castalia Prairie. This material combined with the clay in the same region has yielded many thousands of car loads of good cement. Most of the limestone in this part of America contains so much magnesium as to be unfit for making cement. In the region between Bellevue and Castalia the subterranean waters have dissolved large quantities of a soluble limestone known as the Waterlime, the same formation in which occur the caves in Kentucky and the much smaller caves on Put-In-Bay Island. The material in solution is brought to the surface where the water issues from the ground as at the Blue Hole, the Rockwell Springs, and other springs in the vicinity of Castalia. Before any artificial drainage existed, this water spread over the low surface north and west of Castalia, depositing there much of the lime carbonate which it contained but carrying with it to the Bay and Lake and ocean the magnesium compounds, for they are more soluble than those of calcium. In this way a valuable material for cement was formed from a rock which was not suitable for this purpose. Formation of these compounds has taken place in recent geological times.

Here near Sandusky one can find so many building or structural materials, in addition to farm products. Nowhere else is there clay for brick, tile, and cement; marl for cement; gypsum for plaster and stucco; fine sand for use in foundries; coarse sand for mortar and plaster; gravel for highways and railroad ballast; sandstone and limestone for many purposes. Formerly bog iron ore was dug and smelted in the western part of Erie County. But the greatest of our mineral resources is the soil which produces our grapes, our wheat, and other farm products.

• • •

Of the original flora only a few species contribute appreciably to the present-day food supply, but where the wild grape once flourished, large vineyards of choice varieties are now cultivated, where prairie grass once grew there are now fields of oats and buckwheat, and where the forests stood there are now stands of wheat and corn.

During much of the past century the original plant growth has been of economic importance, not so much by contributing to the food supply as by furnishing wood for fuel and a hundred other uses. The tree whose name is now familiar in connection with the summer resort grew to a larger size both on Cedar Point and the Islands than any specimen to be seen there at present, and the cutting of the cedar wood and shipping it to Cleveland was the first big industry of the inhabitants of the Lake Erie Islands. Later ship building at Fries' Landing, now Abbot's bridge, was made possible by deep water in the river between there and Huron and by a supply of good, white oak timber in the vicinity.

The wood of other kinds of trees was used in the manufacture of articles so valuable that they had a world-wide market. Hickory, in which this region abounds, enabled the Tool Company to supply ladder-rounds for use in the deep copper mines of Lake Superior, the Whip-stalk factory to supply the teamsters of Australia and South Africa, and the Woolworth Handle factory to make axe and pick handles that were in demand all over the country. Planes made in Sandusky, the wooden part out of beach, were sent to Europe and ash hoe handles to the cotton plantations of the southern states. The products of the American Crayon Company, manufactured from gypsum mined near Sandusky Bay, is sent to all parts of the world in boxes which they make of basswood, a tree that formerly grew in abundance in this part of Ohio. Various local industries such as saw mills and basket factories have depended on the neighboring forests for their raw materials.

Of all the many natural resources which have contributed to the prosperity of this community, the one that stands out as prominent is the harbor afforded by Sandusky Bay. It is this that first made it a trading post and afterwards an impor-

Chapter 14 • Sandusky's Scientific and Economic Advantages

tant commercial center. The story of how natural forces formed this Bay and the Cedar Point Peninsula which separates it from Lake Erie, was presented by the writer in his presidential address to the Ohio State Academy of Science at the Cleveland meeting in 1904. Portions of this address appeared in the *Sandusky Register* and the whole was published with accompanying maps in the thirteenth annual report of the Academy (1905).[4]

[Moseley's conclusions in three paragraphs at the end of the publication under the heading, "Looking Forward" contains his prediction for the future of Sandusky Bay. The first paragraph introduces the topic and the second and third are reprinted below with a few editorial modifications]:

• • •

Sandusky Bay with connected marshes is probably twenty per cent larger now than in 1820. So far as the enlargement is due to erosion, it should proceed more rapidly the wider the Bay becomes, for the waves attain greater force. The effect of the waves, however, is diminished by the Bay bridge, by jetties at the entrance to the Bay, by docks and by rocks put on the shore purposely to protect the land. The enlargement of the Bay due to the subsidence of the land may be partly prevented by dikes and may be effected to some extent by changes at Niagara Falls produced by human agency. We may reasonably expect, however, that the Bay will continue to spread over the adjacent lowland much as it has been doing for centuries past.

The rise of the water due to tilting of the land, 2.14 feet in a century, is about the same as the change of lake level that sometimes occurs within a year in consequence of variations in the rainfall and is considerably less than that produced in Sandusky Bay by a single northeast gale. It is, however, cumulative. The present generation is likely to see the water higher than it was in 1858 and in northeast gales the lower parts of Sandusky submerged, but at the present rate of subsidence the Bay at ordinary stages of the water will not extend up Columbus Avenue to as far as Market Street for about eight hundred years. Port Clinton is not so fortunately situated. Northeast gales will cause much trouble there as soon as a period of several years comes when the rainfall is considerably above normal, and before the middle of the next century when the water at such times will go... across the Marblehead Peninsula from Port Clinton to Sandusky Bay. After two or two-and-a-half centuries, the water will cover this part of the Peninsula for months at a time and after three centuries, will do so at ordinary stages. The Marblehead Peninsula will then be an island and, Sandusky Bay will show no resemblance to its present form [see publication note E, page 276].

—Modified and edited by RLS from the following writings of Edwin L. Moseley:

1. 1894-1895. "Attractions for a scientist. Professor Moseley's masterly paper before the Academy of Science." *Sandusky Daily Register*, 30 December 1894, p. 10; *Sandusky Weekly Register*, 2 January, 1895, p. 5; "Attractions for a scientist in the vicinity of Sandusky." (Abstract). *Third Annual Report Ohio State Academy of Science* 1895: 5. 1895.

2. 1895. "Eagles in northern Ohio." *Sandusky Weekly Journal*, 19 January, p. 8.

3. 1896. "The plants and flowers of Erie County." *Sandusky Weekly Register*, 22 April, p. 5.

4. 1905. "Formation of Sandusky Bay and Cedar Point." *Thirteenth Annual Report Ohio State Academy of Science* 1904: 179-238; *Proceedings of the Ohio State Academy of Science* 4: 179-238. (reprinted under the title, *Lake Erie: Floods, Lake Levels, Northeast Storms: The Formation of Sandusky Bay and Cedar Point*. The Ohio Historical Society, Columbus. ii, 64 pp. 1973); "Sandusky Bay and Cedar Point: Their formation — the changes wrought by the hand of time. What the waters have covered in ages past — nature's silent forces." *Sandusky Daily Register*, 20 January 1906, pp. 9-12; *Sandusky Weekly Register*, 24 January 1906, pp. 13-16 (reproduced with permission of the Ohio Historical Society).

5. 1914. "Points of interest around Sandusky, and interesting bits of their history." *Sandusky Register*, 13 June, p. 7.

6. 1922. "Nature played big part in making Sandusky one of the garden spots of the world." *Sandusky Register*, 31 December, p. 14.

7. 1924. "Says Vermilion eagle of *bald* species, quite common near Sandusky." *Sandusky Register*, 7 December, p. 9.

8. 1929. "Huge beast once roamed over this part of State." *Sandusky Register*, 15 April, p. 5.

Notes

9. Noted in the literature as the "most extraordinary artesian spring in the continent," the commercial Blue Hole now closed to the public, is located at the north edge of Castalia, Erie County, Ohio. This spring has been described in many publications, the most authoritative being Karl ver Steeg and George Yunck. 1932. The Blue Hole of Castalia." *Ohio Journal of Science* 32: 425-435. Two anonymous articles are "The Story of the Blue Hole." *Ohio Conservation Bulletin* 2(5): 8. 1938, and "Castalia's Blue Hole." *Ohio Conservation Bulletin* 19(8): 29,30. 1955.

10. Edward Orton, Ohio geologist and second president of the Ohio State Academy of Science, spoke of the spring at Castalia as part of his presidential address presented at the Academy's third annual meeting, 28 December 1893, in Columbus, Ohio. His address, "The Relations of the Ohio Geology to its Water Supply," is not known to have been published, but he did discuss this noble fountain in a later publication: Edward Orton. 1899. "Castalia," pp. 680-682. In "The rock waters of Ohio." *Nineteenth Annual Report of the United States Geological Survey*, Part IV. Hydrogeography, pp. 633-717, 3 pls.

11. The earliest known scientific publications describing these world-known famous grooves are: Charles Whittesey. 1879. "Ancient glacial action, Kelley's Island, Lake Erie." *Proceedings of the American Association for the Advancement of Science* 5: 54-59 and G. Frederick Wright. 1891. "The glacial grooves on Kelley's Island to be preserved." *Science* 17: 358,359.

12. These small grooves, scratches, and polished surfaces were described early in the nineteenth century, but the cause of them was questioned in an article by Ebenezer Granger. 1823. "Notice of a curious fluted rock at Sandusky Bay, Ohio." *American Journal of Science* 6: 179,180.

13. Moseley's definitive floristic study of the area is his "Sandusky flora. A catalogue of the flowering plants and ferns growing without cultivation in Erie County, Ohio, and the peninsula and islands of Ottawa County." *Ohio State Academy of Science, Special Papers*, No. 1. 167 pp.

14. As examples of plants in the lake shore habitat, Moseley listed *Polanisia graveolens* [*P. dodecandra*], *Juncus balticus*, *Scirpus pungens*, and *Panicum virgatum*.

15. Here Moseley listed *Actinella acaulis glabra*, *Nelumbium luteum*, *Opuntia humifusa*, *Arctostaphylos uva-ursa*, *Conobea multifida*, *Gerardia purpurea*, *Isanthus brachiatus*, *Rhexia virginica*, *Helianthus mollis*, *Potentilla supina*, *Pellaea atropurpurea*, *Arenaria stricta*, *Vicia sativa*, *Cassia chamaechrista*, *Meibomia sessifolia*, *Hypericum gentianoides*, and *Eryngium yuccaefolium*.

16. Robert L. Baird. 1901. "Birds of Cedar Point, Sandusky, Ohio." *Ohio Naturalist* 2: 143-145; Lynds Jones. 1909-1910. "The birds of Cedar Point and vicinity." *Wilson Bulletin*, 21: 55-76,115-131,187-204; 22: 25-40,97-114,172-181.

17. The Castalia Prairie, a natural wet prairie and fen, is one of the most diverse floristic areas in northwestern Ohio. It has been the subject of several studies. Alfred Dacknowski. 1912. "Castalia Prairie," pp. 56-58. In "Peat Deposits of Ohio: Their Origin, Formation, and Uses". *Geological Survey of Ohio Fourth Series, Bulletin 16*. 424 pp; Paul B. Sears. 1967. "The Castalia Prairie." *Ohio Journal of Science* 67: 78-88; Stephen Joseph Hurst. 1971. Geographical relationships of the prairie flora element and floristic changes from 1890-1970 at the Resthaven Wildlife Area (Castalia Prairie), Erie County, Ohio, with an appended list of vascular plants. M. S. Thesis, The Ohio State University, Columbus, Ohio. 177 pp.; Karen Adams Foos. 1971. A floristic and phytogeographic analysis of the fen element at the Resthaven Wildlife Area (Castalia Prairie), Erie County, Ohio. M. S. Thesis, The Ohio State University, Columbus. 81 pp.

18. Since 1900 the Castalia Portland Cement Company mined the marl from the Castalia Prairie to make cement. This operation continued into the early 1940s, at which time in 1942, the first land purchases were made by the State of Ohio and continued for several years until 2,210 acres were acquired for the establishment of a State Wildlife Sanctuary, called Resthaven, managed by the Division of Wildlife in the Department of Natural Resources. An early description of the development of the wildlife area was written by Floyd B. Chapman. 1949. "Resthaven Sanctuary development." *Ohio Conservation Bulletin* 13(10): 21.

19. Known as the village pond in midtown Castalia, this artesian "blue hole" spring is the largest one in the area. Many different kinds of birds find winter refuge here, because the pond and outflow stream never freeze, as described by "Doc" Kirby. 1962. "Castalia's duck haven." *Ohio Conservation Bulletin* 26(1): 19,20.

20. Moseley refers to the ancient glacial lake shorelines, which were the earlier stages of Lake Erie created as the glacial ice melted. Ohio route 101, between Castalia and Clyde, is on the Lake Warren Beach (12,800 years ago) at an elevation of 665-680 feet; South Ridge Road, formerly route 175, south of Castalia is on the Lake Whittlesey Beach (13,000 years ago) at an elevation of 735 feet; U. S. route 20, west and east of Bellevue, is on the Lake Maumee Beach (13,500-14,000 years ago) at an elevation of 785-800 feet.

In an earlier article, Moseley ("Original work in high schools." *Ohio Educational Monthly* 52: 367-374. 1903.) explained how he began studying the glacial beach ridges and the streams flowing into Sandusky Bay, after attending a scientific meeting in Detroit. He wrote,

> "By comparing the heights above the normal lake level in 1895 of a benchmark in Cleveland and one at the head of the Welland Canal with the heights of the same as carefully determined in 1858, G[rove] K. Gilbert found that the point near the northeast end of the lake rose as compared with the point in Cleveland. Gilbert's paper on this subject was presented at the Detroit meeting of the American Association for the Advancement of Science, 1897. There too Leverett and Taylor who had traced the old lake beaches and determined their altitude at various points told me of their results, and suggested that the small streams in the vicinity of Sandusky should show in their lower course the evidence of submergence. Inspired by these researchers I returned with a determination to investigate the matter in different ways. Many observations already made harmonized with the idea that the water about Sandusky had deepened."

The geologists Moseley cited published their papers as follows: Frank Leverett. 1898. "Correlation of moraines with beaches on the border of Lake Erie." *American Geologist* 21: 195-199; G. K. Gilbert. 1897. "Modification of the Great Lakes by earth movement." *National Geographic Magazine* 8: 233-247 and "Recent earth movements in the Great Lakes region," *U. S. Geological Survey, Eighteenth Annual Report* 2: 601-647. In the latter paper at page 645, Gilbert added a supplement acknowledging Moseley's studies that showed evidence for a rise in western Lake Erie water level, which Gilbert summarized in a page and a half from the Sandusky Professor's writings. Gilbert also noted that the data Moseley "has gathered consitiute an important contribution to the subject."

Moseley's principal reference for information on the ancient glacial lake beaches would have been Frank Leverett. 1902. "Glacial formations and drainage features of the Erie and Ohio basins." *United States Geological Survey, Monograph*, No. 41. 802 pp. In present-day literature, maps and descriptions are in Jane L. Forsyth. 1959. "The beach ridges of northern Ohio." *Division of Geological Survey, Department of Natural Resources*, Columbus, Ohio. 9 pp., 2 fold-out maps.

For further descriptions see Charles E. Herdendorf. 1989. "Palentology and geomorphology," pp. 35-70. In Kenneth A. Krieger, ed. "Lake Erie estuarine systems: issues, resources, and management." *NOAA Estuary-of-the-Month Seminar Series*, No. 14, United States Department of Commerce, Washington, D.C. vii, 290 pp.

List of Moseley's Lectures at the Sandusky High School

15	February 1890	"On the Philippine Islands." *Sandusky Daily Register*, 13 February 1890, p. 4. [Notice only].
5	December 1890	"Some Popular Delusions." *Sandusky Daily Register*, 5 December, p. 4. [Notice only]. *Sandusky Daily Register*, 6 December, p. 1. [Summary]. "More about Delusions: [Clean Air and Respiratory Diseases]." *Sandusky Weekly Register*, 16 December 1891, suppl., p. 6. [Summary].
30	January 1892	"Peculiar Customs of the Malays, Mongolians and Americans." *Sandusky Daily Register*, 1 February 1892, p. 4. [Notice only].
13	February 1892	"What We Eat." *Sandusky Daily Register*, 15 February 1892, p. 4; *Sandusky Weekly Register*, 17 February 1892, p. 5. [Summary].
18	December 1893	"Sanitary Science." *Sandusky Daily Register*, 15 December 1893, p. 2. [Notice only].
19	May 1899	"The Flora of the Islands and Sandusky's Adjacent Country." *Sandusky Register*, 21 May 1899, p. 5. [Notice only].
28	November 1900	"Sanitary Science: Typhoid Fevers." *Sandusky Register*, 1 December 1900, p. 2. [Notice only].
5	December 1900	"Sanitary Science: Consumption." *Sandusky Register*, 1 December 1900, p. 2. [Notice only].
—	November 1903	"The Resources of Sandusky." *Sandusky Evening Star*, 19 November 1903, p. 4. [Summary].
10	June 1903	"How to Exterminate the Mosquito." *Sandusky Star-Journal*, 10 June 1903, p. 6; *Sandusky Weekly Star*, 11 June 1903, p. 5; *Sandusky Daily Register*, 11 June 1903, p. 2; *Sandusky Register*, 19 June 1903, p. 2. [Summaries].
29	October 1910	"The Philippines." *Sandusky Daily Register*, 29 October 1910, p. 2. [Notice only].

Moseley's tombstone in Oak Grove Cemetery, next to the University campus, Bowling Green, Ohio.

(Photo Service, BGSU)

Illness, Death, and Funeral

Ronald L. Stuckey

CHAPTER FIFTEEN

Twice a year for 20 years, Edwin Lincoln Moseley visited in Dayton, Ohio, with his longtime friend, Carl Schmidt, a drugstore operator and former student he had in Sandusky. On 28 April 1948 while attending the motion picture, *Miracle of the Bells*, at Keith's Theater, Moseley became ill, left the theater, and wandered into a nearby store. From there, Schmidt was called, who came and took the professor to his nearby home.[3]

Moseley, who lived all of his adult life free from illness, "suffered a slight stroke" resulting in paralysis which weakened his heart.[1,2] Another report stated he was suffering "mental depression."[1] Two weeks later, Bowling Green State University President Frank J. Prout dispatched an ambulance to Dayton to bring Moseley to Johnston Hospital on the University campus. Moseley's close friend, Professor Daniel J. Crowley, accompanied the ambulance to serve as an escort en route back to Bowling Green.[4] Frank D. Halleck, M.D., of the hospital staff, treated Moseley, but by 31 May the dying professor refused medication. There Moseley died of a coronary thrombosis on 6 June 1948.[3,5,6,7]

After receiving a telephone message of Moseley's death from the head nurse at the University hospital, President Prout transferred the message to the city and surrounding area through the loud speaker on top of the administration building. Ten minutes later, after the local news editor gave the story to the Associated Press, editors from the *New York Times* and the *San Francisco Chronicle* called for confirmation of Moseley's death.[9,11]

Chapter 15 • Illness, Death, and Funeral

Of the closest family members, only three survived,[6] a cousin, Charles F. Chubb of Pittsburgh, Pennsylvania, son of Lucy (Moseley) Chubb, and two nieces, Mrs. Pearl Ideler of Prospect, Kentucky, daughter of Clara (Moseley) Sutherland, and Mrs. Lillian (Crocker) Brown of Wilmette, Illinois, daughter of Mary (Moseley) Crocker. Attending the funeral were Mr. Chubb and Mrs. Ideler. The latter wrote a letter to her children, and perhaps other family members, describing the events following Moseley's death and his funeral. It was addressed, "Dear Family," dated 9 June, the day following the funeral after she returned home to Prospect.[10]

Dear Family,

This is the saga of my past three days.

Eddie [her husband] *took me to a plane at 5 PM Monday after a day of teaching. Thunderstorms made my flight two hours late by the arriving time in Toledo. Also their time is two hours later than ours,* [as] *we are not on daylight saving. Uncle Ed's good old friend Mr.* [Daniel] *Crowley waited for me all that time at the airport and drove the 20 miles, really crawled along at about eight miles an hour, to the little Ross hotel in Bowling Green. It was interesting having him tell me about his family and Uncle Ed* [Moseley].

I was out on the street for breakfast by 7 am. It is a town of 8,000, and whomever I talked to knew Uncle Ed, 'Old Pete.' Some had tears in their eyes telling me of his kindness to them. An elderly man I had met on the plane told me to say 'hello' to his cousin who sells Mercury cars. I did, and he offered to drive me wherever I wanted to go. We went to a nursery where I got $12 worth of white carnations to make a long lei from all of us, Mother's children. I also got a bouquet from Lillian.

Next I purchased and sent you all the local papers and talked long to Mr. [Ivan] *Lake who wrote the obituary* [for the *Daily-Sentinel Tribune*].[7] *He said Uncle Ed was always very fussy about accuracy but preferred him, Mr. Lake, to any other newspaper man. I was quite moved talking to him.*

Then there was a[n] *hour's visit with Mrs.* [Katherine] *Crowley who is an invalid. She is jolly. Her family has always called Uncle Ed one of her 'boy friends.' She has had him for Christmas dinners, and often for family dinners. He has taken his monographs to her. She said, 'why?' He said, 'Well, you have average intelligence; I want you to read them.' She was a Phi Beta Kappa. She said* [Moseley] *never failed to make his dinner call within a week after being invited.*

I phoned President Prout of the 'U' from there. He said, 'Come right over.' I found Cousin Charlie Chubb there from Pittsburgh,... Mr. Crowley, and the President's right hand man, Mr. [F. Eugene] *Beatty. We sat around the Pres.'s desk, and quickly came to the subject of Uncle Ed's affairs. The Pres. said, 'Lawyer* [Shadwick W.] *Bowman phoned me yesterday to say that he had helped Dr. Moseley make a will not long ago [in 1944]. Of course it would not be very suitable to go into the matter before Dr. Moseley is buried, and we do not know what is in the will.'*

Charlie Chubb reached into his inner coat pocket and said, 'It will be necessary for me to leave immediately after the burial. I have called on the lawyer and have a copy of the will with me.'

We all gasped a little and then he said, 'Cousin Ed has left all that he has to you, Pres. Prout, and your successors to be used in giving financial aid to needy and worthy students.'

I think I said, 'That is what we expected, and we are very sure that it was the most ideal thing to happen.' Then turning to Cousin Charlie I said, 'Do you know what his estate amounts to?' (Uncle Ed owned just one suit of clothes which I had mended in Dayton last month—but which was so tattered and worn that they had to buy him a new suit to bury him in).

Cousin Charlie answered, 'I don't know the maximum but the minimum is at least $50,000.00' Pres. Prout said, 'My very next project is to get a quarter of a million from the state for a building to house Dr. Moseley's collection, to be called after him. Of course, we shall want a room with some of his personal things in it, but if there are any little mementos which you think of [that you want], *you must feel free to ask for them.' Cousin Charlie and I felt we would like some or a memento* [for] *all of us.*

Pres. Prout's correspondence with me, these past weeks, has been as though he were dealing with a vulture. When he discovered that there were no vultures around, there was nothing too good for us two, who represented the family.

There was a fancy luncheon served. In the midst of it he unearthed a letter of May 29th 1948 (This is for your attention, May.) written to Uncle Ed about a lot in Florida which can be sold now for $1125.00, I think—he can't wait to hear from you about the jointly owned property, etc.

At the funeral in the Young Funeral Home, there was a simple service. Then in great state the slow procession of cars followed the hearse through the campus, stopping traffic and saluting policemen, amplified organ music sounding from the chapel tower, and [then] *over to a grave yard lot next to a row of cedar trees.*

[Because of storms] I had not been able to obtain a flight home and was facing a nine-hour grind on the bus, but President Prout sent me as far as Dayton on a University plane, a Cessna 3 seater. More storms and rough weather followed, and then a long wait in Cincinnati, but home at last to exams and more exams. . .student's wedding to play for, and just not home long enough this week to catch my breath. . . .

Chapter 15 • Illness, Death, and Funeral

In some part of the conversation with Pres. Prout and Charlie Chubb I told them how disappointed we had been that Uncle Ed had not helped mother [Professor Moseley's sister Clara] *realize some benefit from the Florida property. Mrs. Crowley said the town gossip was that he owned $75,000 worth of lots there now. How it had been consumed by unpaid taxes, Prout told of a time when Uncle Ed had not heeded his (Pres. Prout's) urgent advice and had lost $30,000 in a bad investment.*

You must all see a copy of the will. Charlie Chubb will see to that. He wants to know more about his genealogy, Lillian–Are there any copies of all that Auntie Bell unearthed? The Bowling Green Sentinel now has the proper names of all of us, Uncle Ed's nieces and nephews. I wish you all could have been there too—to pay him tribute. It was a privilege, and you would have been proud and touched....

Pearl

Prior to the funeral service, an unusual tribute was paid to Moseley, as appropriate organ music was amplified throughout the city from the bell tower on the campus of Bowling Green State University.[8] The service, held Tuesday afternoon 8 June at 2:00 p.m. in the Young Memorial, was conducted by the Rev. Hollis Hayward, director of the Student Christian Fellowship and the Rev. Lyle Loomis, pastor of Trilby Methodist Church. Serving as pallbearers were faculty members Daniel J. Crowley, William C. Jordan, Clare S. Martin, James R. Overman, Claude D. Perry, and John Schwarz. Burial was in Oak Grove Cemetery adjacent to the campus.

In the above letter, Mrs. Ideler identified Ivan Lake, Moseley's close campus friend, as the author of the obituary on the front page of the *Daily-Sentinel Tribune*. With a few editorial changes, Lake eulogized Moseley in these words:[7]

> Time in its relentless progress through the ages today has taken from this community a figure whose scientific contributions to the world's progress will forever be his own memorial. Much of his legend is written in the countless little personal experiences that his thousands of students enjoyed while sitting at his feet, drinking of wisdom from his superior mind. Without a doubt he was one of the most colorful individuals who has ever taught in the halls of any campus. Definitely no student had a complete Bowling Green education..., if he missed taking at least one course under this sage of science who was so demanding in his requirements from his classes, yet was so sympathetic toward those who were evidently making a very sincere effort to learn. He was ever the researcher, the scientist, and the teacher. Moseley was extremely accomodating to those who sought the truth and went at great length to aid them in finding the truth.

References

1. 1948. Anonymous. "Dr. E. L. Moseley is ill in Dayton." *Daily Sentinel-Tribune*, Bowling Green, 3 May, p. 1.

2. 1948. Anonymous. "Bowling Green Scientist's condition reported better. Dr. E. L. Moseley, noted for long-range weather forecasts, is ill in Dayton." [May 4, from an unidentified newspaper clipping in the Paul Jones file of obituaries and related articles; Niederhofer Collection].

3. 1948. Anonymous. "E. L. Moseley, noted for weather forecasts, dies." *Dayton Daily News*, 7 June.

4. 1948. Frank J. Prout. [Memo to faculty that Moseley was brought by ambulance to University Hospital on the BGSU campus]. Typewritten, 1 p. Archives, Bowling Green State University.

5. 1948. Anonymous. "Dr. Moseley, 83, dies and services at Bowling Green," *Sandusky Register Star-News*, 7 June, pp. 1, 10.

6. 1948. [Paul W. Jones]. "Dr. Edwin Moseley, BG[S]U scientist dies; acclaim won for system of predicting periods of floods, drought." *Toledo Times*, 7 June, p. 1.2.

7. 1948. [Ivan E. Lake]. "Dr. Moseley, eminent B.G.U. scientist, dies....;" "Dr. E. L. Moseley's life one of great achievements...." *Daily Sentinel-Tribune*, Bowling Green, Ohio. 7 June, p. 1; p. 2.

8. 1948. [Paul W. Jones]. "Amplify organ music during Moseley rites." *Sandusky Register Star-News,* 8 June, p. 1; "Music is tribute as Dr. Moseley is laid to rest." *Daily Sentinel-Tribune*, Bowling Green, 9 June, p. 1.

9. 1948. Frank J. Prout. "Tribute to Dr. Moseley." *Bowling Green State University Alumni Magazine* 7(4): 2 June.

10. 1948. Mrs. Pearl Ideler. Letter to Family, 9 June 1948. Archives, Bowling Green State University.

11. 1959. Frank J. Prout. "The inquiring mind of Mr. Moseley," *Bowling Green State University Magazine* 4(4): 16-20.

Moseley resting during field excursion.

(Mrs. Ruby G. Engle, Gibsonburg, Ohio; Niederhofer Collection)

Estate Trust Fund of Benefit to Students

Relda E. Niederhofer

The last will and testament of Professor Edwin Lincoln Moseley, made 5 September 1944 in the presence of attorneys Shadwick W. Bowman and Lelan S. Middleton, was filed 9 June 1948, at the office of Wood County Probate Judge, The Honorable Raymond E. Ladd. All debts were directed to be paid, and the remaining property, real and personal, bequeathed to Frank J. Prout, President of the University, in trust for the creation of a scholarship fund estimated to be between $50,000 and $100,000.[9,10,11,12]

Moseley wrote six wills between 1922 and 1944. All of them, except one, are dated as follows: 1922, 1936, 1938, 1941, and 1944. Apparently, the one undated will was prepared between 1922 and 1936. It was written on an examination book, referred to as a "blue book," with the title, "Bowling Green State Normal College," the original name of the school between 1914 and 1929.[13] Moseley inscribed his address on the undated will as "201 N. Maple St., Bowling Green." The Bowling Green city directories listed his residence as 201 N. Maple in 1928, and 122 N. Enterprise in 1930.[5,6] The city directory was not published in 1933, but the college directory for that year listed his residence as 428 N. Prospect.[7] This information narrows the time range from 1922 to about 1929.

The first will of 21 June 1922 was written probably while Moseley was en route to the Hawaiian Islands to visit his only living sister, Mrs. Clara (Moseley) Sutherland of Honolulu.[4] His opening statement indicates his anxiety about the trip. "In case any accident should prevent my returning alive to Ohio, this is a statement of my desire as to the disposal of my estate." Clara was mentioned first in the will as the recipient of his stock in the Diamond Fertilizer Company in Sandusky.

In the 1938 will, no mention is made of the Fertilizer Company's stock, but he bequeathed his half-interest in a Florida property to his sister Clara, if she outlived him. They had inherited this property jointly from an older brother, William A. Moseley, Jr. Clara's death in 1941 eliminated her from subsequent wills.[14] The only other relative mentioned in the wills was his cousin, Charles F. Chubb of Pittsburgh, Pennsylvania, named as the executor in the 1936 will.

The one theme repeated in all of the wills is his desire to establish a trust fund that would be used to assist needy and worthy students toward obtaining a liberal education. In 1922 he restricted the financial assistance to graduates of Sandusky High School. This desire was probably to honor his former school of 25 years. The undated will indicates, in exceptional cases, aid might be given to students still in high school. By 1941, he wrote that aid should go to students who had already completed as many as two years of college work at Bowling Green State University. College freshmen were not excluded from the list of recipients if they needed aid. His last will in 1944 indicated financial aid could be used for those who did not necessarily continue their studies at Bowling Green State University, but who attended other universities.

Moseley wrote that the beneficiaries should be selected not only on the basis of scholarship, but also on the basis of character. Three wills: the undated one, 1941, and 1944, described in detail desirable and undesirable traits to be used as guidelines for selecting worthy students. The undated will had the most complete list of traits, some of which were crossed out and rearranged as if they were being ranked, perhaps from the most important to the least important. Listed in this order of importance, they were: common sense, altruism, originality, ambition, self-control, amiability, industry, perseverance, self-reliance, carefulness, and thrift. Moseley indicated the student should be outstanding in a majority of these virtues and not merely high in two or three of them. No financial aid was to be given for a student who was dishonest, deceitful, quarrelsome, indolent, or extravagant. In 1941, he wrote, "In selecting promising students I believe that the following traits are well worth considering: honesty, dependability, altruism, self-control, freedom from bad habits, intelligence, originality, industry, perseverance, and good sense." In the last will of 1944, Moseley noted that the beneficiaries could be of any race, sex, or creed. He also modified the good and bad characteristics stating briefly that honesty, dependability, self-control, good sense, and especially altruism were important for those who were to receive aid. The following, he considered as insuperable obstacles to success: selfishness, quick temper, indolence, extravagance, poor health, and habitual use of tobacco, alcoholic beverages, or habit-forming drugs.

Moseley's inclusion of tobacco, alcohol, and habit-forming drugs as bad characteristics came from his childhood training. His father, William A. Moseley, Sr., held very strong beliefs about prohibition. William wrote articles and gave speeches about the evils of drinking and smoking.[2] Probably many of the residents of Union City, Michigan believed the same about prohibition, because the newspaper account of Moseley's 1880 high school graduating class bragged: ". . .not one member of the class uses tobacco in any form or drinks malt or alcoholic beverages."[1] Moseley's 1936 will referred to the same topic.

While traveling on the Northern Pacific train en route from St. Paul, Minnesota, to Mandan, North Dakota on 9 August 1936, Moseley composed a will concerned with promoting scientific research pertaining to human nutrition. His greatest concern was the effects of stimulants, narcotics, condiments, beverages, and insufficient or irregular sleep have on one's health. He believed the greatest good could be accomplished by promoting scientific research into how these habits affected good health.

The 1938 will contained the only reference to his natural history museum. The will was written 26 July 1938 about three weeks after he had moved more than 10,000 specimens to Bowling Green from their five-year storage in the Sandusky High School attic.[8] The Sandusky Board of Education had to store the museum items in 1933 to provide more classroom space for students. Probably the driving force to write this will was the anticipation that Bowling Green State University would accept his museum. He indicated that the more than 10,000 specimens should become the property of the University, as well as his books, pamphlets, and magazines.

Moseley wanted to have some control over those who would select the beneficiaries of his trust. In the first will of 1922 he proposed an all Sandusky High School Committee composed of the principal, Frank J. Prout, and three teachers. A separate, undated will suggested making the trustees of the fund distinct from those who would select the beneficiaries. The committee would consist of the high school principal and one or two teachers. Questions on which the committee could not agree were to be settled by the president of the Board of Education. Moseley's last will and testament named Frank J. Prout, President of Bowling Green State University, as the trustee of his scholarship fund. President Prout, with the approval of the Board of Trustees, was to use the fund to benefit worthy students who needed financial assistance. Moseley again suggested that President Prout might appoint a committee of the faculty to assist him in the selection of students. He said ". . .this committee shall not be required as long as the trustee is the President of the University. However, should it happen that the trustee is not the President of the University, then the Committee of not less than three shall be obligatory, and no payments shall be granted by the Board of Trustees without recommendation of the Committee."[3] Acting as Moseley's trustee, Prout took a great deal of pride in managing the trust fund. Funds both large and small were given. One gift as small as 50 cents was rumored to have been administered by this President.

Moseley certainly did not accumulate a fortune large enough to be given to the University as a trust fund on only a teacher's salary. Very early in his career he realized the need to invest his money in real estate as well as in stocks and bonds. At the time of his death Moseley owned a total of 741 shares in companies such as: E. I. DuPont DeNemours & Co., Standard Oil Company, Union Carbide and Carbon Corp., Davis and Company, General Motors Corp., Goodyear Tire and Rubber Company, etc. During his career he owned a property in the city of Sandusky; two farms in Webster Township, Wood County, Ohio; a farm in the Parish of West Carroll, Louisiana, with 500-600 cattle and some hogs; and the Florida property he had inherited jointly with his sister, Clara. He had the good advice of his cousin, Charles Chubb, a banker in Pittsburgh, Pennsylvania, to help him make wise investments.[9]

In the disposition of the will, the Court said the principle could not be invested in the stock market, the result being that little growth occurred in the fund. In 1973 the Internal Revenue Service set two definitions of a foundation: the private and the public. As a private foundation the Moseley Scholarship Fund was subjected to 4% excise tax, and accordingly in December 1973, all of the assets were changed from private to public. This merger of the Moseley Scholarship Fund with the Bowling Green State University Foundation, provided for the fund to be no longer under the 4% excise tax. In the Bowling Green State University Foundation the "corpus" was not used but accumulated interest. The estimated value of the Moseley Scholarship Fund as of 1996 was $322,605.[15]

The will states that awards are to be given to worthy students at the discretion of the University President. The current president, Dr. Sidney A. Ribeau, has delegated the responsibility to the Director of Financial Aid, Mr. Conrad McRoberts. Morally, the University is obligated to follow the guidelines of the will.[15] Since 1990, nineteen students have received a total of $19,580 from the Moseley Scholarship Fund. Ten different student awards were given in the school year 1995-1996 for a collective sum of $7,279.[15]

References

1. 1880. Anonymous. "The orations," *Union City Register*, Union City, Michigan, 10 July 1880.

2. 1892. Wm. A. Moseley. *How to save the nation.* Leaflet published for the author, Union City, Michigan, 4 February. Archives, Bowling Green State University. 1 p.

3. 1922. Edwin L. Moseley. Six wills (1922, 1936, 1938, 1941, 1944, and the undated will) are in Folder 3, Box 4, Edwin L. Moseley File, Archives, Bowling Green State University.

4. 1923. Anonymous. "Seventy-first annual report of the Hawaiian Children's Society," Published by Hawaiian Mission, Honolulu, Hawaii.

5. 1928. Anonymous. *Bowling Green* [City] *Directory*, Bowling Green, Ohio, 1928, p., 109.

6. 1930. Anonymous. *Bowling Green* [City] *Directory*, Bowling Green, Ohio, 1930, p., 110.

7. 1933. Anonymous. *Bee Gee State College, Handbook—Directory 1933-34*. Published by Y.M.C.A., Bowling Green, Ohio, 1933, p. 25.

8. 1938 Anonymous, "Professor Moseley's museum moved to [Bowling Green State] University," *Sandusky Star-Journal*, 2 July 1938, p. 1.

9. 1948. Anonymous. List of Securities received of Bowman, Hanna, and Middleton, 8 June 1948, Folder 4 and 19, Box 2, Edwin L. Moseley File, Archives, Bowling Green State University.

Chapter 16 • Estate Trust Fund of Benefit to Students

10. 1948. Anonymous. "Dr. Moseley wills his estate to aid worthy students." *Daily Sentinel-Tribune*, Bowling Green, 9 June 1948, pp. 1,2.

11. 1948. Anonymous. "Moseley estate will benefit worthy students: Bowling Green State University President named trustee in will." *Toledo Blade*, 10 June 1948, p. 1.

12. 1948. Anonymous. "$100,000 for scholars: Moseley will sets up student trust fund," *Toledo Times*, 10 June 1948, p. 48.

13. 1983. Greg Hadley. "Opened in 1914: University changes over years," *BG News*, 17 February 1983, p. 1, 6.

14. 1983 (procured). Without Date. William Augustus Moseley. [Family list for Genealogical Collection]. Hawaiian Mission Children's Society Library, Mission Houses Museum, Honolulu, Hawaii.

15. 1996. Carl Peschel. Bowling Green Alumni House, Personal Communication with Relda Niederhofer, 15 April 1996.

The Will of Edwin Lincoln Moseley
[5 September 1944]

Be it known that I, Edwin L. Moseley, of Bowling Green, Ohio, do make and declare this my last will.[10]

Item 1. I direct that my debts, if any there be, be first paid from my estate.

Item 2. I give, devise and bequeath all my property, both real and personal and wheresoever situated, to Frank J. Prout, who is now President of Bowling Green State University, in trust, however, for the uses and purposes hereinafter fully set forth.

Item 3. I will and direct that a trust so created of my estate under the administration of the above named trustee, for the benefit of worthy students who need financial assistance.

I direct that the funds of said trust be paid out only on the recommendation of the trustee, with the approval of the Board of Trustees of the Bowling Green State University, by proper action to be shown on the minutes of said Board.

My said trustee may appoint a committee of the faculty to assist him in the choosing of such students as may need assistance, but this committee shall not be required so long as the trustee is the President of the University. However, should it happen that the trustee is not the President of the University, then the Committee of not less than three shall be obligatory, and no payments shall be granted by the Board of Trustees without recommendation of the Committee.

Item 4. The Trustee and the Board of Trustees of the University may decide and follow their judgment as to whether or not the income of the trust only shall be used in carrying out the purpose of the trust or whether a portion of the principal shall be expended; or whether or not assistance shall be by way of gift or loan with repayment to the trust fund. Having full faith in my Trustee and the Board, I leave these matters for them to decide.

Item 5. Those who receive financial aid for this fund need not necessarily continue their studies at Bowling Green, but may go elsewhere, if the faculty committee or officers in charge believe they would make as much or more progress elsewhere. This applies both to graduate and undergraduate study.

Item 6. In selecting beneficiaries, race, sex, or creed should not be an obstacle.

Item 7. While freshmen may not be excluded, it seems desirable as a rule to supply financial aid only to those who have been long enough in attendance at the University for several of the faculty to have learned their capabilities, their characteristics, and their needs.

Item 8. I desire to give some of my notions as to who may qualify for aid from this fund. This may be of some aid to my Trustee and his committee.

Some of the men who have rendered great service to mankind had little schooling and some never read very many books. Reflection, understanding, originality, perseverance, may be as important as getting high grades in examination. Yet those who are not well informed are unlikely to contribute much to human progress.

It is a question whether most good could be attained by limiting financial aid from a university to those students who are among the highest in scholarship. Probably most of the beneficiaries should be selected from those who have high scholarship.

While the following may not be insuperable obstacles to success, the testator regards them as objectionable: selfishness, quick temper, indolence, extravagance, poor health, habitual use of tobacco, alcoholic beverages, or habit-forming drugs.

Important in those who are to receive aid are: honesty, dependability, self-control, good sense, and especially altruism, or a desire to be of service to others.

Prominent among those who have been most useful to their fellow men were: statesmen, judges, authors, editors, lecturers, doctors, engineers, scientists, inventors. The student who is to receive financial aid need not necessarily aspire to be any of those, but he should endeavor to acquire a liberal education and not merely one that is technical.

Chapter 16 • Estate Trust Fund of Benefit to Students

Item 9. In case of the death, resignation or refusal of my Trustee, Frank J. Prout, then I direct that the then President of Bowling Green State University be appointed in his stead; and I direct that if the trust is not exhausted, the President of the University shall function as trustee so long as he can or will act; but in case the President cannot or will not act, the Probate Judge of Wood County shall fill the vacancy, and in that event, I direct that the person appointed be experienced in educational activities.

Item 10. Should Bowling Green State University cease to function as an educational institution before this fund to aid needy students has been exhausted, then the officers or committee who have been administering it, and in that event, the Probate Court shall appoint the President of such designated institution as trustee, and said Trustee shall continue in the same manner and form as designated above.

Item 11. I authorize and empower my trustee to sell at public or private sale any or all of my property and execute and deliver deed or deeds or other instruments of conveyance therefore; to invest and reinvest the funds of the trust; to rent real estate; to make repairs and improvements; and finally to do any and all acts that may be necessary or proper to carry out said trust and keep it earning to the best advantage in his judgment.

I especially want it understood that his acts do not need the approval of the Board of Trustees, except only when extending aid to worthy students.

Item 12. I nominate Frank J. Prout to be the Executor, also, of this Will, with full power to settle and adjust all claims due to or from my estate, and I direct him to administer the estate promptly and then turn all remaining property and assets over to my trustee of the trust created by this Will.

In the case of his death before my decease, or his failure to qualify, then I direct the Court to appoint, following my direction in the appointment of the trustee above.

In witness whereof, I have hereunto subscribed by name at Bowling Green, Ohio, this fifth day of September, in the year nineteen hundred forty-four (1944).

EDWIN L. MOSELEY

Signed by the said Edwin L. Moseley and by him acknowledged to be his last will and testament in our presence, sight and hearing, who at his request have hereunto subscribed our names as witnesses in his presence and in the presence of each other, this fifth day of September, nineteen hundred and forty-four (1944).

S[hadwick]. W. Bowman
Bowling Green, Ohio

Lelan S. Middleton
Bowling Green, Ohio

Commentary on Moseley's Will by *Sentinel* Editor Canary

Spencer A. Canary, editor of the *Daily Sentinel-Tribune* (10 June 1948, p. 4) in Bowling Green, wrote an article describing the rich legacy of Moseley's will. Most of the article repeats phrases from the will, but he expressed his opinion in this statement.

> . . .[The will] directs the continued implementing of the altruism which he [Moseley] felt and practiced in life. By his will, . . . he leaves his entire estate in trust for the future use of deserving students who may need financial assistance.
>
> And his prudence in finances led him to provide for contingences that might arise to thwart the purposes of his gift or give rise to legal misunderstandings. Simple and plain in his language as an author, he was explicit and clear in his will.
>
> The fullest latitude is given his trustee and advisors as to the beneficiaries of his legacy; but, in suggesting qualifications, he discloses the philosophy which guided him in his long life. He makes these suggestions as part of his will, . . . for they are a challenge to young people as to character.

Moseley holding hornets nest, near Wilmington, Ohio.

(Taken by Kelley Hale, two hours before Moseley was stricken with his final illness, 28 April 1948; published in the *Bowling Green State University Alumni Magazine* 7(4): front page. 1948, June; Archives, BGSU)

Tributes From Former Students

CHAPTER SEVENTEEN

These four tributes to Professor Edwin Lincoln Moseley were written by former students of his time. Published, but in somewhat non-readily available sources, they are reprinted here to preserve accounts recalling Moseley as a noteworthy teacher-naturalist. He was their teacher whom they came to know and appreciated many years later.

I. My Greatest Teacher

Donald M. Love [1971]

The greatest teacher of my high school days, and perhaps of my life, was an old-fashioned natural scientist to whom all nature was an open book. The method he used was so simple that one wonders that it has not been more generally imitated. It was based on minute observation and multiple comparisons. We were taught to attend to the smallest details in examining any natural object, to look and look, to photograph the object on the mind's eye, and if it made any sound, to phonograph it in the mind's ear. Again and again, by repeated experience coming at the plant or animal, the rock or the distant star from as many different angles as possible, we were encouraged to know it, and then to compare it with its neighbors until we could identify it unmistakably. Time after time, I have heard the teacher try one simile after another to make clear some scientific fact or relationship—seeking always to find a medium of comparison which would touch the mind of every pupil in the class: "as far as from here to the New York Central Station," "as far as from the Cedar Point dock across to Johnson's Island," "as high as the steeple of St. Mary's Church," and so on and on until the dullest and least interested would feel some reluctant stretching of the mind, and some realization of the nature of the material being presented.

Vivid and impressive as these class sessions were, they drop into second place in my memory when I recall the experience of the field trips to the ravine of Old Woman's Creek in Berlin Heights, or to one of the Lake Erie Islands. If it was to be an island trip, we were up and away early in the morning on the steamer *Frank E. Kirby*, the so-called "Flier of the Lakes," to Put-in-Bay, or Kelley's Island, there to tramp over as much territory as we could cover to see the glacial grooves, the strontium caves, the eagles' nest, the Indian inscription rock, and the fossils imbedded in the limestone. The smell of red cedar still takes me back to a whittling from the root of a decayed stump on Kelley's Island, cut to prove the enduring fragrance of that useful wood. While we stooped to examine some unusual herb, we would be asked to identify a bird call in a neighboring thicket. It was a full day, with first-hand instruction in botany, zoology, dendrology, ornithology, geology, and if we came home on the night run of the Steamer *Arrow*, an astronomy lesson occurred over the placid waters of Sandusky Bay. These are unforgettable experiences.

Years later, I went with this really great teacher and investigator on a daylong expedition south of Norwalk, Ohio, to trace the outline of a pre-glacial valley by ascertaining the depth of farm wells. Measurement of these wells, and a tabulation of distances to the underlying rock, gave a surprising revelation of the buried valley. Similar investigations which he conducted in Sandusky Bay proved the existence of a pre-glacial valley extending the length of the Bay, filled with silt which could be dredged. This discovery removed the chief obstacle to the development of a great inland harbor hitherto thought impossible because of shallow depth and a limestone floor. I can only mention other research projects in the pursuit of which this scientist served the days he could not see. A study of the annual rings of trees made possible the prediction of weather cycles. An analysis of the basic ground structure of the Cedar Point Peninsula explained its successful resistance to the destructive erosion along the other portions of the south shore of Lake Erie. Patient experiments with various floating materials and finally with dyes, proved the connection between the underground stream at Bellevue, Ohio, and the great springs at Castalia. Careful searching in a woodlot pasture south of Sandusky revealed the white snakeroot which had contaminated the milk of cows which fed upon it and had caused undulant fever [milk sickness]. To have known such a reader of the "Book of Nature," and to have seen at first hand some of his work, was in itself an educational experience.

II. A Great Man

R. E. Dillery [1960]

It was with a great deal of interest that I read the speech of Dr. Frank J. Prout on the presentation of the plaque honoring Professor Edwin Lincoln Moseley (see Chapter 4, page 29). I knew Moseley as a teacher for two years and followed his writings with interest over a period of years.

While Prout covered the years at Sandusky with vigor, I do not believe that any one man could cover the great good done by Moseley and for that reason as a man now and as a boy then (1915-1917) I would like to set forth in my humble way a further tribute to that very great man, Moseley.

One of my greatest memories I have of Moseley is of the afternoon when word came that a family living north of Bowling Green had all been taken ill with milk sickness. I met Moseley in the hall of the Science Building and he asked me if I would care to make a trip with him out to the farm, as he wanted to post a cow. Eager to make the trip, I walked with him out to the farm.

I do not remember the farmer's name, but I can see the inside of the barn now and recall how Moseley, after stating who he was, asked to see the cow herd. The man in charge of the farm stated that all the cows were out in the cow lot except one that was sick in the stall. Opening the stall door, Moseley said that this cow was the cow for which he was looking. The cow stood with her head down and was trembling all over.

Having lived in the South, where I saw the effects of malaria and chills, I exclaimed that she had the "buck ague" and Moseley chuckled. He told the farmer that the cow would be dead in a few minutes and he should like to post her. This was agreeable to the man. We sat down to await her death, and Moseley stated that he was certain that we would find a piece of white snakeroot in her rumen.

In about 30 minutes the cow fell over dead and Moseley went to work, while I held a lantern. In a short time Moseley said, "Here it is; look at it." He then explained that the cow, in eating the top of the weed, pulled up the root and it went down with the top. That was the culprit.

On the way home Moseley talked about other things and said, "Dillery, always remember that you can train any animal, but man alone has to be educated. I can train a monkey to pick up a ball or a dog to bring a stick, but man alone can initiate reasoning." As we walked along, he drew a distinction between training and education and I would give almost anything to have that conversation recorded for future teachers. The years that I attended Bowling Green State Normal Collrge I have counted as my most important ones, not so much because of the book material learned, but because of the application of reasoning mostly absorbed from teachers such as Moseley, Holt, Beattie, Cummins, Walker, Biery, and many others. Long may their memory live, for I feel sure that all who were in their classes have hailed their greatness many times.

III. Friend, Teacher, and Naturalist

Seymour Van Gundy [1951]

As I travel the halls of Bowling Green State University, I am daily reminded of a true and dear friend, Professor Edwin Lincoln Moseley. In the Science Building, which has been rededicated, Moseley Hall, there hangs at my left an almost life-sized oil painting of Moseley in appropriate setting. Opposite this painting is a large bronze plate upon which is pictured a full length profile of Moseley beside a tree trunk. At the side is printed this epitaph:

Edwin Lincoln Moseley

Born, March 29, 1865—Died, June 6, 1948

"The most beneficent gift of Science lies in the genius of the Naturalist; it is he who unlocks the secrets of forest and plain, of stream and mountain."

The gift of Addie E. Bettes

The yearbook of the University for 1949 is dedicated to Moseley. It reproduces a very good likeness of him with these words beneath: "34 years of service."

Throughout the building are located cases of Moseley's collections including innumerable specimens ranging from our largest mounted animals to the smallest shells. Some come from ages past, others from our most modern times. One of his most treasured collections was a few passenger pigeon feathers which he had secured from a feather tick composed entirely of these feathers.

Moseley often came to our home varying his stay from several days up to two weeks. Together we spent many hours in the Oak Openings. On one occasion we started quite early in the cool morning. While driving on Route 295 I called his attention to a snake killed on the highway. We proceeded about a quarter of a mile past the snake when his apparent interest prompted me to ask if he would like to go back and take a closer look. The snake was but recently killed and not badly mutilated, so he decided to take it. It was a very hot day and I had no refrigeration facilities along, but he made no particular comments about the snake except concerning the problem of preserving it. Upon returning home he said that it was probably the greatest find of the day. The next time I heard of it was in "a write up" in the local papers stating that Moseley had found the largest hog-nosed snake recorded by any museum.

Moseley was an authority on all plant life, being especially interested in the panic grasses and sedges, often spending many hours identifying and looking for new species. He was very exacting in his identifications never depending upon his own judgement but relying only upon recognized authority. Through his teachings I enjoyed the thrill of finding new and unusual plants and animals.

Moseley's hearing was very keen. One spring morning after a short trip through the woods, he said, "I heard a red-bellied woodpecker, but I was unable to locate it." The next day after he had gone home, I identified three in the general vicinity in which he had heard them. The spring bird census was very important to him. I could always look forward to some profitable trips during spring bird migrations. These trips might include a variety of interests besides looking for birds or plants. He enjoyed meeting other people and especially older folks who knew facts of the earlier days. In fact, I do not know of anything which he did not like to know more about.

When not actively engaged, Moseley wrote letters, made notes or read. He never missed reading a *Reader's Digest* from cover to cover and always read a condensed news magazine. Issues of the *Toledo Naturalists Association, Annual Bulletin* in my library were always a constant source of interest to him. He followed World War II very closely and often commented on the radio "news cast" for many of the places mentioned were familiar to him, even in the Far East.

Moseley enjoyed music and liked nothing better than to spend an evening listening to his favorite compositions. He also enjoyed good food or unusual dishes. My mother cooked a variety of mushrooms at one time which he had gathered on a trip. He remarked that there were some in the group which he was not sure were edible, but, at least, they would not be too poisonous. He was not a fadist. He ate a natural diet with such a variety that he was assured of all essentials of life. He grew old in years, but not in spirit.

Although I did not have the privilege of knowing him in the classroom, Moseley was my greatest teacher. Even while quite small, I enjoyed these trips and the patience with which he taught me shall always be remembered.

IV. No Fear of Bald-Faced Hornets

Richard S. Phillips [1982]

Years ago I was working on a master's degree at Bowling Green State University. At that time, Professor Edwin Lincoln Moseley, a nationally known biologist, had just retired from the faculty of that institution. A man of Moseley's standing does not retire; he just changes from his regular job to the work he has put off for years. Although I never had him as a professor, we became well acquainted in a short time because of our mutual interest in birds. He was writing a lengthy paper on the successful introduction of the ring-necked pheasant in northwestern Ohio. His notes on the birds in Hancock County were a little light, so he used information that I had collected concerning hatching dates and clutch size.

Later I wrote a paper on the golden plover in northern Ohio. My notes for some areas were skimpy. Moseley allowed me to use the information concerning this species that he had collected.

received the Ph.D. in plant pathology (1957). At that time he was appointed as an assistant nematologist at the Citrus Agricultural Experiment Station of the University of California, Riverside. His entire career was there, serving as professor of nematology, dean of research, assistant vice chancellor for research, chairman of the Department of Nematology, and dean of the College of Natural and Agricultural Sciences, and professor emeritus of nematology (1993). Van Gundy was an early recipient of the Moseley Scholarship Fund, and during his research career, he was awarded grants from the University of California, the Rockefeller Foundation, the National Science Foundation, and the United States Department of Agriculture.

Richard S. Phillips (1913-1993), local, well-known ornithologist and interpreter of nature, wrote nearly 1,700 articles for a regular column, "In Nature's Realm" that appeared weekly for over 41 years in the *Courier*, the newspaper of Findlay, Ohio. Born 29 November 1913 in Cygnet, Wood County, Ohio, he received a B. A. from Findlay College and a M. S. and M. A. from Bowling Green State University. For over 30 years Phillips taught general science and biology in the high schools in Cygnet and Findlay, and then for a brief period at Findlay College. As an author of three books, two on birds and one on woody plants, all pertaining to Hancock County, as well as other nature articles in national magazines, he was considered the local revered authority on these and other topics. Among his awards for these achievements and service were: Outstanding Classroom Teacher in Ohio (1960), Outstanding Classroom Teacher of Biology in Ohio (1966), honorary degree of Doctor of Humane Letters from Findlay College (1977), and the Civitan International Conservation Award (1980). At an age of nearly 80, Richard S. Phillips died 2 November 1993 in Findlay and was buried in the Knollcrest Cemetery east of the town.

CHAPTER 17 • TRIBUTES FROM FORMER STUDENTS

Biographical Sketches

Donald M. Love (1894-1974), educator, historian, and administrator, held more administrative positions than any other individual during 36 years at Oberlin College, Lorain County, Ohio. Born 15 September 1894 south of Sandusky in Bloomingville, Erie County, Ohio, he graduated from Sandusky High School (1912) and from Oberlin College (1916) with a B. A. in economics and as an elected member to Phi Beta Kappa. Love also studied at Middleburg College and at Harvard University. His career developed as a teacher of mathematics, history, economics, and English in high school in St. Charles, Illinois, and in Alliance and Youngstown, Ohio, before returning to Oberlin College (1926). There he was appointed as an assistant dean and professor of literature, and served the College further as acting dean, dean, registrar, secretary, and acting president (1959). As the College secretary (1938-1962), he performed his work at a level rarely seen in the educational world, as his minutes were works of art as well as faithful statements of the meetings. He wrote the biography of *Henry Churchill King of Oberlin* (1956), the College's sixth president and was very active in the community and its history, being known as "Mr. Oberlin." For his long dedication to Oberlin College, Love was awarded an honorary Doctor of Letters (1960) and the alumni association presented him with its highest honor, the Alumni Medal (1963). At age 80, Donald M. Love died 13 November 1974 in Oberlin.

R. E. Dillery, who lived at Guthrie, Kentucky, at the time his letter was printed by the *University Magazine*, has not been located, resulting in no biographical sketch.

Seymour D. Van Gundy (b. 1931), retired research pathologist and nematologist living in Riverside, California, developed an enthusiasm for learning plants and preserving herbarium specimens while a teenager. Born 24 February 1931 in Toledo, Lucas County, Ohio, he lived on the family farm near Monclova in the same county. Moseley, a special friend of Seymour's parents, made frequent visits to their home, and instilled his enthusiasm for plants to the young Seymour. Together, they studied the flora of the Oak Openings, only a few miles to the west of the Van Gundy farm. Van Gundy graduated with a B. A. in biology from Bowling Green State University (1953), and while there his interest in plants and fungi led to part-time employment at the Crop Research Department of the H. J. Heinz Company. Here he was introduced to plant pathology, which led to a graduate fellowship in the Department of Plant Pathology at the University of Wisconsin, where he

Chapter 17 • Tributes From Former Students

"Don't run Phillips, Don't run! Stand still and they won't bother you," the professor shouted.

I was not about to stand still and give them another shot at me. I ran for 150 feet or so, until I came to a dense stand of pawpaw shrubs. Without slowing a bit, I dashed into the center of the sizeable clump. The large leaves of the little trees seemed to fend off the pursuing hornets. After a 10-minute wait in the center of the pawpaw trees, I retraced my steps to see what had happened to Moseley. The professor was still sitting on the fence just as he had been when I deserted him, absolutely immobile.

He greeted me with, "Phillips, I told you not to run. What is the condition of this nest?"

I informed him that the insects had quieted down and that not a single one was in sight. Moseley slid off the fence, absolutely unscathed, and walked into the woods.

—Modified and edited by RLS from the following sources:

I. 1971. Donald M. Love. "[My greatest teacher]." In "Professor Moseley, item 80," 3 pp. In Charles E. Frohman. *Sandusky's 3rd Dimension*. The Ohio Historical Society, Columbus. 82 pp. (reprinted, 1973. "About the Author," pp. 61-64. In Edwin L. Moseley. *Lake Erie: Floods, Lake Levels, Northeast Storms*: The Formation of Sandusky Bay and Cedar Point. The Ohio Historical Society, Columbus. ii, 64 pp.) (1; reproduced with permissiom of the Ohio Historical Society).

II. 1960. R. E. Dillery. "[A great man]." In "Letters laud Moseley," *Bowling Green State University Magazine,* 5(1): 22. 1960, February.

III. 1951. Seymour Van Gundy. "Dr. Moseley, friend, teacher, and naturalist," *Toledo Naturalists Association, Thirteenth Annual Bulletin*. 1948-1950: 12,13. April.

IV. 1982. Richard S. Phillips. "Professor Moseley didn't fear bald-faced hornets," *Findlay Republican Courier*, Findlay, Ohio. 25 September 1982.

Anyone who knew the professor can attest to the brilliance of the man. As far as I know Moseley was the first person to suspect that bats hunted their insect food by a sort of ultrasound radar. He was also the first man I ever heard of who studied the annual rings in the trunks of very old trees and used their growth rings to predict average rainfall and temperature in the future.

Moseley also solved the mystery surrounding "milk sickness," a disease that killed many people during the last century. He discovered that the condition, which resembled tuberculosis in several of its symptoms, was not caused by a bacterium. Its causative agent was a chemical poison that originated in the plant known as white snakeroot. The agent caused "trembles" in cattle and horses and was transmitted to human beings who drank milk from the affected cattle.

Despite Moseley's obvious brilliance, he never learned how to drive a car. Because of that situation, he often depended on students to drive him to wood lots so that he might measure the rings in freshly cut stumps.

One summer afternoon I was coming down the steps of Moseley Hall, named after the professor, when I met him coming up the steps. He greeted me with, "Phillips, what are you doing this afternoon?"

"I was planning to study, I replied."

"Why don't you take me out to Whitacre's Woods?" he asked. "There are some new stumps out there that I haven't measured yet."

Well, what do you do when a man of his caliber asks you for a five-mile ride. I was dressed for the outdoors, so I was ready to go. Moseley always wore old-fashioned black suits with long frock coats, and that is the way he went to the woods. He looked like a short, thin, undernourished ambassador looking for a banquet to attend. To get into the woods we had to climb an old rail fence. I went over first and waited for him to cross. As the professor sat on the top rail ready to slide off the fence, I heard a hum, like the drone of a distant aeroplane. Suddenly, bald-faced hornets, the bad kind, were whirling about our heads. A quick look at the fence told me that a grapefruit-sized nest of these insects was hanging under the top rail.

One of the enraged hornets got me in the back of the neck, and I took off, running wildly through the woods.

CHAPTER 17 • TRIBUTES FROM FORMER STUDENTS

Students who Assisted Moseley in His Research Projects

As a component to Moseley's teaching methods, he involved his students in original research investigation. Reflecting upon this aspect of his life, in 1941 Moseley wrote [see Chapter 9, page 113]:*

> When I was teaching in the high school at Sandusky, Ohio, nearly a hundred of the boys helped me at one time or another in tracing buried channels under Sandusky Bay and in determining the age of the ridges [on Cedar Point], which had been thrown up by the waves of Lake Erie at times of great northeast storms. Later, when I became interested in an investigation of the cause of Trembles, which had made trouble for many of the older people who were still living in that region, it was natural that my students should assist in that investigation.
>
> After school, November 26, 1905, I walked part way home with Oscar Kubach, one of the younger boys, who lived some four miles south of town. In the woods we gathered some plants of white snakeroot and he took a few of them home to use in an experiment on his tom-cat [1941, p. 47].

Source, Moseley's Publications

Milk Sickness
Alton Fuchs	*Ohio Naturalist* 6(4): 467. 1906.
Oscar Kubach	*Ohio Naturalist* 6(4): 466. 1906.
August E. Guenther, Ph.D.	*Ohio Naturalist* 6(5): 479. 1906; *Medical Record* 75: 844. 1909.
Walter H. Rieger, M.D.	*Medical Record* 75: 843. 1909.
Fred Schoepfle, M.D.	*Medical Record* 75: 843. 1909.
Henry C. Schoepfle, M.D.	*Ohio Naturalist* 6(4): 467. 1906; *Medical Record* 75: 843. 1909.

Exploration of Daussa's Cave
George Feick	*Sandusky Daily-Star*, 22 May 1902, p. 3.
Frank Daniel	

Potato Beetles
Joseph Ehrmann	*Toledo Blade*, 23 December 1930, p. 9.

Bird Population Fluctuations
Henry Graefe, M.D.	*Wilson Bulletin* 42(3): 192-193. 1930.

* 1941. Edwin L. Moseley. *Milk Sickness Caused by White Snakeroot*. Ohio Academy of Science and the Author. 171 pp.

EDWIN LINCOLN MOSELEY L. H. D.
PROFESSOR EMERITUS OF BIOLOGY
CURATOR OF UNIVERSITY MUSEUM
BOWLING GREEN, OHIO

Apr. 1, 1946

Dear Mr. Campbell:

In Nov. 1945 Frank Keef, who has long owned a dairy barn on the western edge of Bowling Green, told me that a Snowy Owl has roosted there in November or part of the winter for a number of years past.

My article on changes in bird population is almost ready for final typing. If you have any comments on the part I sent you or the few unanswered questions I raised, please let me hear from you.

Yours truly,
E. L. Moseley.

(Gift of Louis W. Campbell; Stuckey Collection)

Commentaries by Natural Science Writers

CHAPTER EIGHTEEN

Three writers on natural science of the Toledo area, Louis W. Campbell (1948), Roger Conant (1982), and Harold W. Mayfield (1984) provide the text for this chapter. They either interacted personally with Moseley or knew him in various capacities. Their published contributions comment on his scientific, educational, or other professional accomplishments. The article by Campbell (1948) is reflective and appeared at the time of Moseley's death. The item by Conant (1982) tells of his visits with Moseley and is extracted from a larger work about the lives of selected naturalists in Ohio. The essay by Mayfield (1984) is the most comprehensive published evaluation of Moseley's career at Bowling Green State University, and represents the summation to his biography of the professor.

I. Gone But Not Forgotten

Louis W. Campbell [1948]

Even those who never knew Professor Edwin Lincoln Moseley must marvel at his accomplishments in the field of natural science. In addition to his great work as a teacher, he was constantly occupied with some extracurricular project. He studied the physical geography of Sandusky Bay and the Lake Erie Islands, made a catalogue of the plants of Erie County, wrote school textbooks, compiled bird migration records for the United States Fish and Wildlife Service, . . .and devoted his declining years to meteorological studies based on tree rings. Although this labor was not completed, he left a basis on which future research may be founded.

To the citizens of Lucas County, Moseley's greatest contribution was his "Flora of the Oak Openings." In this pamphlet he drew the attention of naturalists and ultimately all people who love the outdoors to the unique character of the sand country west of Toledo. With painstaking effort which began in 1897 and ended in 1928, Moseley listed the unusual plants which grow in duneland. He compared the area with the rest of the state of Ohio. He told something of the history and formation of the Oak Openings. Personally, I feel this small pamphlet was one of the greatest contributions to natural science ever to come out of northwestern Ohio.

Indeed Moseley has an impressive list of achievements, but those who knew him remember affectionately his personality as well. Above all else, he was characterized by a never-failing zeal and a most enduring humility. He was utterly free from pose or bombast of any kind. And most important, he was a man who could listen. Even the rawest beginner in the study of nature was received with great attention.

Yes, Moseley has left a legacy in the thousands of students to whom he taught the natural sciences at Bowling Green State University. I am constantly meeting people with some knowledge of birds and plants which they acquired under "Pete" Moseley, as he was called. More than any other person in this area, he sowed the seeds of interest in the outdoors.

II. An Eccentric Genius

Roger Conant [1982]

• • •

Professor Edwin Lincoln Moseley was a genius, and like so many of his kind, he was also quite eccentric. First and foremost he was a naturalist, and his store of information about the plants, animals, and physiography of north central Ohio was profound. He really knew his environment. . . .He was a small frail man in his 60's when I knew him, and he was the personification of the absent-minded professor. He was popular with his students, in whom he had inculcated a deep respect for nature, and over the course of the years many of the boys accompanied him in the field while he was making his investigations, the results of most of which had been published long before I was active in Ohio.

• • •

I first met Moseley at a scientific gathering, and I thought it might be interesting and instructive to invite him along on a short field trip. He agreed to go with us, so I picked him up one afternoon and took him to my home, where he was to spend the night. He retired early, but first he ordered his breakfast for the next morning. As I recall it now, it went something like this: A cup of hot water was to be brought to his bedside at 6:00 a.m. The meal was to be served an hour later, and it was to consist of a dish of five prunes, a poached egg, a slice of whole wheat toast, lightly buttered, and a glass of warm milk. Soon after he had closed the door to his room, I left to hunt up a late-hour convenience store, a rarity in those days. Our larder contained neither prunes nor whole wheat bread.

After breakfast, I picked up two young companions, Barney Gardner and David Delzell, and we were off for what we expected to be a pleasant day. It was, except that Moseley progressed at a snail's pace in the field. Seemingly every blade of grass and every insect had to be examined with care, often with lens in hand. We were polite and patient at first, staying close to him and listening to his wisdom, but we soon tired of that. We decided to take turns, and while one of us remained at his side the others were off exploring all nearby places where snakes or lizards might be lurking. Needless to say, we impatient youngsters didn't invite him to go with us again.

Once, when I visited Bowling Green to examine the small collection of preserved reptiles he had assembled there (he also had prepared a similar collection at the Sandusky High School), I invited him to go to lunch with me at a local restaurant. I expected we would sit at an empty table, but he made a beeline for one, from which the dishes used by previous diners had not been cleared. He promptly extracted a bowl of vegetables that hadn't been touched, several sticks of carrots, a pickle, a roll, and all unused butter. That was the nucleus of his lunch. When the waitress arrived to clear our table I looked up at her, probably with a bewildered expression on my face, but she smiled and winked at me. Obviously she was acquainted with Moseley and his idiosyncracies. His penuriousness was known all over the state. He never went anywhere unless he had free transportation, and he never stayed overnight unless someone offered either to invite him to a private home or to pay his hotel bill. Much less well known was the fact that for years he had been in the habit of personally paying the college tuition of some of his more promising students.

III. An Appraisal

Harold F. Mayfield [1984]

The career of Professor Edwin Lincoln Moseley demonstrates how the scientific temperament can persevere without institutional pressure or financial grants. He was one of the leading natural scientists of Ohio in the early decades of this century, although regrettably, the local public still remembers him more for his eccentricities than for his accomplishments. In his lifetime his colleagues viewed him with a mixture of embarrassment and pride, but in the history of Bowling Green State University he is a bright star. A classroom building on the campus bears his name, the only one named for a faculty member [who was not] an administrator. Moreover, Moseley's scientific publications mark him as one of the first members of the Bowling Green faculty to achieve scholarly recognition in the wider academic community.

Moseley was a naturalist of the old school. Nothing in nature was outside his province. His most enduring claim to fame was his proof of the cause of milk sickness, a dreaded disease that plagued the pioneer farmers of the Midwest. Also early in his career he compiled one of the finest catalogues of plants from a single area by his studies of the flora of the Sandusky region. He dipped into geology, measuring the encroachment of Lake Erie on the Ohio shore and tracing the preglacial drainage patterns there. He was the discoverer of the Oak Openings of northwestern Ohio as a unique biological entity. Finally, in his closing years he attained his greatest public fame for long-term prediction of rainfall based on evidence of past climate as recorded in tree rings. In addition to these major efforts, he published on a host of topics in scientific and education journals, and he wrote four textbooks in natural science.

Moseley probably left his greatest monument in the minds of thousands of students rather than in his published works. Many of these students turned to careers in science or gained a lifelong appreciation of nature as a result of exposure to him. His influence carries on, but the memories are growing dim.

His scientific reputation, on the other hand, rests on his publications. These were marked by wide-ranging interests, meticulous observation, and sustained attention to each topic. His contributions were not marked by brilliance nor conceptual innovations. His *forte* was field biology, aided by an encyclopedic memory for scientific names. For example, he was not the first to suggest that milk sickness might be caused by white snakeroot, but he was the one who proved it beyond doubt. He did not discover that the Lake Erie basin was tilting towards Ohio, but he showed that the process was still continuing, and he measured the progress of it. He did not discover the Oak Openings, but he showed in detail how the area was unique. He was not the first to date former climate by tree rings, but he was the first one to apply the idea to analysis of the rainfall history in this region.

A marvel of his work was that so much of it was a solitary effort. He had casual acquaintanceship with other scientists but little collaboration. His usual field companions were students and laymen. Although he was active in presenting papers for many years at the annual meetings of the Ohio Academy of Science, serving in early times as secretary and president of the academy as well as vice-president of the Wilson Ornithological Society, his papers suggest some intellectual isolation. In science, as in his personal life, he was a loner. He exchanged specimens and brief correspondence with other scientists, but there is no sign that his manuscripts had the benefit of critical reading by eminent specialists. His short papers particularly read like newspaper articles, without references or acknowledgments. His correspondence files reveal no lengthy technical interchanges. Most of his scholarly contributions appeared in regional or minor journals, not the more important national ones, and his scientific reputation hardly extended beyond Ohio and Michigan.

• • •

Moseley's career plays an important role in the evolution of Bowling Green State University. In an age when the Normal College's function was more the transfer of existing knowledge rather than the acquisition of new knowledge, Edwin Lincoln Moseley, unlike most of his colleagues, researched, wrote, and published. In this respect he typifies what the University became in the quarter century after his death rather than what it was during his lifetime. That he accomplished as much as he did with the limitations he faced is a remarkable testimony to his industry, perserverance, and inquisitiveness. People who remember the eccentric professor are fast disappearing, but the record of his solid accomplishments will endure far beyond the fading personal memories.

—Modified and edited by RLS from the following sources.

  I. 1948. Louis W. Campbell. "Dr. Moseley gone but not forgotten." *Ohio Conservation Bulletin* 129(8): 15. August. (also, *Toledo Times*, 13 June).

  II. 1982. Roger Conant. "Mostly about people and collections," pp. 43-48 . In *Herpetology in Ohio. . .Fifty Years Ago*. Special Publication of the Toledo Herpetological Society, Toledo. 65 pp.

  III. 1984. Harold F. Mayfield. "Edwin Lincoln Moseley, naturalist and teacher, 1865-1948." *Northwest Ohio Quarterly* 56(1): 3-17. Winter.

Louis W. Campbell (b. 1903), a retired transportation engineer for the Toledo Community Traction Co., was an outdoor writer of the column "Waters and Woods" for the *Toledo Times* until it ceased publication in 1975. A field naturalist, Campbell began as a fisherman, but later focused on birds, and for decades has been the acknowledged authority on the birds of northwestern Ohio. He has published, *Birds of Lucas County* (1940) and *Birds of the Toledo Area* (1968), both recognized as models for reports on birds of a restricted region. He is an honorary curator of birds for the Toledo Museum of Science. Campbell had a principal role in the establishment of parks and nature preserves in the Oak Openings area, one of which is named the "Louis W. Campbell State Nature Preserve." His most recent book is *The Marshes of Southwestern Lake Erie* (1995).

Roger Conant (b. 1909), curator of reptiles, and later general curator at the Toledo Zoological Gardens (1929-1935), conducted a field survey of Ohio reptiles during the early 1930s. This survey led to the publication of two books, *The Reptiles of Ohio* (1938, reprinted 1951 with a lengthy revisionary addenda), and a *Field Guide to Reptiles and Amphibians of Eastern and Central North America* (1958). The former book is based on extensive and detailed locality data, coupled with ecological information; whereas the latter is better known as one in the Roger Tory Peterson Field Guide Series. It is his best known work, which had the widest use in the United States of any book on herpetology, having sold a half million copies. In 1935, Conant returned to his native Philadelphia where he was curator of reptiles and, later, also director of America's first zoo at the Philadelphia Zoological Garden, where he served for 38 years. Since retirement from there in 1973, he has lived in Albuquerque, New Mexico, where he is an adjunct professor in the Department of Biology at the University of New Mexico. His publications, numbering almost 250, include *Herpetology in Ohio. . .Fifty Years Ago* (1982), a small book of his experiences while in Ohio conducting field work, from which are taken his comments about Moseley. Conant is the recipient of numerous honors and accolades, among them an honorary Doctor of Science degree from the University of Colorado, the R. Marlin Perkins Award for Professional Excellence from the American Zoo and Aquarium Association, and most recently the David S. Ingalls, Jr. Award for Excellence from the Cleveland Museum of Natural History (1996).

Harold F. Mayfield (b. 1911), a retired director of personnel relations for Owens-Illinois, Inc., Toledo, and an adjunct professor of biology at the University of Toledo, has pursued dual careers in business and ornithology. A graduate of Shurtleff College (now Southern Illinois University), he earned a master's degree in mathematics at the University of Illinois, Champaign-Urbana, and then joined Owens-Illinois, Inc., the world's largest glass and packaging company, where he was in charge of functions concerned with the human aspect of business in more than 100 of their factories worldwide. Since retirement in 1971, Mayfield has devoted much time to active research in conservation and ornithology, authoring more than 200 publications. The most notable of these works is his definitive book on one of America's rarest birds, *The Kirtland's Warbler* (1960), published by the Cranbrook Institute of Science. For this effort, he was awarded the highest honor in American ornithology, the Brewster Memorial Award, for "the most important recent work on the birds of the Western Hemisphere." Mayfield is the only individual to have served as president of the three major professional societies in American ornithology, the American Ornithologist's Union, the Wilson Ornithology Society, and the Cooper Ornithological Society. His field work on birds has taken him on expeditions into the arctic, Mexico, and Central America. Other honors received are the Arthur H. Allen Award at Cornell University, the Ohio Conservation Hall of Fame, the United States Forest Service 75th Anniversary Award, the W. E. Clyde Todd Award of the Audubon Society of Western Pennsylvania, and the Conservation Award of the Detroit Audubon Society. For his contributions and scholarly achievements he was awarded honorary doctor of science degrees from Occidental College, California, and from Bowling Green State University.

Organisms named for Moseley: Fish, *Gonorhynchus moseleyi*; Bird, *Actenoides moseleyi*; Plant, *Thalictrum moseleyi*.

(From references 6 and 12, respectively, at the end of this chapter, and from Nathaniel L. Britton and Addison Brown. 1913. *An Illustrated Flora of the Northern United States, Canada and the British Possessions.* vol. 2, Charles Scribner's Sons, New York. p. 120; the latter reproduced with permission of the Lu Esther T. Mentz Library of the New York Botanical Garden)

Commemorated in Names

Ronald L. Stuckey

CHAPTER NINETEEN

I. Plant and Animal Names

As a field naturalist and preserver of museum specimens, Edwin Lincoln Moseley collected many animals and plants for this purpose during the early years of his life. He distributed many of his specimens to various individuals, museums, and herbaria throughout the world. Among the major museums to whom he sent specimens of animals were the American Museum of Natural History (New York), the British Museum of Natural History (London), the Field Museum of Natural History (Chicago), the National Natural History Museum at the Smithsonian Institution (Washington, D.C.), and the Imperial Museum (Vienna).[11]

The most extensive collection of Ohio plants obtained by Moseley is in the herbarium at Bowling Green State University (BGSU). This collection is Moseley's original herbarium that once was a part of the Sandusky High School Museum, which he moved to Bowling Green in 1938. "A Checklist of Ohio Species in [the] Moseley Herbarium" was compiled by Nathan William Easterly for the Ohio Flora Project (typescript, 77 pp.). Prepared during the early 1950s, this document was used by E. Lucy Braun during the writing of her two books on the vascular flora of Ohio: *The Woody Plants of Ohio* (1961) and *The Monocotyledonae* [of Ohio] (1967). Easterly's *Check List,* a part of Braun's records for the Ohio Flora Project kept in the Herbarium at The Ohio State University, is retained in the Moseley file of

245

Ronald L. Stuckey. The majority of the specimens in Moseley's herbarium are from Erie County, but many were obtained also from the Oak Openings in Lucas County. The collection contains some specimens which are quite rare in the state flora.

Other herbaria, according to Vegter (1976),[13] having specimens of Ohio plants collected by Moseley are: the Carnegie Museum of Natural History, Pittsburgh (CM); the Field Museum of Natural History, Chicago (F); the Gray Herbarium of Harvard University Herbaria (GH); the herbarium of The University of Michigan, Ann Arbor (MICH); the herbarium of the Missouri Botanical Garden, St. Louis (MO); the herbarium at New Mexico State University, Las Cruces (NMC); the New York Botanical Garden, Bronx (NY); the herbarium of The Ohio State University, Columbus (OS); and the herbarium of the National Museum of Natural History at the Smithsonian Institution (US). His plant specimens from Louisiana are at CM, F, MO, and US.

On occasion, an investigator would determine that one of Moseley's specimens represented a species new to science. A bird, two plants, a fish, and a coral have been named in Moseley's honor. Below in chronological order is a short commentary relative to each one of these species.

While with the J. B. Steere Zoological Expedition to the Philippine Islands in 1887,1888, Moseley found on Negros Island a new species of kingfisher. Steere (1891)[1] named this bird *Actenoides moseleyi*, but later this species was considered a variant of *Halcyon lindsayi*, the spotted wood-kingfisher. The scientific name then became *Halcyon lindsayi moseleyi* (Steere, 1891), as used in the book *Philippine Birds* (du Pont, 1971).[12]

The currently used name is *Actenoides lindsayi moseleyi* Steere, 1891, according to Dickinson, *et al*. (1991).[15] The type specimen is BGSU582 collected 14 February 1888 at Sibulan on Negros Island in the Philippines by E. L. Moseley. The bird is an immature female on permanent loan to the Museum of Zoology at The University of Michigan.

Moseley's specimen, the type of the spotted wood-kingfisher, named by Steere was discussed by Trautman [see Chapter 8, page 93] and as noted above, now is located at The University of Michigan. How was it that this rare specimen was in Moseley's museum at Sandusky and later at Bowling Green, rather than with the Steere collection of birds from the Philippines, where it would be suspected to have been retained? The answer appears in a story in the Sunday *Sandusky Register* of 18 February 1894.[2] The occasion for the article was the arrival from the British Museum of a registered parcel containing the kingfisher. A portion of the account is as follows:

> It is a beautiful kingfisher, which was shot by Prof. Moseley in the Island of Negros, Philippines. . . .It is not as large as our American kingfisher but has a greater variety of colors, the breast being buff and white with bars of black and the back green, blue, buff, black and brown, arranged in such an intricate pattern that a full description would occupy a column. It was shot at dark from a bamboo on the bank of a little stream about a mile from the ocean. It was alone and none like was seen during the remainder of the expedition. . . .Professor Steere, the leader of the first expedition, on arriving in this country and comparing the specimen with other kingfishers from the East Indies and the descriptions in works on ornithology, decided it to be a new species and named it . . . [for E. L. Moseley].

Not knowing that it was really distinct from other species of kingfishers already known, Moseley took it to the British Museum, which contained the largest collection of birds in the world. The chief ornithologist, R. B. Sharpe, who had made a special study of the kingfishers, pronounced the bird distinct from any previously described ones. Sharpe, offering liberal exchange, tried to induce Moseley to let the British Museum have it. Not succeeding in this effort, he obtained consent to keep it long enough to have an engraving made of it. Then afterward the specimen became misplaced until a few weeks ago when it was located and returned to Moseley for the Sandusky High School museum.

Two specimens of plants Moseley obtained in 1895 from the Oxford Prairie in Oxford Township, Erie County, were described as new to science and named in his honor. Merritt L. Fernald (1908)[3] of Harvard University named a goldenrod, *Solidago moseleyi* Fernald, based on Moseley's specimen collected 5 September 1895 (GH). Edward L. Greene (1912)[4] whose herbarium is at the University of Notre Dame named a meadow rue, *Thalictrum moseleyi* Greene, based on Moseley's specimen collected 8 June 1895 (ND-G). Because later investigators have not recognized specific differences between these named entities and their closely related species, both names have been treated as synonyms of earlier described species. *Solidago moseleyi* has been placed in synonymy with *S. remota* (Greene) Friesner (1933) and in the most recent treatment of *Solidago* in Ohio by Fisher (1988),[14]

Chapter 19 • Commemorated in Names

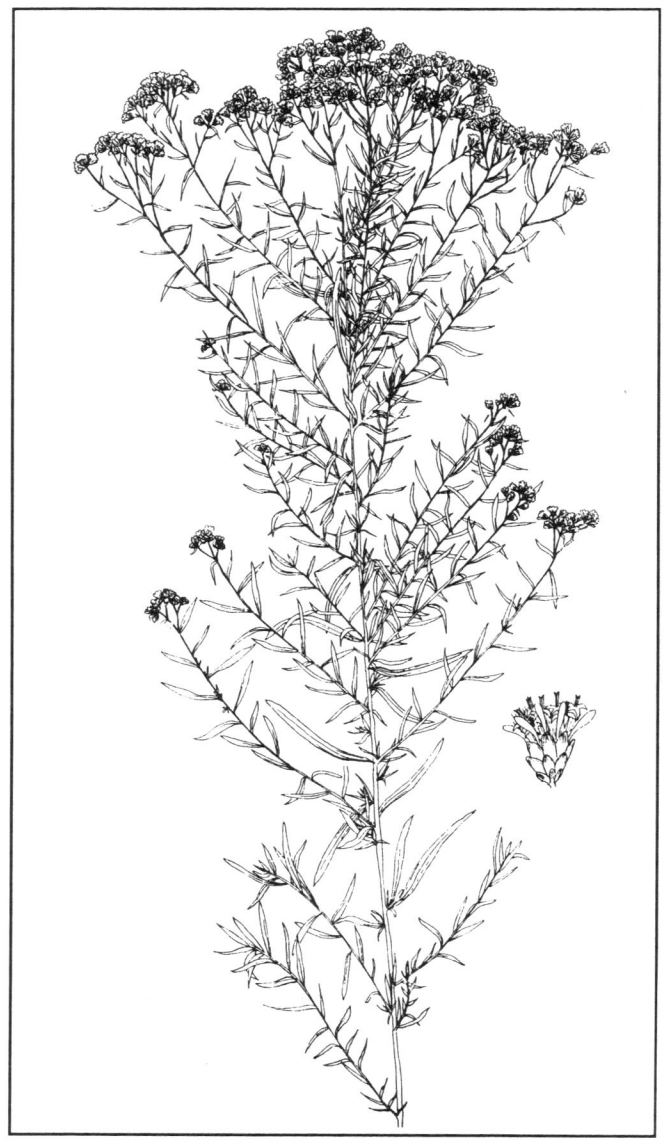

Solidago moseleyi, a goldenrod named for Moseley by the
Harvard University botanist, Merritt L. Fernald (*Rhodora* 10: 93. 1908).

(T. Richard Fisher, 1988. *Part 3. Asteraceae of Ohio*.
The Ohio State University Press, Columbus. p. 52.)

both *S. moseleyi* and *S. remota* are listed as synonyms of *Solidago gymnospermoides* (Greene) Fernald. This species is known in Ohio from only four counties, all bordering Lake Erie. *Thalictrum moseleyi* has been relegated to synonymy under *Thalictrum dasycarpum* Fish., Mey. &. Lall. (Boivin, 1944).[10]

The report that Edward S. Steele of the Smithsonian Institution had named a button snakeroot or blazing star for Moseley is an apparent error. Steele (1913)[5] was studying this group of plants as reported by him in 1913, but no taxonomic work on this genus is known to have been published by him.

While vacationing and visiting relatives in the Hawaiian Islands during the summer of 1922, Moseley made an extensive collection of fishes. Most of these fishes came from the market places of the Japanese. Upon returning to San Francisco in the United States, he left his collection at Stanford University with Dr. David Starr Jordan (1851-1931), the most noted authority on the fishes of the Pacific Ocean. Moseley pointed out to Jordan the belief that one of the fishes was a new species. A year later Jordan and his associate John O. Snyder described the fish as new to science with the name *Gonorhynchus moseleyi* (Jordan and Snyder, 1923).[6] They commented that "this dainty little fish was found by Moseley in the market of Honolulu, where he made a valuable and interesting collection of fishes." The *Bee Gee News*[7] noted that "The college... has in Prof. Moseley a man who is high authority in the biological sciences. It is indeed a privilege to work under such an authority."[7]

"A coral has also been named after Moseley by Charles K. Swartz, professor of geology at the Johns Hopkins University," as reported in the *Sandusky Register* (8 December 1923).[8] No further information has been located on this topic, despite considerable research effort.

References

1. 1891. Joseph B. Steere. "*Actenoides moseleyi*," p. 306. In "Ornithological results of an expedition to the Philippine Islands in 1887 and 1888." *The Ibis*, Sixth Series 3: 301-306, pls. VII–VIII.

2. 1894. Anonymous. "A rare treasure added to Professor Moseley's collection at the high school." *Sandusky Sunday Register*, 18 February, p. 1.

3. 1908. Merritt L. Fernald. "*Solidago moseleyi*," p. 93. In "Notes on some plants of northeastern America." *Rhodora* 10: 46-55,84-95.

4. 1912. Edward L. Greene. "*Thalictrum moseleyi*," pp. 294,295. In "Western meadow rues–1." *American Midland Naturalist* 2: 290-296.

5. 1913. Edward S. Steele. "An investigation of *Laciniaria scariosa*." *Torreya* 13: 78,79.

6. 1923. David Starr Jordan and John Otterbein Snyder. "*Gonorhynchus moseleyi*, a new species of herring-like fish from Honolulu." *Journal of the Washington Academy of Sciences* 13(15): 347-350.

7. 1923. Anonymous. "New fish named in Moseley's honor." *Bee Gee News* 5(3): 7. (reprinted in *School Science and Mathematics* 24: 523. 1924).

8. 1923. Anonymous. "Moseley is man of many biological discoveries." *Sandusky Register*, 8 December, p. 3.

9. 1933. Ray C. Friesner. "*Solidago remota*," p. 62. In "The genus *Solidago* in northeastern North America." *Butler University Botanical Studies* 3: 1-64.

10. 1944. Bernard Boivin. "*Thalictrum dasycarpum*," pp. 480-487. In "American *Thalictra* and their old world allies." *Rhodora* 46: 337-377,391-445,453-487.

11. 1950. Anonymous. "Edwin Lincoln Moseley," p. 159. In *National Cyclopaedia of American Biography*...vol. 41. James T. White & Co., New York. 611 pp., index.

12. 1971. John Elenthere du Pont. "*Halcyon lindsayi moseleyi*," p. 206, pl. 45-D. In *Philippine Birds*. Delaware Museum of Natural History, Monograph Series No. 2. Greenville, Delaware. x, 480 pp. (The illustration of Moseley's kingfisher in this book is reproduced on page 244 with permission from the Delaware Museum of Natural History).

13. 1976. L. H. Vegter. "Index Herbariorum Collectors M." *Regnum Vegetabile* 93 (Part II, 4): 475-576.

14. 1988. T. Richard Fisher. "*Solidago gymnospermoides*," p. 56. In *The Dicotyledoneae of Ohio, Part 3. Asteraceae*. Ohio State University Press, Columbus. xiv, 280 pp.

15. 1991. Edward C. Dickinson, Robert S. Kennedy, and Kenneth C. Parkes. *The birds of the Philippines: An annotated check-list*. British Ornithologists' Union, Zoological Museum, Tring, Herts HP23 6AP, United Kingdom. 507 pp.

CHAPTER 19 • COMMEMORATED IN NAMES

II. Place Names

Moseley has been recognized by having two places "Moseley Hall" and "Moseley Channel" named in his honor, as described on the next two pages.

Science Building erected in 1916 on Bowling Green campus; named Moseley Hall in 1951.

(Archives, BGSU)

1951. Science Building on Bowling Green State University Campus Named "Moseley Hall," in Honor of its First Professor of Biology.

The Science Building adjacent to the original administration building on the Bowling Green College campus was constructed in 1916 and housed the classes in science, agriculture, industrial arts, and the upper grades of the teacher training school. Here Moseley taught all of his classes in the various sciences. In 1950, at the suggestion of the faculty in the Department of Biology, the building was named "Moseley Hall," chosen to honor its first professor of the natural sciences. The building underwent renovations in 1951, 1962, 1967, and 1977. Beginning in 1951, Moseley Hall was home for the Department of Biology and the Moseley Museum, until 1967 when that Department moved to a new Life Science Building. The Computer Center occupied the building for the next several years. At the present time, Moseley Hall is the center for off campus students and a writing and study skills laboratory.[16,20,22]

Identification sign in front of Moseley Hall.

(Taken by Relda Niederhofer, summer 1996; Niederhofer Collection)

1959. Outer Channel of Sandusky Bay Named for Moseley.

The natural outer channel of Sandusky Bay, a channel about 1.6 miles long, was officially named "Moseley Channel" in the Professor's honor. This channel provides access to Sandusky Bay from Lake Erie, between Cedar Point and Bay Point. Moseley Channel connects to the glacially and post-glacially buried valley which Moseley and his students discovered and mapped in the early 1900s. Approval of the channel name was made by the domestic committee of the Board of Geographical Names contained in Decisions List No. 5904, 10 December 1959, according to J. D. Kilmartin of the Department of the Interior (published April 1960, p. 39). The natural Moseley Channel carved by the glacier in the bedrock was known as early as the 1840s and from various studies has remained virtually unchanged to the present.[21]

The project was sponsored by Frank J. Prout, president emeritus of Bowling Green State University; Nicholas Catri, the Sandusky Lions Club; and other local organizations of Sandusky.[17,18,19]

References

16. 1951-1977. Anonymous. "[Newspaper articles about Moseley Hall." Archives, Bowling Green State University.

17. 1959. Anonymous. "Channel finally named for Dr. Moseley." *Sandusky Register*, 21 December, p. 7.

18. 1960. Anonymous. "Ohio," pp. 38,39. In *Decisions on Names in the United States: Decisions Rendered from September 1959 through December 1959. Decision List No. 5904*. United States Board on Geographic Names, Department of the Interior, Washington, D.C.

19. 1969. Anonymous. "Sandusky outer channel named for Moseley." *Bowling Green State University Magazine* 5(1): 22. February.

20. 1967. James Robert Overman. *The History of Bowling Green State University*, Bowling Green University Press, Bowling Green, Ohio. 234 pp. (p. 130).

21. 1975. Charles E. Herdendorf. "Shoreline changes of Lakes Erie and Ontario: With special reference to currents, sediment transport, and soil erosion. *Bulletin of the Buffalo Society of Natural Sciences* 25(3): 67-73.

22. 1982. Anonymous. "People build institution: Faculty names tell history of Bowling Green." *Monitor* 5(21): 1,2. 22 February.

CHAPTER 19 • COMMEMORATED IN NAMES

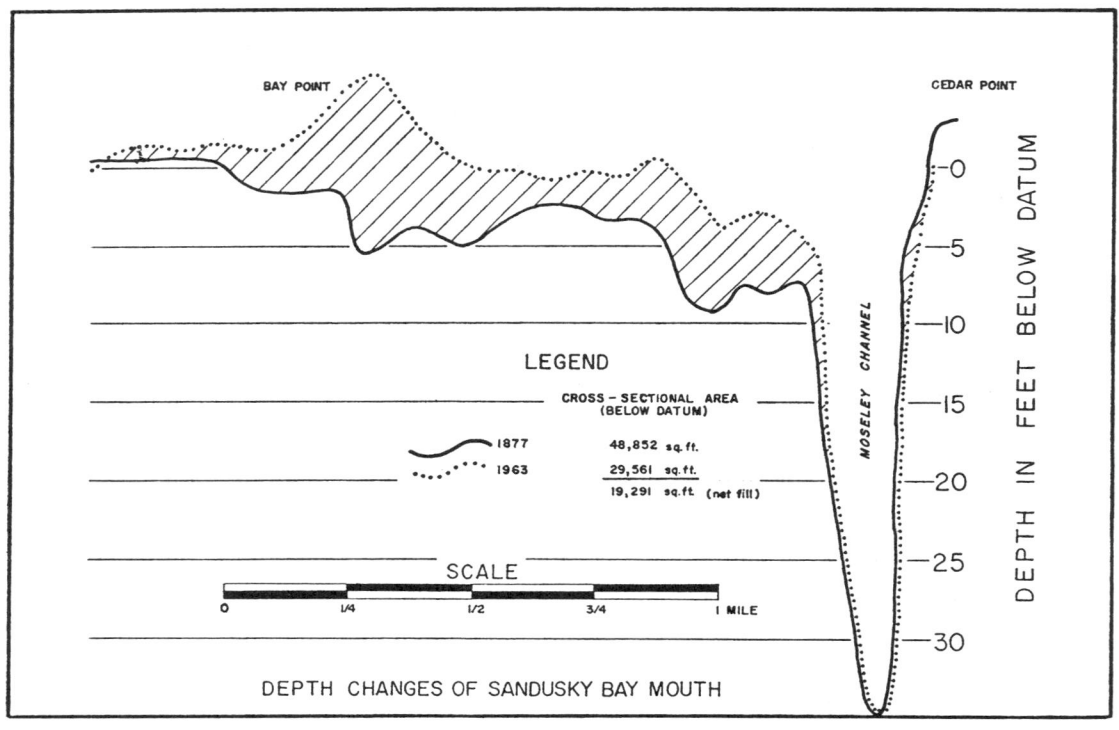

Cross-sectional view of mouth of Sandusky Bay showing Moseley Channel.

(Charles E. Herdendorf. *Bulletin of the Buffalo Society of Natural Sciences* 25(3): 70. 1975)

CHAPTER 19 • COMMEMORATED IN NAMES

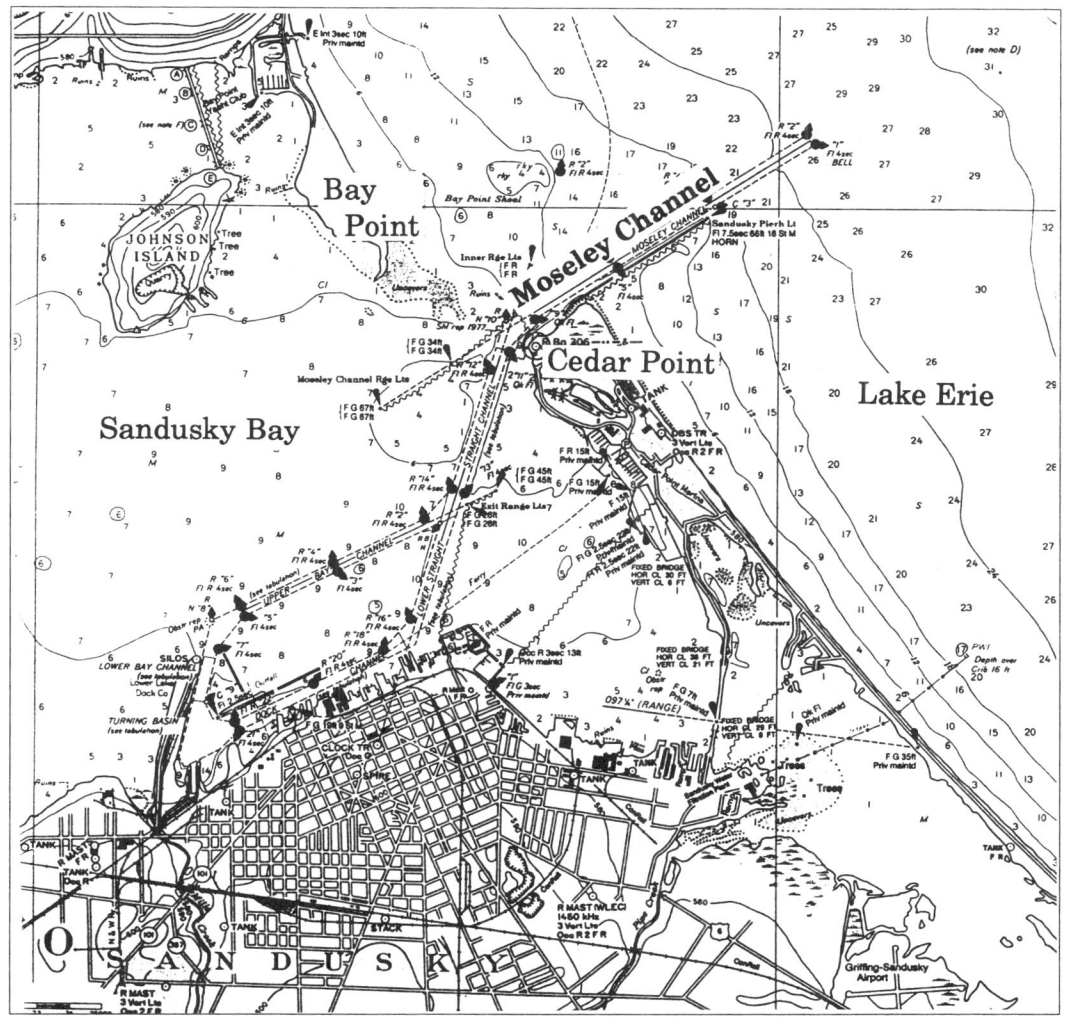

**Location of Moseley Channel between Bay Point and Cedar Point,
extending from Sandusky Bay to Lake Erie.**

(Map No. 14844. *Islands in Lake Erie*. U.S. Department of Commerce, Washington, D.C.
23rd Edition. 9 June 1979)

Floral mound in Washington Park in the center of downtown Sandusky, Erie County, Ohio.

The mound honors the centennial of Moseley's arrival in the city as the science teacher in the high school, shown in the background. Here is where Moseley taught classes to many students.

(Taken by Dennis Horan, 24 July 1989; Sandusky Library Archives)

Recognitions and Tributes

CHAPTER TWENTY

Ronald L. Stuckey

During Moseley's lifetime various honors and recognitions came to him because of his scientific and educational achievements. At this time in history, during the first half of the twentieth century, these kinds of awards were few and rarely given by scientific societies or educational institutions. Moseley's receipt of these awards was the exception. The attitude towards the awarding of accolades was expressed by Homer B. Williams, first president of Bowling Green State University, who was not favorable towards a policy of granting honorary degrees. Although the trustees in 1929 granted authority for the conferring of these degrees, none was awarded until after his retirement in 1938. At that time Williams was awarded the first honorary degree by Bowling Green State University. Acknowledgment must be made that the honors and recognitions accorded Edwin Lincoln Moseley were truly justifiable and deserving. Following his death, as in life, Moseley continued to receive tributes and memorials for his accomplishments. Two components comprise this chapter:

I. Honors and Recognitions that were given Moseley during his lifetime, and
II. Memorials and Tributes that posthumously celebrate his life.

Those recognitions and tributes that are known are reported here as an annotated list. The format chosen is a description, comment, or quoted item about the event, and its source of information.

CHAPTER 20 • RECOGNITIONS AND TRIBUTES

I. Honors and Recognitions

1914. Recognition Paid to Science Teacher Who Leaves Local School Work [8 June].

On the occasion of the commencement exercises of the Sandusky High School at the Opera House, Moseley was recognized for his past 25 years of service to the high school as its science teacher. The recognition statement was delivered by school principal Roy E. Offenhauer.

> Professor Moseley is a man who hates all the shams of life. He believes in honest efforts, and his pupils during his many years of service were always sure of his sympathy when, after trying, they were unable to master difficulties. We are more than sorry that he is about to leave us, but we hope that in his new field he will be more able to carry on the work which he has started here. Moseley is recognized as one of the highest authorities in his line, in the country, and when writing to colleagues of the country, we always took pride in mentioning the fact that he was a member of our teaching staff.
>
> In reply to the words of Principal Offenhauer, Moseley said that he had been benefited by his years of service in Sandusky and sincerely hoped that he would be of service to this community, even when discharging to his duties at the state normal school at Bowling Green, to which he has been called.

(Sandusky Star-Journal, 19 June 1914, p. 14).

1929. Has Not Missed a Day of Class Through Illness in 50 Years

Moseley was recognized in *Ripley's Believe It Or Not!* for his excellent class attendance record. This achievement was also subject of articles in the newspapers. Moseley wrote about why he enjoyed an excellent life without illness, as follows:

> I attribute my long continued vigor in large measure to abstinence from medicine and various other harmful substances. . . .Many young people would form the habit of getting regular sleep if they knew its value. . . .I rarely let a day pass without being out of doors the greater part of an hour. Except in winter, I am usually outside much longer. The outdoor science instruction, which my pupils [have participated, and] in which so many of them rendered assistance, have been continued since I went to Bowling Green, where in pleasant weather about one-third of my time with classes is spent out of doors.

(Sandusky Sunday Register, 21 July 1929, p. 5).

1931. Recognized For 45 Consecutive Annual Reports of Bird Migration.

Moseley was one of seven individuals to receive an engrossed testimonial from the Biological Survey of the United States, headquartered in Washington D.C., for his annual reports on bird migration. His recognition was for 45 years of reports.

(The Auk 48(2): 333. 1931).

1937. Honored at Retirement-Birthday Dinner as Teacher, Author, Scientist [30 March].

Officially honored by fellow faculty members and a number of former students, Moseley gained the "praise of the world" at a special 72nd birthday dinner held in the dining room of Shatzel Hall on the campus of Bowling Green State University. The event honored him as the first faculty member to retire with the appointment of Professor Emeritus of Biology which became effective in the fall of 1936.

About 100 participants were present to enjoy the three-course dinner, featured by the presentation of a lovely birthday cake with 72 tiny lighted candles. Moseley ably blew them out. The college-girl waitresses lined up behind him and sang "Happy Birthday To You." Misses Riley and LaVern of the Department of Music furnished instrumental music during the meal.

Moseley's close friend, Professor Daniel J. Crowley, served as toastmaster and introduced the speakers. The featured speaker, President Homer B. Williams, lauded Moseley as a teacher, author, scientist, and paid glowing tribute to him as a man [see Chapter 3, page 19]. Williams formerly was superintendent at Sandusky High School when Moseley taught there.

Other speakers were Ralph Schaller, biology teacher in the local high school, and former student of Moseley who spoke briefly of the alumni's appreciation of him as an internationally known scholar. Crowley unveiled a portrait of Moseley given to the University by an anonymous donor, which was painted by Ralph H. McKelvey, a former student of Moseley's at Sandusky, and a member of the American Artists Professional League in Bradenton, Florida. Dr. Charles Otis of the Department of Biology spoke briefly and presented Moseley a packet of letters written for the occasion by former students. [These letters have not been located].

The final commentary was given by Moseley who expressed his gratitude for the honor. He then said:

> If I had my life to live over I should try to avoid one mistake. I believe that is a mistake to fail to let any pupil know when I thought they had done a good piece of work. The pleasure that I have enjoyed from this meeting and from this fine tribute tonight convinces me that there is much good done to a man by a little praise.

Moseley then announced some of his discoveries concerning the 46-year weather cycle, and closed with a prophecy to the effect that "we are about to enter a period of wet weather." [see Chapter 10, page 127].

(*Bee Gee News* 21 (26): 1, 2, 3, 4. 31 March 1937; *Daily Sentinel-Tribune*, Bowling Green, 31 March 1937, p. 4,5; *Sandusky [Daily] Register*, 4 April 1937, p. 11).

1943. Receives Honorary Degree of Doctor of Humane Letters from Bowling Green State University [13 August].

Moseley must have been asked on a number of occasions why he did not continue his education to obtain a Ph.D. degree. He wrote a reply that is retained in the Archives, Bowling Green State University: "The U. of M. granted me the A.M. degree in 1885 when I was twenty years old. I have been too busy since to work for a doctor's degree." (Box 3, Folder 7)

Moseley's honorary degree was the first the University awarded to one of its own faculty members. Although all the credits mentioned in the degree citation have been written elsewhere, for the record, it is quoted here in its entirety:

> **Edwin Lincoln Moseley:** In acknowledgment of your long and valuable service to Bowling Green State University, of which you have been a faculty member since the opening of the institution and are now professor emeritus of biology and curator of the University Museum; in tribute to such distinguished contributions as proof that white snakeroot caused the disease called trembles in animals and milk sickness in humans and the establishment of accurate long-range weather forecasts based on your research with tree rings, sun spots, and alternating periods of rainfall and drought; in consideration of your professional attainments as president, secretary, charter member, and honorary life mem-

ber of the Ohio Academy of Science, chairman of the botanical section of the Michigan Academy of Science, vice president of the Wilson Ornithological Club, and charter member of the American Society of Mammalogists; in view of your versatility in teaching biology, geography, hygiene, physics, geometry, astronomy, physiology, geology, English, and Latin, and in appreciation of your numerous scientific publications, your collections of botanical, zoological, and geological specimens, your generosity with time and money in behalf of your students, and your constant struggle to make life more worthwhile, I now present you to the President of the University for the award of the degree of Doctor of Humane Letters.

(News Release, BGSU, 16 July 1943, 2 pp.; *Sandusky Register Star-News*, 19 July 1943, p. 10; Degree Citation, BGSU, Typewritten, 1 p.).

University President Prout (right) congratulates Moseley (left) upon receiving Honorary Degree, 13 August 1943.

(Archives, BGSU)

Chapter 20 • Recognitions and Tributes

Dinner Party for those awarded honorary degrees, August 1943.

Back row: l. to r., Mrs. Ralph G. Harshman, Ralph G. Harshman, **Edwin L. Moseley.** Front row: Daniel J. Crowley, Ervin J. Kreischer.

Banquet room in the Student Union, the Falcon's Nest.

(Photo Service, BGSU)

II. Memorials and Tributes

1948. Moseley's Admirer's Saddened by His Death; Praised as a Genius and Humanitarian [6 June].

On the day of Moseley's funeral, 8 June, the editorial page of the Bowling Green newspaper carried the following editorial titled, "Dr. Moseley," which was believed to have been written by the newspaper's editor, Spencer A. Canary.

> Dr. Moseley's many admirers who were privileged to know him personally, as well as by the great reputation he had won as a scientist, . . . [are saddened by his death Sunday 6 June] . . . Since boyhood, his life had been filled by active pursuit of knowledge afield and in his studio.
>
> His thirst for knowledge was not quenched by the fountains and streams where it might best be found in satisfying his curiosity; but he searched the creeks and rivulets that swelled to hither, lest some of the flavor might be lost. He was a good teacher, as well as keen observer, collator, and writer. Those who thought they had something to contribute found him furtive. To his vast storehouse he was ready to add their best and never gave them the impression of inwardly smiling over their naivete.
>
> Thus the master was sunk in the learner and students were encouraged by his generosity of intellect to invite him to learn of their own explorations. His was an intelligence that was humble because he realized how much that remains to be learned.
>
> Oddly impervious to many things of life that seem important to others, his thinking was so concentrated on the subject of the time that he often appeared abstracted and oblivious to surrounding things; and a stranger would have been startled to learn that this apparently unalert man was a genius. The vista about him was for the time-being lost in the fathom of speculation. Over his eyes there then seemed drawn a film to shut out anything else.
>
> But Dr. Moseley was far from being merely a scientist to whom earth, stream, and stars confided their secrets. He was wide awake to the needs of humanity and the call of friendly interest, as his sponsorship of the campaign for clothing for the naked overseas and of students in sickness or financial straits attest.
>
> He had won the rest that is now his.
>
> *(Daily Sentinel-Tribune*, Bowling Green, 8 June 1948, p. 4).

CHAPTER 20 • RECOGNITIONS AND TRIBUTES

1948. President Prout's Tribute to Moseley as Reported to the University's Alumni [June].

A one-page tribute to Moseley by President Frank J. Prout is printed in the June 1948 issue of the University's *Alumni Magazine*, of which selected quotations from this tribute follow:

> His greatness lay in a keen, inquiring, analytical mind. He was determined on getting the facts about a proposition. . . .Many students developed in some degree, this most valuable habit and have ever blessed him for it. . . .
>
> His philanthropy is well known, [and] literally scores of students have been helped through college by his generosity. . . . his philanthropy insures that his name shall forever be carried in the active rolls of this university. Thus, will he continue to live with us, doing good.

(*Bowling Green State University Alumni Magazine* 7(4): 2. 1948).

1948. Moseley's Influence as Professor-Botanist Continues, Frank J. Prout told Bowling Green Kiwanians [9 September].

President Prout rated the scientist outstanding in creating love of nature on the part of his students and endeavoring to find out why a particular. . . [phenomenon exists]."

(*Toledo Blade*, 10 September, 1948, p 29. News Release, BGSU).

1949. Moseley's Life, written by Frank Seidel of "The Ohio Story," on Radio Broadcast Stations [7 March].

(News Release, BGSU, 3 March, 2 pp; *Sandusky Register-Star News,* 3 March 1949, p. 13; also News Release, BGSU, 4 April 1952).

1949. Posthumous Lecture by Moseley Given at Meeting of the Ohio Academy of Science [22 April].

Kelley Hale, M. D., a physician of Wilmington, Ohio, presented a recorded "Lecture on Longevity" by Edwin L. Moseley, and showed kodachrome slides made on field trips by him. The tribute was one of the contributed papers given at the fifty-eighth annual meeting of the Ohio Academy of Science held 21-23 April 1949 at

Denison University, Granville, Ohio. The location of these items, if they survived, has not been investigated.

(OAS Meeting Program, p. 9).

1950. Bronze Plaque in Memory of Professor Moseley Given to Bowling Green State University by Michigan Woman [30 May].

Received during an Honors Day assembly, the plaque was placed inside the main entrance of the Science Building, where Moseley taught since 1916. The then new building, first occupied at that time, was later named Moseley Hall, with the fourth floor containing his mounted collection of birds, once part of his museum at the

Bronze plaque given in memory of Moseley, 30 May 1950.

(The full inscription is printed on page 228; Photo Service, BGSU)

Sandusky High School. The inscription on the plaque is quoted by Seymour Van Gundy as part of his tribute to Moseley [see Chapter 17, page 228].

(News Release, BGSU, 30 May 1950).

The donor, Miss E. Bettes of Grand Rapids, Michigan, explained the meaning of her gift in a letter of 22 May 1950 to the University, which in part follows:

> [*Moseley's*] *career commands the respect of all interested in youth and in the success of the democratic principles of our country. In this era of wavering standards of integrity, loyalty, and achievement, we cannot honor too highly such leadership as Dr. Moseley's way of life offers nor give it too much need.*
>
> *With a master's degree at the age of 19 he came to Central High School in Grand Rapids as instructor in natural science. I was a member of the junior class.*
>
> *In his science courses through field trips, then an innovation, Mr. Moseley made his students responsible for their own observations and conclusions. He was a leader more than an instructor, insisting upon individual investigation, evaluation, and work. Always friendly in suggesting and directing our studies, he inspired our confidence....*
>
> *It is in recognition of the way of life chosen by Dr. Moseley, his contribution to science and education and his humanitarian leadership, that the plaque has been given.*

1958. Tribute Given Moseley by Frank J. Prout at Sandusky's Zion Couples Club. [24 September].

Retired President of Bowling Green State University, Prout said, "Moseley could and should be a legend among all youth, especially in Sandusky." He also noted that "no mention of this great man or reminder of his great contributions are to be found in Sandusky." Prout "told some of eccentricities, habits and his occasional absent mindedness, but above all these, he stressed his greatness of mind and spirit."

(*Sandusky Daily Register*, 25 September, p. 8).

Chapter 20 • Recognitions and Tributes

1959. Memorial Service Honors MOSELEY, FORMER SCIENCE TEACHER, with portrait at Sandusky High School [14 April].

An artist's painting of Moseley, the work of Miss Carol Creason of Cleveland, Ohio, and a graduate student and assistant in the art department at Bowling Green State University, was presented to the school by the Sidney Frohman Foundation. Charles E. Frohman, Sandusky resident and official representing the Hinde and Dauch Division of the West Virginia Pulp and Paper Company, made the presentation. The painting was hung in the lobby of the city's new high school.

(*Sandusky Daily Register*, 3 April 1959, pp. 1, 8.; *Sandusky Daily Register*, 14 April 1959, pp. 1,10.).

A plaque to Moseley presented by the Sandusky Lions Club was placed in the school's science laboratory. The plaque has the following inscription:

> *He taught students to search for the wonders and*
> *secrets of field and forest, of hill and stream.*

Portrait of Moseley and memorial plaque at Sandusky High School.

(Taken by Relda Niederhofer; Niederhofer Collection)

267

Former student and school superintendent of Sandusky High School, Frank J. Prout, was the principle speaker at the memorial program. His topic was "My Association With Edwin Lincoln Moseley, 1898–1948."

(*Sandusky Daily Register*, 14 April 1959, pp. 1,10.).

Prout's speech was published in the *Bowling Green State University Magazine* 4(4): 16-20. November, 1959, most of which is reprinted here [see Chapter 4, page 29].

1971-1974. Charles E. Frohman, Sandusky Lawyer-Historian, Leaves Important Moseley Legacy.

A great admirer of Moseley was his student Charles E. Frohman (1901-1976), who became a lawyer, businessman, and historian of Sandusky. He wrote eight small books on the town's history. Short articles about Moseley's work appeared in two of them, *Sandusky's 3rd Dimension* (1971) and *Sandusky Potpourri* (1974), both published by the Ohio Historical Society, Columbus. Frohman also published *Lake Erie: Floods, Lake Levels, Northeast Storms* (1973), which is a reprint of Moseley's published paper by the Ohio State Academy of Science, "Formation of Sandusky Bay and Cedar Point" (1905). This paper was Moseley's presidential address delivered at the 13th annual meeting of the Academy held at Adelbert College, Cleveland, Ohio, 25 November 1904. Frohman's reprint not only brought Moseley's research to public attention, but it also provided a lasting reminder of the devastation created along the area's shoreline by the Lake Erie storm of 13-14 November 1972.

Frohman's most important, but least known, work toward Moseley's legacy is his index of those items written by or about Moseley in the Sandusky newspapers principally the *Sandusky Register*. This index, retained in the Frohman Collection at the Rutherford B. Hayes Presidential Center, Fremont, Ohio, has 170 titles, spanning a 70-year period from 1889-1959. From other newspapers in Erie County, Frohman indexed 78 articles. The importance of Frohman's index can be stated further, in that without it, this book could not have been written with this great a comprehensiveness [see publication note F, page 277].

1972-1989. Moseley's Contributions to Bowling Green State University Recognized Decades Later.

Moseley's contributions to Bowling Green State University have continued to be remembered into the 1970s and 1980s with short articles written about him. These items, appearing in local newspapers or campus magazines, continue to remind readers of his legacy to the University campus. These articles discuss his estate financial contribution to aid worthy students, his main teaching objective of creating independent thinking by students, his scientific discovery that the white snakeroot plant causes milk sickness, his fame as a long-range weather prophet predicting years of droughts and floods, and not to be forgotten are his eccentric dietary habits and frugal lifestyle ways that he lived. These accounts were written by Don Wolfe, assistant managing editor of the *Toledo Blade* (1972), Randy Morrison, a student assistant editor and 1974 graduate of BGSU (1974), and Jim Nieman, a reporter for local newspapers (1984, 1985). Wolfe wrote: "And long after Dr. Edwin Lincoln Moseley is gone, his good works remain."

1972. Don Wolfe. "The legend and legacy of a farsighted professor." *Toledo Blade Sunday Magazine*, 9 April, pp. 20, 23,24.

1974. Randy Morrison. "Dr. Moseley: The eccentric professor." *At Bowling Green, News for Alumni* 4(6): 15,16. December.

1984. Jim Nieman. "Moseley contributed more than funds to BGSU." *BG News*, 23 October, p. 5.

1985. Jim Nieman. "Edwin Moseley: BG's eccentric scientist." *Daily Sentinel-Tribune*, Bowling Green, 23 August, p. A-11.

1985. Relda E. Niederhofer. "Edwin Lincoln Moseley: An internationally known scientist, a locally known eccentric." *At Bowling Green* [an alumni magazine] 4: 14(14). Winter.

1981-1984. Former Sandusky Student Remembers Moseley with Photos and Stories in the *Register*.

Wilbert Ohlemacher (1892-1987), a former student of Moseley's who graduated in 1911 from Sandusky High School, was one of the individuals interviewed in Chapter 5. According to the interview, Ohlemacher worked for 40 years as plant engineer at the American Crayon Company in Sandusky. In retirement, he wrote

Chapter 20 • Recognitions and Tributes

a column, "The Elderlies" that appeared for six years in the *Sandusky Register*. He remembered Moseley to the newspapers' readers in four stories each accompanied with a choice photograph, all of which are printed in this book as follows: Frontispiece to Chapters 5, 12, and 17, and the one introducing the third section of this book. The newspaper citations of the articles are:

1981. "The Elderlies: Sandusky's Professor Moseley." *Sandusky Register*, 8 November, p. A-4. [see Section III, page 177].

1981. "The Elderlies: More about Moseley." *Sandusky Register*, 6 December, p. A-4. [see Chapter 12, page 164].

1982. "The Elderlies: Learning science the Moseley way." *Sandusky Register*, 31 January, p. A-4. [see Chapter 11, page 156].

1984. "Sandusky Revisited: B G instructor finds interesting facts on Professor Moseley." *Sandusky Register*, 19 February, 4-A. [see Chapter 5, page 38].

1989. Floral Design Is Tribute to Moseley's Arrival in Sandusky One Hundred Years Ago.

In beautifully groomed Washington Park in downtown Sandusky, Ohio, commemorative floral mounds are displayed each summer. In 1989, a floral mound was designed to honor the memory of Edwin L. Moseley who came 100 years previous to teach all of the sciences in Sandusky High School. The design was created by Relda Niederhofer and Tom Ott, the latter, superintendent of the Sandusky City Parks. The plants, *Alternathera* and *Santolina* were used for the lettering, PROF. EDWIN L. MOSELEY. Centered below his name were the years 1889-1989, with a mortar board placed between the years. The third line was TEACHER--NATURALIST. To maintain the letters, the plants were trimmed every other week during the summer months. The south side of the Moseley mound was in an excellent location, because the former high school building, where he taught for 25 years, is in the background. The two objects make an appropriate photograph (see frontispiece of this chapter). Relda Niederhofer's study, "Moseley's inspiration knew few bounds" appeared at this time in the *Register* [see below].

In 1855, downtown Sandusky was a cow yard and later a drill ground for the militia. Since the city's inception in 1818, these grounds were designated for public use as a promenade, walk, or parade. In about 1875 the first Park Commission was appointed to improve the site. The early landscaping consisted of flat flower beds, but in 1910 raised floral mounds were first designed. Today the city commissioners accept requests from local organizations for the six floral mounds to recognize their anniversaries. The city finances the cost of planting and maintaining the mounds.

(*Sandusky Register*, 13 August 1989, pp. B1, 2, 5).

A Final Summation

If the reader is to capture and understand Edwin Lincoln Moseley's total personality, unusual life-style, teaching methodology, and research drive toward understanding the natural world, perhaps all or part of his characteristics will emerge by reading this entire book. This chapter has highlighted many of his attributes through the various recognitions and tributes that have honored him through life and after death. Like all human beings he was a product of his family heritage and environmental surroundings, and combined with these aspects and through whom he interacted, he became the person that we have attempted to know through an objective and positive research approach.

Although much is written in this book about Moseley's frugal lifestyle, we have expanded beyond the description that Moseley was "abstemious to an extreme in matters pertaining to the comforts of life," who lived "almost the life of a recluse." These words were written in Moseley's obituary (*Ohio Journal of Science* 49: 168. 1949) by Charles H. Otis (1886-1979), his long-time colleague in the Biology Department at Bowling Green State University. Moseley's lasting contribution to scholarship and knowledge are now his most important legacy.

Besides his parents and close family members, Moseley's biographers have written that a third grade teacher interested him in plants while on outdoor excursions. At The University of Michigan, he would have interacted with Joseph B. Steere (1842-1940) professor of zoology, but he made no mention of Volney M. Spalding (1849-1918), the acting professor of botany. Later he credited the botanists at Michigan State College, East Lansing, for aid in identification of plants. Other acknowledgments to individuals for assistance with his research projects are named in his books and other major publications. Many of these names are given in Chapters 9 and 10.

Chapter 20 • Recognitions and Tributes

Moseley undoubtedly became the most noted naturalist and scientist of the first half of the twentieth century in northwestern Ohio. In reality, he was the only one actively working at that time in that part of the state. Of frail physique throughout life, he completed a prodigious amount of work. Because of his indefatigable efforts in teaching and research, he developed a reputation that spread locally and later became one of national and international note. His original observational and experimental approaches to scientific study in both the field and laboratory, which also involved the use of high school and college students, were pioneer methods in his day. Because of his unorthodox personality of never-failing zeal and most enduring humility, he developed a kind of rapport with the local citizenry that always attracted attention. They continually supported his teaching philosophy and research endeavors.

Moseley's scientific studies were frequently noted in the local and national newspapers, and in many instances he published his own articles in the local newspapers. His published writings were in a style somewhat conversational and simplistic that contained familiar words and short paragraphs. This writing style made science interesting and allowed for an understanding by individuals representing most degrees of intellect and professional life-styles. The practical applications of his research were often stressed, particularly to farmers, especially in the conservation of birds, guidelines for healthful living, control of white snakeroot to prevent milk sickness, and predictions of rainfall as related to the cultivation of crops. Regardless of whatever techniques were employed, his work, at times controversial, certainly attracted attention. Truly Moseley's work received wide attention, perhaps more publicity than any other Ohio scientist has ever received. In his time, he was one of Ohio's greatest all-around naturalists and certainly one of Ohio's most competent scientists.

> To one whose keen observations and careful scientific investigations have won him international renown in science, to our first Professor Emeritus, Edwin Lincoln Moseley, we gratefully dedicate this book, The 1937 Key.

Dedication of 1937 BGSU Yearbook to Moseley.

(Dedication, *The Key*, BGSU; Archives, BGSU)

List of Publications about Moseley by the Authors

I. Publications by Relda E. Niederhofer

1983. "Edwin L. Moseley, internationally known naturalist, as viewed by those who knew him." *Ohio Journal of Science* 83(2): 8. [Abstract].

1985. "Edwin Lincoln Moseley: An internationally known scientist, a locally known eccentric." *At Bowling Green* [an alumni magazine] 14(4): 4. (Winter).

1988. "Edwin Lincoln Moseley: An internationally known naturalist." *Bartonia* 54: 74-82.

1989. "Moseley's inspiration knew few bounds." *Sandusky Register*, 13 August, pp. B-1,2,5.

1997. "Edwin Lincoln Moseley's botany class field trips." *Ohio Journal of Science* 97(2): A-24. [Abstract].

II. Publications by Ronald L. Stuckey

1983. "Edwin Lincoln Moseley's contributions to science." *Ohio Journal of Science* 83(2): 8-9. [Abstract].

1997. "Drought in 2037: Forecasted by Edwin L. Moseley." *Ohio Journal of Science* 97(2): A24. [Abstract].

1997. "Edwin Lincoln Moseley," pp. 559-561. In Keir B. Sterling, Richard P. Harmond, George A. Cevasco, and Lorne F. Hammond. *Biographical Dictionary of American and Canadian Naturalists and Environmentalists*. Greenwood Press, Westport, Connecticut. xix, 937 pp.

Chapter 20 • Recognitions and Tributes

p. 21. A. No documentation has been seen to verify that any members of an International Fish Commission under the leadership of David Starr Jordan came to study fishes in Sandusky Bay; neither has any evidence been seen to show that Moseley interacted with any of these members.

p. 77. B. A major source of information for the Moseley and Bingham family histories comes from an unpublished manuscript written in 1940 by Mrs. Lillian (Crocker) Brown, Edwin Moseley's niece. The manuscript was provided by Mrs. Brown's daughter, Mrs. Elizabeth (Brown) Brooks, Edwin's grandniece of Wilmette, Illinois. Now believed not living, Mrs. Brooks is the only family member who supplied information by letter or telephone conversation during 1981-1984.

Additional information has been provided by Mrs. Marjorie Glesmann, historian from Union City, Michigan. She has researched the life of Edwin L. Moseley and supplied information about Union City and Moseley's boyhood.

Mrs. Richard Lee, an author and researcher of Hawaiian history, lives in Honolulu, Hawaii. She is the first cousin once removed of Relda E. Niederhofer.

p. 107. C. Nathan W. Easterly published the following papers on the flora of the Oak Openings, Lucas County, Ohio.

- 1969. "The oaks of the Oak Openings." *Castanea* 34(4): 335-351.
- 1972. "The Compositae of the Oak Openings." *Ohio Journal of Science* 72(1): 11-21.
- 1973. "A list of the grasses and grasslike plants of the Oak Openings, Lucas County, Ohio." *Ohio Journal of Science* 73(5): 272-296.
- 1975. "Plant communities of the Irwin Prairie and adjacent wooded areas." *Castanea* 40(2): 201-213.

1975. *The Oaks of the Oak Openings.* Department of Biological Sciences, Bowling Green State University, Bowling Green, Ohio; The Metropolitan Park District, Toledo, Ohio. 23 pp.

1976. *Woody Plants of the Oak Openings.* Department of Biological Sciences, Bowling Green State University, Bowling Green, Ohio. 143 pp.

1979. "Rare and infrequent plant species in the Oak Openings of northwestern Ohio." *Ohio Journal of Science* 79(2): 51-58.

1984. "Some Rare and infrequent flora of the Oak Openings: Addenda to Professor Moseley's findings. *Northwestern Ohio Quarterly* 56(1): 18-20. Winter.

p. 114. D. The complimentary items Moseley received on his research in milk sickness are excerpted from letters that were printed in a newspaper story, "Prof. Moseley's latest book, 'Milksickness,' wins praise." The name and date of the newspaper is not identified with the article, which is in the Center for Archival Collections, Bowling Green State University.

p. 203. E. In the fall of 1972, the water level of Lake Erie was unusually high for that time of year, and following the severe northeastern storm of 14 November, considerable flooding, shore erosion, and destruction of property occurred along the southwest shoreline. This event prompted a *Sandusky Register* reporter* to write about Moseley's predictions of high water in the Sandusky and Port Clinton areas. He reminded that Moseley had predicted that due to natural evolution of the lake, Port Clinton would be regularly under water by the year 2050. Marblehead would be an island, and Sandusky's Columbus Avenue will be under water as far as Market Street in 750 years.

---

*Abner John Katzman. 1972. "Geologist predicted Erie flooding in 1904: Port Clinton under water by 2050?" *Sandusky Register*, 16 February 1973, pp. 15,16.

Two forces are involved in the shoreline modification, (1) the upward tilting of the eastern end of the Lake, which Moseley determined to be 2.14 feet per century, and now measured to be 0.72 feet per century, and (2) the erosion of the shoreline by violent storms during high lake water levels. As Moseley wrote in 1904, the water piles up during northeast gales and causes "much trouble there as soon as there comes a period of several years when the rainfall is considerably above normal, and before the middle of the next century the water at such times will go quite across the peninsula from Port Clinton to Sandusky Bay."

p. 268 F. Frohman's comprehensive index to articles by and about Moseley in Sandusky newspapers totals 248. The list of articles for each newspaper is by title, date, month, year, and page number. For the *Sandusky Register* the index is hand printed on seven cards plus two additional cards. The earliest item is dated 26 December 1889 and the last one is noted 21 December 1959, for a total of 170 items. The *Sandusky Star-Journal* is indexed on five cards, from 2 August 1898 to 9 October 1939, for a total of 55 entries. References to articles in four Erie County newspapers date from 31 December 1890 to 6 August 1925, for a total of 23. All 78 of these entries are typewritten on cards. As stated in the text, Frohman's Moseley index is in the Rutherford B. Hayes Presidential Center, Fremont, Ohio.

In various libraries, we obtained and read articles by and about Moseley taken from various newspapers, the *Daily Sentinel-Tribune* (published at Bowling Green), the *Cleveland Plain Dealer*, the *Detroit News*, the *Toledo Blade*, and others. Articles by and about this celebrated naturalist in these and other newspapers have not been indexed.

This book was composed in New Century Schoolbook on a Power Macintosh 8500 Series Computer using Adobe PageMaker Version 6.5 software.

LIBRARIES CONSULTED

Bentley Historical Library and The Herbarium Library, The University of Michigan, Ann Arbor, MI 48109.

Biological Sciences & Pharmacy Library, The Herbarium Library, the Main Library, and other Departmental Libraries, The Ohio State University, Columbus, OH 43210 and 43212.

Botany Library, University of North Carolina, Chapel Hill, NC 27599.

Firelands College Library, Bowling Green State University, Huron, OH 44839.

Hayes Presidential Center, Spiegel Grove, Fremont, OH 43420.

Jerome Library, Bowling Green State University, Bowling Green, OH 43403.

Marston Science Library, University of Florida, Gainesville, FL 32611.

Mission Houses Museum, Collections of the Hawaiian Mission Children's Society, 553 South King Street, Honolulu, HI 96813.

Oberlin College Archives, Oberlin, OH 44074-1532.

Sandusky Library and Follett House Museum of the Sandusky Library, Sandusky, OH 44870.

Tiffin Public Library, Tiffin, OH 44883.

Toledo Public Library, Toledo, OH 43611-2100.

PHOTOGRAPH AND ARCHIVE CREDITS

Archives, BGSU	Center for Archival Collections, Jerome Library, 5th Floor, Bowling Green State University, 1001 East Wooster Street, Bowling Green, OH 43403.
Archives, Oberlin College	Oberlin College Archives, 420 Mudd Center, 148 West College Street, Oberlin, OH 44074-1532.
Archives, OSU	University Archives, Libraries, The Ohio State University, Library Book Depository, 2700 Kenny Road, Columbus, OH 43210.
Bentley Historical Library	Bentley Historical Library, The University of Michigan, 1150 Beal Avenue, Ann Arbor, MI 48109-2113.
Mission Houses Museum	Collections of the Hawaiian Mission Children's Society, 553 South King Street, Honolulu, HI 96813.
Niederhofer Collection	Mrs. Relda E. Niederhofer, 2707 East Perkins Avenue, Sandusky, OH 44870 (Niederhofer's archives for this book are to be transferred to the Archives of Bowling Green State University).
Photo Service, BGSU	Office of Public Relations, Bowling Green State University, 806 Administration Building, Bowling Green, OH 43403.
Sandusky Library Archives	Sandusky Library and Follett House Museum, 114 West Adams Street, Sandusky, OH 44870.
Stuckey Collection	Ronald L. Stuckey, Herbarium, Museum of Biological Diversity, The Ohio State University, 1315 Kinnear Road, Columbus, OH 43212 (Stuckey's archives for this book are to be transferred to the Hayes Presidential Center, Fremont, Ohio).
Yale University Art Gallery	P.O. Box 208271, New Haven, CT 06520-8272.

ACKNOWLEDGMENTS

The authors gratefully express their appreciation and thanks to the following who willingly contributed information, assistance, and encouragement for this book.

Bowling Green State University, Bowling Green, Ohio: Clifton Boutelle, director of public relations; Ann Bowers, archives; Stephen M. Charter, archives; Charles Codding, physical facilities; William Easterly, biological sciences; Elaine Ezell, archives; T. Richard Fisher, biological sciences; Jane Forsyth, geology; Stewart Givens, history; Ernest Hamilton (deceased), biological sciences; Kenneth H. McFall, liberal arts; Gardner A. McLean, Jr., public relations; Charles R. Middleton, provost/vice president; Reginald D. Noble, biological sciences; Carl E. Peschel, director/foundation accounts; Evelyn Steidtmann; Jacob Verduin (deceased), biological sciences.

Bowling Green State University, Firelands College, Huron, Ohio: John W. Chun, humanities; William W. Currie, library; JoEtta Crupi, faculty secretary; Kenneth R. Hille, natural and social sciences; Sue Joy, typist; Julius Kosan, humanities; D. David Sapp, humanities; Julie A. Rogers, computer services.

Contributors to Chapters: Louis W. Campbell, Roger Conant, Harold F. Mayfield, Mrs. Richard S. Phillips, Milton B. Trautman (deceased), Josephine (True) Dehn, Seymour Van Gundy, individuals listed in Chapter Five.

Erie County: John Blakeman, biologist; Diane Ernst; Dennis Horan; Roger Kleckner; Georgia Russell; Barbara Toft.

Erie County Historical Society: Janet Senne, president; Katherine Wunderly, historian/author.

Mission Houses Museum Library, Honolulu, Hawaii: Pali Lee, historian/author; Marilyn L. Reppun, librarian; Margaret S. Schleif, curator/registrar.

Oberlin College: Roland M. Baumann, archivist.

Ohio Dept. of Natural Resources, Old Woman Creek State Nature Preserve: H. Eugene Wright, administrator.

The Ohio State University: John Condit, ornithologist; J. Perry Edwards, Donald Les, and Nancy Ryan, student assistants; Charles E. Herdendorf, geologist;

Bruce Leach, librarian; Kathy Royer, museum secretary; David H. Stansbery, zoologist; Thomas M. Stockdale, biologist.

Reviewers: William R. Burk, Parker Bower, Guy L. Denny, T. Richard Fisher, Charles E. Herdendorf, Ricki C. Herdendorf, Harold F. Mayfield, Carolyn Ratz, Andrea Schlageter, Thomas M. Stockdale.

Sandusky City Government: Frank Link, former city manager; Thomas Ott, parks superintendent.

Sandusky City Schools: A. Troy Bouts, treasurer; Robert Fial, photography teacher; class members April Karbler, Tom Loris, Tara Webb; Craig Holcomb, clerk of board of education; Fred Leffler, former principal; Kevin Lutz, biology teacher.

Sandusky Library, Sandusky, Ohio: Helen Hansen, former curator Follett House Museum; Virginia Steinemann, Follett House; Cyndie Roberts, administrator of special collections; Susan Schwerer, special collections.

Union City, Michigan: David Evert, photographer/lecturer; Mrs. Marjorie Glesmann, historian.

The University of Michigan: Matthew T. Schaefer, archivist; Edward G. Voss, botanist.

INDEX

Abbot, Charles G. 128, 135
Agassiz, Louis, 23
American Artists Professional League in Bradenton, FL, 259
American Association for Advancement of Science, 101, 103, 104
American Board of Commissioners for Foreign Missions, 80
American Crayon Company, 54, 201, 264
American Museum of Natural History, New York City, 6, 168, 245
American Society of Mammalogists, 115
Andover Seminary, 77, 80
Animals
   Abrornis olivacea, 13
   Actenoides moseleyi, 13, **244**, 246
   Cassis cornutus, 166
   Cryptolopha nigrorum, 13
   Gonorhynchus moseleyi, **244**, 249
   Halcyon lindsayi moseleyi (kingfisher), 93, 246
   Helix pulchella, 166
   Lungworms in deer, 92
   Macropetalichthys sullivantii, 172, 191
   Noturus trautmanii, (darter), 97
   Onochodus, 191
   Tridacna, 172
Ann Arbor, MI, 72, 93, 94, 103, 108, 130
Arthur, J. C., 105
Atkinson, George F., 103

Bailey, Liberty H., 103
Beal, William J., 107
Beecher, Henry Ward, 11
Berlin Heights, OH, 47, 60, 197, 226
Bessey, Charles E., 103, 104
Bettes, Addie, 228, 266
Bingham Family
   Ancestry of family, 79
   Hiram, Sr. and Sybil, **76**, 77, 80
   Hiram, Jr., 81
   Hiram III, 83

   Lydia, 2, 83
   Naomi, 83
   Sophia, 11, 77, **81**
   Thomas, 77
Biographical Sketches
   Campbell, Louis W., **236**, 242
   Conant, Roger, 242
   Dillery, R. E., 233
   Fisher, T. Richard, xii, **xiii**
   Lake, Ivan E. "Doc", 159
   Love, Donald M., 233
   McKelvey, Ralph Huntington, 74
   Mayfield, Harold F., 243
   Niederhofer, Relda E., 291
   Offenhauer, Roy E., 25
   Phillips, Richard S., 234
   Prout, Frank Jay, 36
   Stuckey, Ronald L., 291
   Trautman, Milton Bernhard, 96
   True, Josephine, 8
   Tudury, Moran, 140
   Van Gundy, Seymour D., 233
   Williams, Homer B., 24
Biological Survey of United States, Washington, DC, 259
Bistline, Morris, 154
Bittikofer, Lelia, 41
Black Swamp, 44
Bloomingville Cemetery, 32
Books
   Bible Stories in the Gilbertese by Clara Bingham, 83
   Birds of Buckeye Lake, Ohio by Milton B. Trautman, 96
   Fishes of Ohio by Milton B. Trautman, 96, 97
   Hawaii by James A. Michener, 82
   Ideal Teacher by Palmer, 20
   Manual of Poisonous Plants by Louis H. Pammel, 113
   Michigan Flora by William J. Beal and Charles F. Wheeler, 107
   Nature Study by E. L. Moseley, 149
   New-World Science Series by the World Book Company, 146

Other Worlds by E. L. Moseley, 151
Our Wild Animals by E. L. Moseley, 42, 116, 149, **150**
Phytogeography of Nebraska by Roscoe Pound and Frederic E. Clements, 104
Residence of Tewnty-one Years in the Sandwich Islands by Hiram Bingham, Sr., 83
Trees of Michigan by Charles H. Otis, 184
Trees, Stars, and Birds, by E. L. Moseley, 7, 42, 59, 62, **144**, 146, **147**, 148
Botanical Society of America, 104
Botanical Survey of Nebraska, 104
Botany, 101, 103, 104, 191
Bowling Green, OH, 3, 6, 40, 52, 55, 57, 61, 62, 64, 105, 192, 215, 217, 227, 239
Bowling Green State Normal College, 52, 62, 168, 215
Bowling Green State Normal School, 6, 228
Bowling Green State University, **xxiv**, 3, 5, 7, 19, 21, 29, 30, 41, 47, 48, 50, 53, 54, 56, 93, 107, 127, 130, 135, 138, 153, 155, 157, 167, 179, 216, 217, 222, 228, 230, 238, 240, 241, 245, 257
   Administration Building, **xxvi**
   Biology Laboratory, 2, 44, 162
   Board of Trustees, 157
   Campus, **163**
   Chemistry Department, 157
   Department of Biology, 259
   Director of Financial Aid, Mr. Conrad McRoberts, 218
   Foundation, 218
   Hanna Hall (former Practical Arts Building), 52
   Johnston Hospital, 209
   Life Science Building, 252
   Museum, 49, **176**
   Science Building (Moseley Hall), **9**, **37**, 52, 53, 56, **162**, **251**, **252**
   Shatzel Hall, 259
Bowman, Shadwick W., attorney, 215, 223
Braithwaite, Howard, 41
Braun, E. Lucy, 245
British Museum of Natural History, 245
Britton, Lord Nathaniel, 103
Brooks, Mrs. Elizabeth (Brown), 12
Brown, Mrs. Lillian (Crocker), 77, 81, 210
Buffalo, NY, 103, 104, 108, 192
Bureau of Plant Industry, 113

Campbell, Louis W., 107, 115, 237, 238, 242
Canary, Spencer A., 223, 263
Carpenter, Dr. of Castalia, 32
Case Institute of Technology, 53
Castalia, OH, 20, 47, 60, 226
   Blue Hole, 31, 32, 68, **75**, 102, 190, 194, 195, 200
   Cemetery, 32
   Prairie, 194, 200
   Sporting Club, 194
Cedar Point, OH, 5, 32, 34, 67, 68, 101, 102, 109, 128, 192, 193, 201, 202, 226, 253
Cedar Point Amusement Park, 54
Central High School, Grand Rapids, MI, 4, 13
Chapin, Deacon Samuel, 77
Chicago drainage canal, 93
China, 13, 166, 172
Chippewa Indians, 168
Chubb, Charles F., 210, 216, 218
Chubb, Lucy (Moseley), 210
Churches
   Congregational Church, Union City, MI, 86
   Episcopal, Rochester, NY, 49
   Kawaiahao Church, Honolulu, HI, 82
   Presbyterian Church, Bowling Green, OH, 53
   St. Mary's Catholic, Sandusky, OH, 226

Clark, Clarence, 44
Clements, Frederic E., 104
Cleveland, OH, 49, 53
Coan, Titus, 12
Colleges
    Adelbert, Cleveland, OH, 110
    Amherst, 77
    Bowling Green State Normal, 52, 62, 168, 215
    Defiance, 44
    Harvard, 77, 247
    Kenyon, 49
    Massachusetts State, 46
    Michigan Agricultural College, 105
    Middleburg, 80
    Oberlin, 57, 74, 108
    Smith, 58
    Western Reserve, 49
    Yale, 77
Columbus, Christopher, 35
Columbus, OH, 16, 93, 101, 192
Conant, Roger, 238-240, 242
Cooperrider, Tom S., 107
Coulter, John M., 103
Crane, Ichabod, 39
Crawford, Albert, C., 113
Creason, Miss Carol, 267
Crocker, Mary (Moseley), 210
Crowley, Daniel J., 209, 212, 259, **262**
Cullen, Glen, 49

D. Appleton and Company, New York, 149, 151, 152
Darwin, Charles, 12, 42
Davidson, Wilbur C., 114
Davis, Watson, 152
Deam, Charles C., 114
DeLury, Ralph E., 133
Delzell, David, 239
Department of Hygiene and Bacteriology, University of Chicago, 21
Department of Natural Resources, 44
Dexter, Ralph, 46
Deyo, Dr. of Bellevue, 32
Diamond Fertilizer Company, 216

Dillery, R. E., 227, 228, 233
Doctor of Humane Letters, 7, 131, 260
Dominion Observatory, Ottawa, Canada, 133
Douglass, Professor Andrew E., 6, 129, 135
Drake, Dr. Daniel, 111
Drewsen, Ellen, 184
Dudley, Thomas, 77
DuPont, E. I. DeNemours and Company, 218

Eagle, 59, 114, 115, 166, 172
Easterly, N. William, 107, 245
East Harbor, 193
Elderlies, The, 54, 269
Erie County, OH, 103-105, 172, 190-193, 196, 237
    Historical Society, 171
    Medical Society, 111

Feick, George, Sr., 170
Fenton, Carroll T., 148
Fernald, Merritt L., 247
Field Museum of Natural History, Chicago, 245
Finney, Mr., 74
Flora and fauna (see Plants and Animals)
Flycatcher, 114
Franz Theodore Stone Laboratory, Put-in-Bay, OH, 45, 94, 97
Fries' Landing (Abbot's Bridge), 201
Frohman, Charles E., 108, 110, 267, 268
Fuertes, Louis Agassiz, 148

Gardner, Barney, 239
Geology, 103, 107, 190
Gilbert, Gore K., 108
Goslin, Charles, 115
Gough, John B., 11
Graefe, Charles, M.D., 165
Grand Rapids, MI, 13, 30, 99, 103, 167
Great Blue Heron Rookery, 47, 61
Grunder, Hazel B., **57**

Hale, Edward Everett, 11
Hale, M.D., Kelley, 264
Halleck, Frank D., M.D., 209
Hamilton, Stuart, 20, 30, 31
Hansen, Albert A., 21, 113
Hause, Lewis, 47, 48
Hayward, Rev. Hollis, Student Christian
    Fellowship, BGSU, 212
Hills, Norman E. and Ruth, 184
Hinde and Dauch Paper Company, 170
Hine, James S., 96
Holzhauser, Ruth (Milkey), 41, 48
Honolulu, HI, 77, 80
Hornet's nest, 231
Horn, Stella, 180, 181
Hotel Victory, 60
Huron High School, 57
Huron School, 54

Ideler, Mrs. Pearl, 210
Imperial Museum, Vienna, 245
Internal Revenue Service, 218
International Fish Commission, 21
Interurban station, 60, 61
Islands
    Bass Islands, 45
    Catawba, 68
    Eagle Island, 193
    Erie Islands, or Lake Erie Islands, 67,
      108, 172, 201, 226, 237
    Gilbert Islands, 83
    Green Island, 68, 191
    Hawaiian Islands (Sandwich Islands),
      80, 172, 215, 249
    Negros Island, Philippines, 13, 93,
      114, 246
    Johnson's Island, 67, 198, 226
    Kelleys Island, 32, 59, **75**, 184, 190,
      192, 193, 199, 226
    Middle Bass Island, 59
    Philippine Islands, 13, 93, 114, 165,
      167, 172, 246
    Rattlesnake Island, 68, 191
    South Bass Island, OH, 94, 108
    Spit Island, 34, 35
    West Sister Island, 45, 181, 182

Japan, 13, 166, 168, 172
Johnny Bones, 169
Jones, Lynds, 115
Jones, Paul W., 131, 138
Jordan, David Starr, 21, 249
Jordan, William C., 212
June bugs, 193

Kaahumanu, Queen, 81
Kamehameha, King III, 82
Keith's Theater, Dayton, OH, 209
Kellerman, William A., 103
Kelsey, Professor, 74
Kent Scientific Institute, Grand Rapids,
    MI, 13, 99, 101
Kiefer, Mrs. Charles, 32
Kingfisher, 93
Koch, Inez (Reinheimer), 49, 50
Kraus, Edward H., 113
Kreischer, Ervin and Marge, 50, 51, **262**

Ladd, Raymond E., Wood County Probate
    Judge, 215
Lakes
    Erie, 4, 21, 34, 35, 45, 93, 95, 102-104,
      108, 114-116, 128, 129, 131, **132**,
      190, 195, 199, 202, 240
    Great Lakes, 34, 93, 127, 130
    Huron, 198
    Loraine, Shelby County, 45
    Maumee, 195, 199
    Michigan, 128
    Superior, 34, 201
    Warren, Lucas County, 105, 195, 199
    Whittlesey, 195, 199
Lake, Ivan E., 128, 133, 135, 152, 159
Lake Shore Depot, 72
Lake Shore Electric Railroad
    (Interurban), 60, 67, 199
Lange, Norbert, 170
Letters Moseley wrote to:
    Drewsen, Ellen, 184, 185
    Horn, Stella M., 180, 181

Ideler, Pearl, 210-212
Pratt, Ione R. 179, 180
Weier, LeRoy, 183, 184
Leucocytozoon in waterfowl, 92
Leverett, Frank E., 108, **188**
Lincoln, Abraham, 5, 11, 16, 32
Long-range weather forecasting, 3, 4, 6, 32, 93, 101, 138
Looking Forward, 202
Loomis, Rev., Lyle, Trilby Methodist Church, Bowling Green, OH, 212
Love, Donald M., 225-227, 233

MacMillan, Conway, 103
McCartney, E. S., 114
McDougal, Daniel T., 103
McKelvey, Ralph H., 72, 74, 259
Marblehead Peninsula, 104, 172, 190-193, 199
Martin, Clare, 52, 157, 212
Mayfield Harold F., 115, 240-242, 243
Mayflies, 193
Medical science, 110-114
Men's Literary Club, 109
Meteorology, 101
Michener, James A., 82, 83
Michigan Academy Science, Arts, and Letters, 92, 108, 130, 145
Michigan School Masters' Club, 145
Middleton, Lelan S., attorney, 215, 223
Milan, OH, 60, 68, 69, 190, 197
Milk sickness, 5, 6, 21, 32, 33, 96, 101, 110, 113, 227, 231, 241
Miller, William, 49
Miracle of the Bells, motion picture, 209
Moore, Hollis A., 50
Morse, Samuel F. B., 80
Moseley Family
   Ancestry of Moseley Family, 78, 79
   Channel, 34, 253, **254**, **255**
   Edwin Lincoln, iii, 1, 2, 10, 14, 18, 28, **38**, 43, 44, 51, 55, 59, 66, 89, 90, **126**, **177**, 208, 214, 224, **261**, **262**, **265**, 267
      Signature, 112

Teaching Certificate, **161**
   John, 77, 78
   Museum, BGSU, 192, 252
   Progeny of William A. Moseley and Sophia (Bingham), 84
   Scholarship Fund, 218
   Sybil, 80
   Thomas, Colonel, 11
   William A., Jr., 216
   William A., Sr., 11, 84, 217
Museum of the Kent Scientific Institute, Grand Rapids, MI, 13
Museum of Natural History, Chicago, 6
Museum of Zoology, University of Michigan, 92, 93

National Aeronautics and Space Administration, 41
National Natural History Museum at the Smithsonian Institute, Washington DC, 245
National Museum, Washington, DC, 6
Newcombe, Frederick C., 103
Newspapers
   Bee Gee News, 7, 23, 159, 249, 260
   Cleveland Plain Dealer, 125, 131
   Daily Sentinel-Tribune, 125, 127, 128, 133, 142, 152, 159, 210, 223, 260, 263
   Erie County Reporter, 102, 108, 114, 125
   International News-Special Service, 131
   New York Times, 30, 93, 130, 138, 140, 210
   Peninsular News, 41
   San Diego Union, 159
   Sandusky Daily, 110
   Sandusky Daily Register, 102, 108, 109, 110, 125, 260, 266-268
   Sandusky Daily-Star, 109, 125, 235
   Sandusky Register, 54, 67, 74, 102, 104, 105, 111, 115, 131, 148, 149, 166, 167, 169, 189, 202, 258, 261, 268-271
   Sandusky Register Star News, 261, 264

Sandusky Star-Journal, 108, 109, 111, 115, 116, 125, 127, 151, 258
Sandusky Weekly Register, 102, 104, 109, 110, 114
San Francisco Chronicle, 30, 210
Toledo Blade, 111, 125, 235, 264, 269
Toledo Times, 142
New York Botanical Garden, 103
New York State 35, 139, 141, 142, 146, 149-151, 180
Nichols, John T., 148
North Carolina Agricultural Experiment Station, 113
Norwalk, OH, 60, 226

Oak Grove Cemetery, 212
Oak Openings, near Toledo, OH, 47, 56, 104-107, 183, 229, 240, 246
Offenhauer, Roy E., President of BGSU, 22, **25**, **177**, 258
Ohlemacher, Helen and Wilbert, 53, 54, 269
Ohio State Academy of Science, 5, 33, 46, 69, 91, 101-103, 105, 108-111, 113, 114, 180, 181, 189, 190, 202, 241
Ohio Conservation Hall of Fame, 97
Ohio Historical Society, 110
Ohio State Fish Hatchery, 59
Old Woman Creek Reserve, Huron, OH, 41, 226
Oration (Moseley's, Union City High School, Union City, MI), 16, 17
O'Roke, Earl, 92
Orton, Dr. Edward, 190
Osburn, Raymond C., 45, 46, 96, **178**, 181, 182
Otis, Charles, 42, 56, 184, 259, 271
Ottawa County, 94, 104, 105, 191, 193, 196
Ott, Tom, 270
Overman, Dr. James R. 212, 252
Oxford Prairie, Oxford Twp., Erie County, 247

Pammel, Louis H., 113
Periodicals
 American Fruit Grower, 124
 American Naturalist, 104, 114, 124, 125
 American Schoolmaster, 125
 Annual Report of the Ohio State Academy of Science, 124
 Annual Reports Michigan Academy of Science, 124
 Auk, The, 125
 Bird Lore, 125
 Botanical Gazette, 104, 124
 Cappers Farmer, 125
 Country Gentleman, 125, 138, 139
 Elementary School Journal, 125
 Fram, The, 167
 Ibis, The, 125
 Journal of Infectious Disease, 21
 Journal of Mammalogy, 115, 123
 Journal of the Royal Astronomical Society of Canada, 124
 Lakeside Magazine, 108, 114, 125
 Medical Record, 111, 113, 125
 Monthly Weather Review, 109, 124
 Mulford's Veterinary Bulletin, 111, 125
 National Geographic Magazine, 108, 109, 125, 180
 Nature Magazine, 184
 Ohio Conservation Bulletin, 125
 Ohio Educational Monthly, 108, 109, 125, 145
 Ohio Farmer, 21, 111, 125
 Ohio Journal of Science, 56, 124
 Ohio Naturalist, 111, 113, 124
 Papers of Michigan Academy of Science, Arts, and Letters, 124, 130
 Popular Astronomy, 124
 Reader's Digest, 230
 School Science, 123
 School Science and Mathematics, 123
 Science, 104, 123
 Scientific American, 124, 151
 Special Papers of the Ohio State Academy of Science, 124

Toledo Naturalists Association,
    Annual Bulletin, 123, 230
United States Department of
    Commerce, Weather Bureau, 141, 143
Wilson Bulletin, 114
Perry, Bliss, 20
Perry, Claude, 212
Perry's Cave, South Bass Island, 60, 190
"Pete", Moseley's nickname, 40, 41, 43, 54, 238
Phi Beta Kappa, 58
Phillips, Richard S., 230-232, 234
Pittsburgh, PA, 129, 139, 180, 216, 218
Pittsfield, MA, 11
Plants
    American lotus, 107
    Carex, aurea, 107
    Ceanothus herbaceus (narrow-leaved New Jersey-tea), 107
    Chara, 194
    Eupatorium (see White snakeroot)
        ageratoides, 113
        rugosum, **98**, 110, **122**
        urticaefolium, 110
    Gentiana puberulenta (prairie gentian), 107
    Hymenoxys herbacea (Lakeside daisy), 107
    Lady's tresses orchid, 107
    Lance-leaved, buckthorn, 107
    Nelumbo lutea (water lotus), 107
    Opuntia humifusa (prickly-pear), 107
    Poison hemlock, 107
    Rattlesnake master, 107
    Solidago
        moseleyi, 247, **248**
        remota, 247
        gymnospermoides, 249
    Symphoricarpus albus (snowberry), 107
    Thalictrum
        dasycarpum, 249
        moseleyi, **244**, 247
    White snakeroot (see *Eupatorium*), 32, 33, 110, 113, 269

Port Clinton, 94, 191
Pound, Roscoe, 104
Pratt, Ione R., 179, 180
Premo, Clem, 153
Prout, Frank J., President of BGSU, 4, 29, **36**, 65, 138, 157, **177**, 193, 209, 215, 217, 218, 227, 253, **261**, **262**, 264, 266
Prout, A. H., 193
Put-In-Bay, OH, 45, 59, 182, 190, 192, 200, 226

Ramaley, Francis, 103
Ransom, Ross, 29, 33
"Reader of the Rings", 138
Reinheimer, Bartel, 49
Report of the Michigan Academy of Science, 108
Ribeau, Dr. Sidney A., President of BGSU, 218
Ringling Bros. and Barnum & Bailey Circus, 169
Ripley's Believe It or Not!, 3, 11, 258
Rivers
    Connecticut, 78
    Huron, 69, 190, 197, 200
    Illinois, 195, 199
    Maumee, 64
    Mississippi, 93, 195
    Niagara, 199
    Ohio, 127, 129, 130
    Portage, 56
    Preglacial rivers, 32, 33, 101, 226
    Sandusky, 95
    Vermilion, 73, 200
    Wabash, 195, 199
Rochester, NY, 49, 129
Rockwell Springs Club, 195, 200
Rocky Mountains, 72
Rowlee, Willard W., 103
Rye Beach, 34, 197

Sackett, Walter G., 21, 113
Sandusky, OH
    Adams Junior High School (former

Central Building), 47, 166, 167, 169
Bay, 4, 5, 21, 33, 34, 50, 58, 67, 101, 104, 108, 109, 145, 170, 191, 193, 199, 201, 202, 226, 237, 253
Biemiller Theater, Sandusky, OH, 30
Board of Education, 29, 166, 167, 217
City, 3, 4, 22, 40, 47, 49, 54, 55, 57, 60, 94, 102-104, 107, 109, 111, 129, 155, 181, 182, 189, 227
Concretion, Washington Park, **171**, 198
County, 68
Flora, 5, 67, 101, 105, **106**
Floral design, Washington Park, **256**, 270
High School, **xiv**, 1, 14, 19, 23, 32, 35, 36, 41, 48, 53, 54, 57, 58, 60, 67, 68, 72, 89, 94, 102, 167, 169, 170, 179, 189, 191, 216, 217, 239, 258
High School Faculty, 1, **89**, **177**
High School Laboratory, **156**
High School Museum, 13, 41, 49, **164**, 165, 245, 247
Hinkey's Blacksmith Shop, 170
Monroe Elementary School, 54
Opera House, 258
Public School, 47, 48, 54
Revisited, 54
Soldiers' Home (Ohio Veterans Home), 68
Soldiers' Memorial Building, 167
Sand Hill Cemetery, 32
Saybrook, CT, 77, 79
Schaller, Ralph, 259
Scheid, Edna, 57
Schmidt, Carl, 209
Schultz, Louis, Sr. and Jr., 58
Schwartz, John, 212
Science field excursions, 71
Sears, Paul B., 101
Seidel, Frank, 264
Seminary, Miss Emma Willard's, 84
Sharpe, R. B., 247
Sheats, "Caterpillar Bill" of Washington, NJ, 140

Sheffield, England, 77, 79
Shepard, Rev. Samuel, and Sarah, 80
Ships
  Arrow, steamer, 59, **65**, 226
  Chippewa, 182
  Erie, steamer, 68
  Frank E. Kirby, steamship "Flier of the Lakes," 226
  Thaddeus, brig, 80
Sine qua non (an indispensable condition), 20
Sink holes south of Castalia, 195
Skookum, Joe, 140
Small, John K., 103,
Smith, Erwin F., 105
Smithsonian Institution, Washington, DC, 138
Snake, fox, 22, 31
Sones, George D., 165
Spalding Volney, M., 105, 271
Spencer, Herbert, 42
Standish, Miles, 77
Steele, Edward S., 249
Steere, Joseph B., 13, **14**, 93, 114, 165, 246, 271
Steward Observatory, 6, 129
Stewart, C. S., 12
Stockdale, Hazel, 41, 58
Stroud, Charles E., 169
Strouse, Don, 133
Students who assisted Moseley in research projects, 235
  Daniel, Frank
  Ehrmann, Joseph
  Feick, George
  Fuchs, Alton
  Graefe, Henry
  Guenther, August E.
  Kubach, Oscar
  Rieger, Walter H.
  Schoepfle, Fred
  Schoepfle, Henry C.
Sunspots, 35
Sunderland, J. T., 11
Sutherland, Mrs. Clara (Moseley), 210,

289

215, 218
Swartz, Charles K., 249

Thomas, Edward S., 96
Thurston, Asa, 80
Toledo, OH, 7, 47, 53, 56, 104, 128, 180
Trautman, Mary Auten, 94, 97
Trautman, Milton, 91, 96, **97**, 115, 246
Trautman's Riffle, 97
Tree rings, 35, **134**
Trembles, 5, 21, 32, 96, 101, 110, 113
True, Josephine, 8, 129, 135
Tschantz, Rose (Steiner), 62
Tudury, Moran, 130, 138, 140, 141
Turton, Charles M., 149
Twain, Mark, 11

Underwood, Lucius M., 103
Union Carbide and Carbon Corp., 218
Union City High School, **12**
United City, MI, 11, **85**, 217
United States
    Biological Survey, 140, 181
    Civil Service Commission, 41
    Department of Agriculture, 107
    Geological Survey, 108
    Fish and Wildlife Service, 115, 237
    Weather Bureau, 140
Universities
    Arizona, 129
    Bowling Green State, 41, 47, 48, 50, 53, 54, 56, 167, 216, 217, 222
    Chicago, 20, 21, 33, 103, 148
    Columbia, 54, 103
    Cornell, 103
    Duke, 114
    Johns Hopkins, 249
    Kent State, 46, 54
    Miami, OH, 44
    Michigan, 12, 20, 49, 92, 94, 103, 105, 113, 114, 165, 184, 246
    Minnesota, 103
    Nebraska, 103
    Ohio State, 44, 52, 58, 94, 103, 245
    Purdue, 21, 105

Stanford, 21, 74
Yale, 77
Upper Sandusky, OH, 54
    High School, 62

Van Gundy, Robert, 183
Van Gundy, Seymour, 228-230, 233, 266
Van Tyne, Dr. Josselyn, 93, 94
Visscher, J. Paul, 115

Waggoner Farm, 47
Walker Museum, 148
Washington, DC, 113, 180
Waterlime, 200
Wehr, Dr., 183
Weier, Leroy, 94, 183
Wenger, George, 94
Wheeler, Charles F., 105, 107
Wheelock, Ralph, 77
Wherry, Edgar T., 107
Whiting, Lucy, 83
Wickliff, Edward L., 96
Willard, Frances, 11
Williams, Homer B., President of BGSU, 1, 6, 19, 23, **24**, 50, 56, **89**, 113, 157, **177**, 257, 259
    Residence, BGSU, **27**
William Wood and Company, New York, 111
Wisconsin glacier, 108
Wilson Ornithological Club, 114, 115
Wilson Ornithological Society, 241
Witte, Mrs. Cynthia (Otis), 56
Wolf, Curtis and Kaup, 113
Wolf, Frederick A., 114
Woodbridge, Benjamin, 77
Woodcraft League, 149
Woolworth Handle factory, 201
World Book Company, 146, 149
World War II, 230
Wright, G. Frederick, 108

Youngman, Henny, 63
Young Memorial, Bowling Green, OH, 212

Zoology, 101, 103, 114-116, 192

Relda E. Niederhofer

Relda Elaine Grunder, born 15 April 1928 in Creston, Wayne County, Ohio, graduated from Creston High School (1946). She earned a B. S. in Education (1950) and an M. S. in Education (1956) from Bowling Green State University. Her high school teaching experiences included Pontiac, Michigan; Mansfield, Ohio; Sandusky Public Schools (1953-1965). In 1957 Mrs. Niederhofer taught part-time for Bowling Green State University, Sandusky Academic Center as a full-time instructor (1969) and assistant professor (1983) at Firelands College. After 40 years of teaching, Mrs. Niederhofer retired Emerita in 1991.

Niederhofer's research include medical history and horticultural therapy. She has had a horticultural therapy program for geriatric residents at Erie County Care Facility since 1982. Her interest in Moseley has resulted in publications and presentations.

She married James W. Niederhofer in 1952, the couple had a daughter, Sandra (Niederhofer) Douglas. Mrs. Niederhofer was widowed in 1997.

Ronald L. Stuckey

Ronald L. Stuckey, born 9 January 1938 in Bucyrus, Crawford County, Ohio, is a country farm boy who lived his first 18 years in Lykens Township. He graduated as valedictorian from Lykens High School (1956), earned a B. S. *cum laude* (1960) in Biology from Heidelberg College, Tiffin, Ohio, and an M. A. (1962) and Ph.D. (1965) in Botany from The University of Michigan, Ann Arbor.

From 1965-1991 he served as Professor of Botany in The Ohio State University, Columbus, where he taught courses in Local Flora, Aquatic Flowering Plants, and Plant Nomenclature. Stuckey is an internationally recognized authority on the identification and geographical distribution of aquatic and wetland plants in North America. He has also written extensively on the botanical history and exploration of eastern North America.

Stuckey is past president of the OSU Chapter of Sigma Xi, the Ohio Academy of Medical History, and the Ohio Academy of Science.

Relda E. Niederhofer and Ronald L. Stuckey at Moseley Hall, Bowling Green State University, 26 April 1997.

(Taken by William R. Burk; Stuckey Collection)